THE BIG BIGFOOT BOOK

ETHAN HAYES

FREE REIGN

ISBN 13: 979-8-89234-052-6

Free Reign Publishing, LLC
San Diego, CA

FREE REIGN

Publishing

CONTENTS

INTRODUCTION

Welcome, intrepid explorer, to *The Big Bigfoot Book*—a compendium like no other. Herein lie 100 extraordinary tales of encounters with the elusive giant known as Bigfoot, each a glimpse into the mysterious world of this legendary creature. These stories, carefully selected from my *I Saw Bigfoot* and *Encounters Bigfoot* series.

For decades, tales of Bigfoot have captivated the imagination of adventurers, skeptics, and believers alike. These accounts stretch across isolated forests, hidden valleys, and the untamed wildernesses of North America, painting a picture of a world just beyond the reach of modern civilization. The stories in this book have been chosen not just for their intrigue and mystery, but for their ability to challenge our understanding of the natural world.

As you turn these pages, you will meet eyewitnesses who have come face-to-face with Bigfoot. You'll read of close encounters in twilight woods, harrowing experiences in the dead of night, and fleeting glimpses that have turned the most ardent skeptics into believers. Each story is a thread in the larger tapestry of Bigfoot lore, contributing to a narrative that is as wild and diverse as the landscapes where Bigfoot is said to roam.

The Big Bigfoot Book is not just a collection of stories; it is an invita-

INTRODUCTION

tion to ponder the possibilities that lie in unexplored corners of the world. Whether you are a lifelong Bigfoot enthusiast or a newcomer to these mysterious tales, there is something in this book for you. So, prepare to embark on a journey into the unknown, where the lines between myth and reality blur, and the primal wilderness holds secrets waiting to be uncovered. Let the adventure begin.

- Ethan Hayes
2024

CHAPTER ONE

LET me take you back to a memorable camping trip I had just a few months ago, in the beautiful wilderness of South Carolina. It was September, a time when the colors of nature begin to change, and the air carries a hint of anticipation for the approaching fall season. Little did I know that amidst the serenity of the remote campground, an encounter awaited me that would defy all expectations and leave an indelible mark on my mind.

As the evening settled upon the campsite, and the sky transformed into a canvas of twinkling stars, a peculiar tapping sound reverberated from above—the roof of my trusty camper. It was as if unseen finger-tips were gently rapping against the metal surface, creating an eerie symphony that disrupted the tranquil night. Curiosity mingled with a tinge of apprehension, urging me to investigate the source of this mysterious disturbance.

Stepping out of the camper, the cool night air enveloped me, carrying with it a sense of anticipation and the faintest whisper of something out of the ordinary. And then, I heard it—a soft, rhythmic sound that seemed to mimic the act of breathing, but with an enig-matic quality that defied explanation. It was an ethereal, elusive melody that tantalized my senses, making it difficult to put into words.

I strained my ears to grasp its essence, to decipher the nature of this elusive phenomenon.

In the dimly lit surroundings, barely 15 to 20 feet away, stood a figure that seemed to have emerged from the realm of myth and mystery. It was a creature, unmistakably female, bearing a striking resemblance to both a gorilla and a person. My eyes widened in disbelief as I took in its surreal appearance—the gorilla-like breasts juxtaposed against the partially human face. It was a sight that defied the boundaries of what I believed to be possible, challenging my perception of the natural world.

As if sensing my presence, the creature emitted a soft, soothing cooing noise—a sound that resonated deep within my being. It was a tender, maternal murmur, reminiscent of a mother comforting her young. In that moment, time seemed to stand still as the creature turned gracefully, disappearing into the protective embrace of the nearby treeline. I stood there, awestruck and bewildered, grappling with the sheer strangeness of what had just unfolded before my eyes.

The sheer size of the creature added to the surrealness of the encounter. Standing at a towering height of approximately 8 feet, it possessed a majestic presence that commanded attention and respect. Its massive form, shrouded in the veil of the night, left an indelible imprint on my memory. I had entered the wilderness with a sense of adventure and a longing for the unexpected, but I could have never fathomed coming face to face with such a marvel.

The cooing noise, reverberating in the air, lingered like a haunting melody. It was unlike anything I had ever heard before—an enigmatic chorus that seemed to resonate from the depths of the creature's being. Its unique timbre evoked a sense of both familiarity and unease, leaving me pondering the mysteries of the natural world.

As the creature gracefully retreated into the darkness, a profound sense of wonder engulfed me. I struggled to comprehend the enormity of what I had just witnessed—a glimpse into a realm where the boundaries of reality blur, and the extraordinary coexists with the ordinary. It was a moment that defied explanation, leaving me humbled by the vastness of the universe and the countless wonders it holds.

In the days that followed, I found myself revisiting the memory, contemplating its significance and seeking solace in the company of fellow campers who shared the experience. Each retelling of the encounter only deepened the mystery, as others recounted their own encounters with strange tree formations in the forest—a puzzle that remained unsolved, leaving us all yearning for answers.

As I sit here now, recounting the tale, the memories still vivid in my mind, I am left with a profound sense of gratitude for the remarkable experiences that the natural world has to offer. It is a reminder that, no matter how much we think we know, there will always be mysteries that elude our understanding, inviting us to embrace the unknown and approach life's adventures with an open heart and a curious spirit.

CHAPTER TWO

IT WAS SEPTEMBER 17TH, 2005, and I'm sitting in my deer blind, minding my own business, when out of nowhere, I start hearing this bizarre gibberish hollering. I mean, seriously, it sounded like a bunch of nonsensical noises coming from behind me, roughly a hundred yards away.

Now, you might think, "Ah, it's probably just some wildlife or maybe some rowdy teenagers messing around." But let me tell you, this wasn't your ordinary woodland creature or prankster. This gibberish hollering, it started moving, y'all. It was heading from east to west, getting closer and closer to where I was sitting. And let me tell you, that's when things started to get real unsettling.

Feeling a mix of curiosity and nerves, I unzipped the back of my deer blind and grabbed my trusty field glasses. I wanted to get a glimpse of whatever was causing such a ruckus and scaring away the deer. But guess what? When I peered through those glasses, there was nothing to be seen. Nada. Zilch. It was as if this bizarre noise had no visible source. Now, that's enough to make anyone's heart skip a beat.

As if the situation wasn't unnerving enough, the sound kept getting closer, and my anxiety levels started to skyrocket. Mind you, I had all the proper permissions to be hunting in that area, but that didn't stop the fear from creeping in. And that's when it hit me—literally hit me—the most peculiar stench I've ever encountered. It was a mix of damp, musty roadkill and, believe it or not, dirty diapers. Yeah, I know, it sounds repulsive, and trust me, it was.

The combination of the advancing noise, the invisible presence, and the ghastly odor forced me to make a quick decision. I had to prioritize my safety above all else. Without wasting a moment, I readied my bow, nocked an arrow, and made a swift exit from the deer blind. Fear wrapped its icy fingers around my heart as I made a beeline away from the disturbance, not daring to look back.

But here's the kicker, folks. As I emerged from the woods, heading toward my trusty vehicle parked approximately twenty-five yards away, I heard it again. That gibberish hollering was still going on, but this time it was coming from the parallel woods, about twenty yards from where I was. Can you imagine? It felt like I was being trailed by an invisible tormentor, and let me tell you, that sent shivers down my spine like nothing before.

At that point, panic took over, and I wasn't taking any chances. With my bow firmly drawn and ready for action, I sprinted towards my truck. I was ready to defend myself against whatever unseen force was doggedly following my every move. Yet, despite my heightened senses and the intensity of the situation, there was still no sign of anything—no movement, no figure lurking amidst the trees. It was as if I was being pursued by a ghost.

Finally, I reached my truck, my heart pounding in my chest. I quickly released my bowstring without letting the arrow loose, placing my bow carefully in the back seat of my trusty Suburban. With adrenaline coursing through my veins, I fired up the engine and wasted no time in making my exit. I can tell you this, folks, in all my years of hunting bears, wild pigs, and deer, never had I experienced such a gut-wrenching need to flee the woods.

So, there you have it, folks, the unforgettable tale of my eerie encounter in the swamp bottoms of West River. It was a day that forever changed the way I view the wilderness, reminding me that even amidst the beauty and tranquility of nature, unseen forces can stir, evoking fear and uncertainty.

CHAPTER THREE

MY SON-IN-LAW and I were out running our hounds on a coon hunt that night. The area we were in stretched far beyond Green Lake, extending into the Hickey Marsh and eventually reaching the Seney. Little did we know that this particular night would be etched in our memories forever.

As we parked our vehicles, preparing for the hunt, I couldn't help but notice the remains of partridges scattered around. It didn't strike me as anything out of the ordinary at the time. Our hounds, full of energy and excitement, were eager to get started. I released a young and proven hound, both displaying immense determination and fear-lessness. Something in my gut told me that we might not be chasing coons that night; it felt more like a bobcat was on the prowl.

Sure enough, after about twenty minutes, the hounds signaled they had treed. We made our way towards them, but just before we reached the tree, the creature bailed, much like a cat would when it catches sight of lights at night, or a bear when we pursue them. Undeterred, the dogs pulled themselves together and resumed the chase, leading us deeper into the wilderness.

Sensing the need for caution, my son-in-law decided to return to the truck, ready to call me out if necessary. I kept the tracker with me, venturing further into the marsh, where a dense blend of spruce, cedar, bog, and popple surrounded me. The dogs had treed deep within this maze of foliage. In search of a vantage point to better hear their barks, I climbed a high spot—a thickly wooded ridge. My radio tracker struggled to pick up their signals, as well as the extra collar left at the truck. Its range in such densely forested areas was limited to around 7 miles. I slowly swung the tracker, hoping to catch a stronger reading.

Amidst the hunt, a foul odor wafted through the air. At first, I dismissed it, assuming it was simply my own scent after multiple encounters with swamp muck. But as I swung the tracker, its moonlight illuminating the path of the antenna, my gaze fell upon a pair of eyes nestled among the spruce trees, right next to a deer trail on the ridge. As a seasoned coon hunter, I had seen my fair share of eye shine in the darkness. However, this sighting gave me pause. I shrugged it off momentarily and swung the tracker back, only to find the trail before me filled with a creature standing merely twenty feet away.

This being stood at an astonishing height of around 8 feet, boasting long arms with distinct fingers, a barrel chest, and a potbelly. Its eyes, deeply set and intense, locked onto mine, while its mouth hung open. Strangely enough, its ears appeared small in proportion to its massive frame. Time seemed to stand still as I stood frozen, my hounds' call forgotten in the face of this surreal encounter. I couldn't tear my eyes away as the creature wrapped its hand around a large spruce tree. Its hair, a blend of black and brown, was neither long nor short, while its nose appeared flat, and its face lacked the same hair coverage as its body. I can't quite recall how it departed from the scene, but the lingering smell followed me almost all the way back to the truck, where my son-in-law met me. He jokingly commented about me passing gas, unaware of the terror that had just unfolded.

Shaken to my core, I struggled to regain composure as we made our way back, doubting the accuracy of my tracking system and questioning the reliability of my compass. The path we took back wasn't the straightest; the encounter had left me disoriented. To this day, I haven't mustered the courage to run my hounds in that area again, whether it be for coons or bears. Moreover, it remains the only time I have left my beloved hounds alone in the woods. The following morning, after getting some much-needed rest, I ventured back up there, my nerves on edge, in a desperate attempt to locate my hounds by myself, as my son-in-law had to go to work. Thank the Lord, I found them treed in the beechwoods, just 30 feet off the gravel road, with the most beautiful sleeping bobcat perched in the tree.

CHAPTER FOUR

I HAD LIVED on those mountains for five years before the incidents began. There was nothing notable at first, little things here and there. Things moved around the property; animal carcasses left hanging in trees. They started in spring and continued into winter before I left. The big thing that happened that caused me to move out of my home and live back in the city happened one especially cold winter weekend.

I woke up early Friday morning. Staring up at the wooden ceiling for a bit before I sat up. The fire from last night died down but the heat still hugged the air like a blanket. I stood and stretched, walking into the living room, and adding some wood to the fireplace. I stoked the fire, made sure it took again before I made my way over to the kitchen. I decided to splurge a little and made bacon, eggs, toast, and some pancakes. Whilst I was eating, I looked out at the complete whiteout from the large window. The storm had been raging for a couple days at that point, the snow was halfway up my calves. I finished breakfast and washed up the dishes before I got into my snowsuit and pushed open the door. The blast of cold could be felt down to my bones, shivering. I trudged out, fighting against the snow. Each step felt heavier than the last. It took me a while to make it across the clearing to the small shed where I kept the snow blower. I was trying to open the shed when I noticed something strange off to my right. I squinted trying to make it out. After a while, I still could not see it clearly and started to trudge towards it. When I got to the tree line, I was shocked to see a deer hanging in the tree. I was used to this by now, but it was never anything as big as a deer. I felt my mouth run dry, deep tracks in the snow left by a bipedal creature. I twisted the deer, trying to pull it down, I fell back when I noticed a jagged hole in the stomach. I took a few deep breaths before making my way back to my feet. I grabbed the carcass and pulled it down, putting it over my shoulder. I carried it back to the shed, pulling the door the rest of the way open. I dropped the deer onto the butchering table and grabbed my knife. I had spent many days hunting and learnt many skills when it came to skinning and cleaning animals. I took care to check on the skin and insides, once I made sure it was safe, I tied its legs together and hung it up in the corner on a hook.

Grabbing the snowblower, I started it up and pushed my way out of the shed. The storm kept dumping more snow, falling in large clumps. Even as I made a path to my front door, the snow was settling, my thoughts roamed back to the deer carcass. The deep tracks, even in the tree line, looked fresh. I did one more pass with the snow blower before putting it away. Grabbing a bit of firewood, I headed back inside. I shook off the snow and tossed the wood to the side. I got out of my snow gear and made my way to the window. I looked out, but could no longer see the trees, simply a white sheet. I watched for a while, putting on some coffee. The snowfall slowed for a bit while I poured myself a cup, I could start to make out the tree line as I took a tentative sip of the hot drink. I leaned forward as it came into view; it was at this moment that I saw the creature for the first time. I could barely make out anything other than an outline. But what I saw was ingrained into my memory forever. It walked on two legs; it was also tall with thick arms and legs. I couldn't make out what it was wearing. Although it looked like it had fur clothes. I watched as it walked along the tree line towards the shed. It was at this time that I noticed he did not have clothes but thick fur. My breath started to increase, watching closely as the creature walked up to the shed and stopped in front of the door. It raised its arm and swung it at the shed door. The cold wood easily shattered under the force of the punch. I could hear a roar come from the creature as he entered the shed. The creature returned after a minute; the deer carcass was being dragged from behind. As the creature stepped outside, it looked towards the house and I could have sworn we locked eyes, it was for a moment but through the storm, I saw a flash of two dark eyes staring at mine. I took a step back, quickly turning to the bedroom and going for the satellite phone I keep in my nightstand. I took it out and turned it on, walking back to the window. At this point, the storm had picked back up and the creature was gone. I heard the beep of the phone finishing its startup sequence, bringing it up. My heart dropped, there was no signal. The storm clouds were blocking the signal. I tossed the phone on to the couch. A fear of what I had seen creeps inside. I have never frightened easily but the way that creature looked at me, its sheer size, terrified me. I walked up to the front door and checked that it was bolted. I slid a dresser in front of the door. There was no way to get down the mountain in this storm and I couldn't call for help. Barricading myself inside and waiting for the storm to die was the safest option. I checked outside before closing the blinds. I walked over to the couch, kneeling, I reached under and pulled out a case, I opened it to find my hunting rifle. I took it out and loaded up a cartridge. I made my way over to the bedroom, placing a chair in the corner. I sit down and lean the rifle against the wall. Rubbing my hands together, I blew into them. Trying to calm myself down. I don't know how much time passed while I sat there. I could not sit still and kept fidgeting the entire time, waiting for the creature to return. A few times during that wait, I would hear creaks at the front of the house, groans as the wind pushed against the aging wood. Each sound made my heart skip a beat. My thoughts continued to run wild until I eventually passed out in the chair.

I abruptly woke up in the middle of the night, I was shivering and could feel a bitter cold wind blowing through the cabin. I grabbed the rifle and stood up; I aimed it forward as I approached the bedroom door. I slowly peaked out at the dark cabin, as the cold wind cut at my skin like a knife. I didn't hear any other sounds other than the wind as I slowly made my way further in. The fire had died down and so I put down the rifle, I added some wood to bring it back to life. The flames flickered against the bitter cold as the light danced against the walls, leering shadows made it seem as though others were in the room. I approached the table and grabbed my lantern, As I lit it, the shadows faded, and my heartbeat steadied. It was at this point when I noticed a large hole in the main window. A stick had crashed through. My breath catches in my throat, even as the storm raged outside, it was impossible for a stick that size to fly through that window on its own. I approached the window and lifted the lantern, trying to peer into the darkness, but all I saw was falling snow. I felt my hands start to freeze against the bitter wind. So I put the lantern down and Reached for some garbage bags and duct tape. I patched up the window as much as I could, the plastic rippling against the force of the storm.

I put on some soup, rubbing my hands together to warm them up, and waited for it to heat up. I placed my cold hands against the heated metal and greedily drank the soup. My eyes went wild, darting at each little movement in the shadows. I got up and went to grab the chair, bringing it out, I set it next to the fire and sat down. My back was to the wall to keep an eye on the whole cabin. I finished drinking my soup and put it down above the fire. Grabbing the rifle, I cradled it to my chest, finding strength in the cool wood. The fear kept me alert for a few more hours until the bright light of dawn started shining through the cracks not covered by the garbage bag. My head started to droop with the coming day. The tension slowly left my body until I fell asleep.

I woke up with a slight jolt. My rifle fell to the floor, causing me to jump out of my seat. I looked around in a panic, still half out of it. It took a moment for me to get my bearings. I picked up my rifle and set it on the table, I took a few deep breaths before looking out the window. I couldn't help but smile when I saw the blue sky. I quickly ran to the couch and grabbed the satellite phone. I fumbled it as I turned it on, it fell to the floor with a loud crunch and as I lifted it, I noticed a large crack on the screen. I watched in suspense as the screen turned on, I took a deep breath, lifting it up as I waited for a signal. As soon as the phone connected, I quickly dialed up the park rangers who had a station at the bottom of the mountain. When I got through, I explained what happened. Luckily a friend of mine, who I would sometimes hang out with at the cabin when going around, answered. He listened to everything quietly, I finished explaining everything and waited for the response. There was some static before his scratchy voice could be heard. He apologized and explained that they were totally snowed in, and it would have taken a few days to clear a path up. Unless I could come down, I would be stranded. He tried to make me feel better, saying it was probably just a bear, it was easy to mistake these things when you didn't see what I saw. I told him it was not a bear and he said fine, but that didn't change anything. I was still stranded. He told me he would try to get people up as quickly as possible and to stay inside until they could.

After we hung up, I did a quick once over of the cabin to make sure I had everything I needed. There was plenty of food left since I had just recently restocked. The taps were working fine, and I had a couple of jugs as backup. The one thing I did not have a lot of in the cabin was firewood. That was kept in an overhand about 50 feet from the front door. I walked over to the broken window from last night and peered outside through the small parts not covered by the garbage bags. After a few minutes of looking around and not seeing the creature, I decided to run out and grab some wood. I put on all my outdoor gear and made my way to the door. I looked back at my rifle and chose to leave it. I would need both hands to bring the wood back quickly, if anything happened, I would simply run. I took a few deep breaths before I opened the door and stepped outside. The cold hit me like a punch and a shiver shot through my entire body. I began trudging through the snow, keeping my eyes peeled for any movement. My racing heart started to calm down slightly as I reached the overhang without incident. I started placing a bunch of the cut-up wood onto a sled that I kept there, making sure it was full before I began tugging it over the deep snow. I was halfway back when a loud crack like a gunshot rang out beside me. I turned and watched as a large tree fell over some twenty feet beyond the clearing.

It was not uncommon for trees to snap like that in the colder temperatures, but as though it was a warning, whilst I was looking in the direction that the sound came, I once again saw the creature, the trees shaking as it pushed through the underbrush. I began to hyperventilate, tugging hard at the sled trying to move faster. I was almost at the door when I heard the snap of a cord and fell into the snow. I scrambled up and saw that the creature was now in the clearing with me, I completely forgot about the wood and ran back inside, slamming the door shut. I pushed a dresser in front of the door and sat down in my chair holding up my rifle. I waited quietly for some sounds that the creature was trying to get in, but as seconds turned into minutes, turned into an hour, nothing ever came. I put down my rifle and put in the last few pieces of wood I had inside. I slowly opened the door and checked back where I saw it before, but it was gone. I took a few tentative steps out, continuing to closely scan the tree line. I thought I saw movement at one point and dove back towards the door, but it turned out to be nothing. I quickly ran over to the wood and noticed deep fissures in the snow that were not there before. I looked in the direction they went, I could not see anything and began pulling the sled with all my strength until it slid the last few feet to the door. I looked around one more time before starting to pile the wood inside. Once it was all in, I quickly shut the door and barricaded myself inside. I added a couple pieces to the fire and made myself some food. I wasn't very hungry but in that kind of situation, eating to have energy can save your life.

I ate next to the fire, my eyes darting between the door and the window. I looked down, my hands were shaking. Not from the cold, but from the fear and being tense for so many hours. I curled my hands into fists and got up from my seat. I grabbed my rifle and walked over to my room, I grabbed the blankets off the bed and brought them to the couch. I put the rifle down next to the couch and wrapped myself up. I sat there watching as the sun slowly began to set, the day feeling like a blur.

I don't know when I passed out, but the next thing I remembered was being shaken, I slowly opened my eyes and in the blurriness all I could see was brown fur. My mind was engulfed in fear, I tried to reach for my rifle, screaming. But a hand grabbed my wrist, I tried to fight it off, but it didn't let go no matter how hard I tugged. It was at this point that I heard someone calling my name and stopped fighting. I looked up and was surprised to see the ranger telling me to calm down and that it was ok. I stared at him dumbfounded and asked what he was doing there. He let go of me and explained how another storm was fast approaching and so he and a few others grabbed the skidoos and made their way here. When there was no answer at the door, he came in and found me there. I explained to him what happened and as I finished, he nodded, explaining how throughout the years, others have also claimed to see this same creature. I quickly got on all my gear and asked him what they thought it was. He said that no matter how many different people told stories, it always had one name, sasquatch. I looked down at the ground as we made our way out of the cabin, locking it behind us. We went to the skidoos and there were three others waiting for us. I recognized them and we all exchanged pleasantries before making our way down the mountain.

I stayed at the ranger station for the rest of winter. A few of the rangers went up to investigate but were unsuccessful in finding anything. As the snow began to melt, I struck a deal with the men at the station and sold them the cabin to do with as they saw fit. I purchased a small house by the city and never again went back to that cabin. Visiting the rangers was as close as I got.

CHAPTER FIVE

IT WAS AROUND ten years ago when I had an encounter that has stayed with me ever since. Our family has always been fond of camping in the majestic mountains of Alberta, and on this particular trip, we decided to take our trusty old motor home and set up camp in a remote area near David Thompson. It was the kind of place so secluded that we were the only ones there at the time, surrounded by the beauty and tranquility of nature.

Just beyond our campsite, there were numerous bike trails, rolling hills, and vast stretches of forest. Those hills, I would describe them as mini mountains, were quite challenging to climb and surprisingly large in size. My brother, being at that age when relaxation took precedence over exploration, preferred to stay back at the campsite. This left me with the freedom to venture out on my own, biking and hiking to my heart's content.

On one occasion, I decided to grab my Walkman and hop on my bike to explore what I dubbed the "mini mountains." It took me about 20 minutes to reach a point quite far from our campsite. As I pedaled along, lost in the music blaring through my headphones, little did I know that an unsettling moment was about to unfold—one that still haunts me in my nightmares.

I was jamming to some music when suddenly, an eerie sensation washed over me—a distinct feeling of being watched. Startled, I brought my bike to a halt and glanced to my right. At first, all I saw was a large tree stump. But then, out of nowhere, a head peeked out from behind that stump. Time seemed to come to a standstill as I found myself locked in a stare-down with this mysterious figure. It kept shifting its gaze from side to side, as if contemplating its next move. I was frozen, unable to tear my eyes away from the sight.

And then, it happened—the figure stood up. The stump that had initially caught my attention turned out to be as tall as me when this enigmatic being rose to its feet. The sight of it sent shockwaves through my entire being. Something deep inside me screamed to run, to escape from whatever this thing was. In my terrified state, I even lost my balance and tumbled off my bike, leaving a scar on my knee that serves as a constant reminder of that harrowing moment.

The fear coursing through me was palpable, and my pounding heart seemed to drown out all other sounds. When I finally managed to make my way back to our campsite, tears streaming down my face, I couldn't help but pour out my emotions to my parents throughout the entire night. My dad, in his attempt to understand what I had experienced, asked me to take him back to the spot where it had occurred. But the mere thought of returning to that place filled me with such overwhelming dread that I simply couldn't bring myself to do it.

Even to this day, I refuse to camp in that general area. The memory of that encounter, etched deep within my psyche, has left an indelible mark on me, forever altering my perception of the wilderness. It serves as a constant reminder of the unknown mysteries that lie hidden in the woods and the unexplained entities that may inhabit the very places we find solace in.

CHAPTER SIX

WHEN I GREW UP, I lived in a cabin in the middle of the woods in Alaska. Back in the nineteen seventies when I was a kid, it really was like living feral. We had an outhouse and I remember at a very young age having electricity put into the place for the first time. My parents were simple people, and I was one of seven kids. I was child number five and the loner of the bunch. While my siblings were content to go on all sorts of adventures, in the woods and otherwise, with my parents or each other, I felt much more comfortable in the woods alone. I have since made my living as a writer and author and I guess the making up of strange and oftentimes dystopian worlds and societies started in those woods that surrounded my house when I was little. My parents still live in that house, and I don't live too far from them but nowadays a lot of the land they owned they've since sold off and the place just isn't the same. Not to mention how modernized the house is now. When I was growing up, I had many strange experiences with many things that I still to this day can't explain but one of the strangest and the first was the one I am about to tell you all about now. I always knew that bigfoot existed because even back then there were rumors of the beast among the adults around me. I heard them talking and thought for sure if I hung out in the woods for long enough, I could prove its existence one way or another. My quest started at thirteen and it would take two long years of hanging out in those woods, which I would have been doing otherwise anyway, for me to find what I was looking for. Needless to say, though I greatly underestimated what I was dealing with and never captured proof for anyone but myself.

The day it happened is one I will never forget. I've since seen bigfoot in those woods about a handful of times, but that first time was by far the strangest and it's a memory that sticks out not only because of how odd it all was but also because I know what catching sight of one means, especially nowadays. I packed myself lunch and grabbed some buckets. I was going to try and catch some worms for fishing while I was out there. I had a tree out there that I built a little tree house, which wasn't much of a house really, using sticks and larger pieces of wood that I found. The tree house was quite high, and it overlooked the shore that if you walked through the woods, you would eventually get to. I never expected I would see bigfoot anywhere other than directly inside of the woods too, but that was another shocker. I was digging for worms, and I was close enough to the little beach that I could hear the waves crashing onto the shore, but it was still a long way away from where I was at that point. Everything was normal until I felt like there was someone standing behind me and I started to smell a horrible stench. I looked around but didn't see anyone or anything. I really felt like something was behind me and watching me but for the life of me I saw nothing at all. While looking around to see the reason why I was no longer alone in the forest, I noticed something else odd as well. I noticed that the entire forest seemed to have gone silent. I don't remember noticing exactly when it actually happened, but I noticed it when I felt another presence there with me. It was really creepy and the hair on the back of my neck and on my arms was standing straight up on end. I considered running back home, but I hadn't caught that many worms yet and something inside of me told me that then was my chance to see something out of the ordinary. Remember for two years up until that point I had been trying to obtain evidence that bigfoot existed. I stood up and walked over to a nearby giant tree that had been downed and sat on the stump. I just waited, watched, and listened. There was still total silence and I still felt like I wasn't alone out there anymore.

I tried to pretend like I didn't notice something was wrong or amiss and just started looking at the ground like I was about to go back to digging for worms at any moment. I saw the grass moving to the right of me even though there wasn't any breeze that day at all and from where I was sitting, I couldn't see anything there that would be parting it the way it was. It looked like something large was walking through it all but again, there was nothing there at all. I was scared and my heart started pounding because it was at that point, I knew for a fact that I wasn't alone out there. However, my mind couldn't make sense of what my eyes were seeing or of what it clearly knew at that point; that something invisible was there. Suddenly the birds were chirping again, nothing seemed to be moving around anymore and the feeling of being watched or of not being alone went away altogether. Once again, I thought that I should just go home but I was a precocious and curious teenager, and I wasn't about to just let it go. I needed to figure out what I was dealing with. I heard a really loud whooping noise. It sounded like something hollering and it almost sounded human. Once I heard the first sounds, which were coming from the direction of the shore, I heard the same noises echoing across the forest and through the trees, coming from all over the place. Whatever it was, there were several of them and they were communicating with one another. I ran over to my tree house and climbed up. I was as high as I could possibly go and looked all around. I didn't see anything until I looked over at the beach.

I couldn't believe my eyes as I watched a gigantic beast stand there as it looked around at first. It almost looked like it was making sure it wasn't being seen. It kept turning quickly from one side to the other before it would bend down and pull something out of the water and bring it to its mouth. It was either grabbing small fish, crabs, or clams. I couldn't be sure, but I watched in shock and sheer amazement at the sight. It had to have been about twelve feet tall and maybe five or six feet wide. I could see it very clearly from my vantage point, but it hadn't yet spotted me. I didn't think it would have been able to see me from where it was as I was really far away and so I boldly just stood there, without trying at all to conceal myself, watching this fantastic creature grab its food from the water. It was covered in brownish red fur, all over its body except for its face. Its face was tan colored but had no fur or hair on it. I could see it had large eyes and I think that they were black, but I really couldn't be sure because I wasn't close enough and I still have no real idea. I watched for about ten minutes before it stopped what it was doing again and looked directly at me. I really thought there was no way that it could see me, so I didn't duck or try to hide or anything I just stood there staring at it. It could see me though because it hollered over in my direction and, as though it were talking to or otherwise trying to communicate with something I couldn't see, it pointed up at me. I wanted to duck or get down from the tree stand and run as fast as I could back home, but my legs didn't seem to want to work. I was terrified and my heart sank as I realized it could see me. I bent over for a moment to try and stop myself from passing out and when I looked back up the creature was gone. Well, I could no longer see it anyway. I wanted to go to the beach and look and see if there were any fresh footprints before the tide came in and washed them all away. I didn't have a camera or anything with me but at that point I just needed to prove to myself that I wasn't crazy or seeing things. I needed to prove it to myself that bigfoot existed. There was no question in my mind at that point either of what I had just seen.

I climbed quickly down from the tree and started the somewhat treacherous hike to the beach. I noticed the path I was taking was the same one where I had seen the grass and trees parting and moving earlier, as though someone were walking through it when there was no one and nothing else there. It took me about twenty minutes but finally I made it to the beach. The second I exited the tree line and stepped a foot onto the shore, I felt that strange feeling again like I was being watched. There was no one and nothing there though. That horrible stench was back as I looked around and saw dozens of gigantic footprints all over the sand. There weren't any where I had seen the bigfoot though because the water had already washed them away. It had been standing with its feet in the water as it caught its meal. I was afraid to walk forward because I felt once again like I was being watched and like I wasn't alone. However, there were no other human beings and no animals as far as the eye could see. I heard a loud grunting noise coming from right about where I had seen the bigfoot before and that's when I knew that it was still there, that it had been there all along and that if I went any closer, I would then be approaching it. I also didn't think it was alone and knew somehow deep down inside that it had been a bigfoot that had invisibly walked past me while I was sitting on the stump, and it was more than likely just watching me as I dug for worms as I first recognized that I wasn't alone anymore in the forest.

I turned and ran as fast as I could back to my house. I left the bucket and all the worms I had collected, along with my lunch, in those woods. I never got them back. I was excited but I knew my mom and siblings might not believe me but was hopeful that my father would. However, by the time he got home from work that night it was too late to go trekking through the dark forest and so we waited until morning to walk together to the beach. When we got there nothing was left of the footprints, I had seen there the day before but both of us felt extremely uncomfortable in that area and like we were being watched. Also, I will never forget how strong that horrible smell was when we were out there that day and so many other times too when we were in the woods together or when I was all alone. That's how I always knew a bigfoot was around, even when I couldn't see one with my eyes. My dad believed me, and he would tell the story about when I saw bigfoot on his land, on the shore in the forest, to anyone who would listen. No one dared question or mock him because it would have been considered disrespectful, but I don't think many people believed him. He believed me though and before long he was joining me on my excursions into the woods as much as possible and it didn't take long for us to see one of them while we were together. It was absolutely fascinating and while I know they exist all over the world nowadays, I think Alaska is the perfect place to find one because it really is the last frontier and there is so much untouched land here, even today. I think I figured out and bore witness to a lot of the reason why no one can ever seem to catch a good picture or video and why they aren't able to catch any sort of evidence of its existence and that's that it can disappear or phase out at will. I also believe they make their own portals wherever they stand if they need to and that that's how they get out of there when they feel like a human is threatening them or even just trying to capture photographic or video evidence. Honestly, I think someone trying to catch any evidence of them is threatening in and of itself to a bigfoot but that's just my opinion. I will write about more of my encounters and experiences as well. Just thought that my first experience would be a great place to start.

CHAPTER SEVEN

BACK IN AUGUST OF 1985, during the tranquil evening hours around twilight, an extraordinary event unfolded while my brothers and I were strolling along the railroad tracks behind our house, heading towards Fort Wayne. Now, Fort Wayne may seem like an unlikely place for a bigfoot sighting, but regardless, I'm here to recount what we witnessed that day.

As we leisurely walked, engaged in animated conversation, and indulged in the classic boyish pastime of throwing rocks, little did we know that our usual track exploration was about to take an unexpected turn. I was just twelve years old at the time, and my oldest brother's keen eyesight caught something peculiar, something that stood out amidst our familiar surroundings. We were well acquainted with these tracks and could instantly tell when something didn't belong. Curiosity piqued, we continued walking towards the enigmatic sight, still oblivious to the significance of what lay before us.

In the waning light of the evening, it appeared to be nothing more than a large mound of black dirt nestled on the left side of the tracks, not far from the rails. Without giving it much thought, we approached it while engrossed in our chatter, absentmindedly kicking stones along the way. Drawing closer, perhaps within a range of 100 to 150 feet, an astonishing sight unfolded before our eyes, shattering our sense of normalcy. To our utter surprise, the mound abruptly stood up, towering on two legs—a colossal figure, easily reaching a height of 7 to 8 feet. With an incredible display of power, it effortlessly cleared a double set of railroad tracks in just two massive strides, swiftly vanishing into the depths of the wooded ravine on the right side of the tracks.

The magnitude of what we had witnessed struck us like a bolt of lightning. It was as if time had slowed down, imprinting every detail of that awe-inspiring moment into our memories. The creature we saw was undeniably tall, standing at a towering height of 7 to 8 feet, its imposing figure defying any logical explanation. Its upper body was massive and robust, leaving an indelible impression on our young minds.

In a surge of adrenaline-fueled terror, we instinctively turned on our heels and sprinted home as fast as our legs could carry us. Bursting through the door, we breathlessly recounted the encounter to our father, seeking solace and reassurance. As fathers often do, he offered a plausible explanation, assuring us that it was probably just a deer. In the moment, I accepted his explanation, despite the fact that I had never witnessed a deer standing upright on two legs, effortlessly traversing a double set of railroad tracks. However, even to this day, I cannot conclusively claim that it was indeed bigfoot that we encountered. The fleeting glimpse we caught of the creature didn't provide us with a clear view, nor did it emit any of the spine-chilling howls or distinctive sounds commonly associated with such encounters. Nevertheless, one thing remained undeniable—it was an entity unlike any animal we had ever seen before. Perhaps it was merely a man, but if so, he should have secured a place in the record books for his extraordinary abilities.

Allow me to paint a picture of the surroundings to give you a better sense of the setting. The area encompassed the railroad tracks, which were accompanied by gentle slopes and adorned with patches of grass and clusters of small bushes on the left side. On the right side, a stretch of woodland flourished, complete with a slight ravine adding depth to the landscape. There, nestled amidst the woods, you could find a small creek meandering its way alongside a serene pond, enhancing the natural allure of the area.

Once our father was notified of our astonishing encounter, he, like any concerned parent, listened attentively to our tale, offering both his support and a sense of rationality. But deep down, we knew that what we had witnessed that fateful evening went far beyond the realm of ordinary. It left an indelible mark on our young lives, forever fueling our curiosity and leaving us with a sense of wonder about the mysteries that lie just beyond the veil of the known.

CHAPTER EIGHT

AS A LAW ENFORCEMENT OFFICER, my commitment to truth and integrity is unwavering. I have no reason to fabricate or exaggerate what I witnessed, and quite frankly, I couldn't care less if anyone believes me. Throughout my career, I've come across stories and rumors of strange phenomena, but I never paid them much attention. It's not that I didn't believe, but rather, I adopted a "seeing is believing" approach.

It happened on a sweltering evening, just after or before Labor Day in 2007. The darkness had descended, roughly around 8:30 or 9:00 PM, although the western sky still retained a faint glimmer, characteristic of that time of year. I was on patrol, driving westbound on Highway 128, leaving Cloverdale behind, responding to a routine alarm call at a ranch property. Such calls were commonplace in my line of work.

As a law enforcement officer, you develop an acute awareness of your surroundings. You notice things that are out of place—a car parked where it wasn't the day before, a person walking along a desolate road, lights emanating from a closed business. These details catch your eye, often escaping the notice of ordinary passersby. And so, as I was driving westbound, something caught my attention—a figure emerging from the ravine and stepping onto the roadside. I can't quite describe it, but I caught a glimpse of movement amidst the brush and instantly knew it was a person. People frequently try to evade us, so my initial thought was that I had startled someone who might be cultivating marijuana in the woods—a common occurrence in these parts. I could discern the outline of a body, and as my headlights reflected off its eyes, it swiftly retreated into the undergrowth before I could pass by.

Believing it to be someone attempting to avoid detection, I slammed on the brakes and promptly reversed my vehicle. That's when I witnessed it in the beams of my headlights. Standing at a height of approximately 6 to 7 feet, it possessed a thick, matted coat of brown fur and walked upright. Although I didn't catch a glimpse of its face as it was facing away from me, the sight left me dumbfounded, just like everyone else who has had a similar encounter. I couldn't believe my eyes. It was certainly not something I was willing to relay over the radio. There were dense branches and overgrown foliage obstructing my view, but there was no mistaking what I had witnessed.

Two details remain etched vividly in my memory. Firstly, the creature had small leaves and grass entwined within its fur all over its back. I observed this as it slowly walked away from me. The image remains seared in my mind. Secondly, I distinctly remember its deliberate and unhurried movements. It proceeded with calculated steps, using its arm to brush aside small branches and twigs obstructing its path. I had the creature in my line of sight from the rear for a significant 4 to 5 seconds before it vanished once again into the thick vegetation. I found myself stepping out of my car, standing there in silence for approximately 2 to 3 minutes, with the engine turned off. I could hear the same measured movements, the unmistakable crunch of leaves and twigs, echoing from the depths below. It seemed to be making its way toward the nearby creek area. Each time the sounds ceased and I contemplated returning to my vehicle, a distant "crunch" would reach my ears, compelling me to linger a little longer, listening intently.

The ravine harbored a creek, and it was evident that the creature had retreated back to that secluded enclave.

Needless to say, I kept my encounter to myself. It was not a matter to be discussed during briefings or recorded in the patrol blotter. Sharing such an experience would undoubtedly have made for an uncomfortable and challenging career. I toyed with the idea of reaching out to one of our Fish and Game Officers, but considering that he was acquainted with many of my colleagues, I decided to maintain my silence. Reading the accounts of others on various forums reassures me that I'm not alone. While I've never encountered a ghost, UFO, or anything of that nature, this experience has opened my eyes to the possibilities that lie beyond the realms of our everyday understanding. It begs the question of what else is out there, lurking just beyond the boundaries of our laughter and skepticism.

CHAPTER NINE

IT WAS that time of the year again, my visit to my summer home in Nakina. Being where I grew up, I made a point to visit at least once a year to go camping, fishing and enjoy the lush forests and lakes. It started off as every other trip did but finished unexpectedly.

I drove into town, music blaring loudly as my girlfriend, and I sang along to the lyrics we knew by heart. We turned down the side road leading to the subdivision where our house resided. Seeing the playground there brought back many fond memories from when I was younger. We pulled into the driveway, and I started to unpack everything while my girlfriend went into the house to air out the place. I brought in our suitcases and set them at the top of the stairs, making my way behind my girlfriend looking out the large front window. I wrapped my arms around her and kissed her head. I could feel her smile as she grabbed my arm. We spoke for a bit to make plans on what we were going to do before splitting off. I chose to run to the northern store in town to pick up some things while she would stay at the house and tidy up. I took a minute to drive there as the wave after wave of nostalgia ran over me. An old restaurant I would hang out at, the train station cafe and many others.

I walked into the Northern, where I was greeted by an old friend of my grandfather. My grandfather spent most of his life there and that was the main reason I was there as well. The friend recognized me from a few years back and asked how I was doing and wanted to know what I had been up to. I explained how I was going camping up on stinger lake. It was my favorite place to fish growing up. He told me a story about when he was younger and driving down the road that led to stinger. He was going fast, but he was sure he saw sasquatch. I thought it was crazy but said how cool that was and that I would keep my eyes open. We said farewell and I went back to shopping. It didn't take me long to get everything before I went back home.

After I got back, I brought everything into the house, kissed my girlfriend and headed back out to get the boat into the back of the truck. Luckily the small twelve-footer we used was light and I had no problem lifting it in and strapping it down. I put in the gas tank and motor before going in and grabbing all our stuff to bring it out. Once everything was loaded, we locked the house again and shot off towards our launch site. It was a bit of a drive, but with the windows down and more music, it felt quick, we arrived and backed down the slope, getting out, I unstrapped the boat and slid it off the truck and into the river. My girlfriend parked the truck off to the side as I got everything ready. My girlfriend came down, hopped into the boat and I pushed us off, jumping in.

The short trip through the river was one of stingers best qualities, all the lush greenery untouched by anyone. We reached the mouth of the river, marked by two trees crossed over. As soon as we cleared it, I lowered the engine fully into the water and we took off. It was around a thirty-minute boat ride to our usual campsite, we saw a couple of moose, a cow and a calf, along the way. But otherwise, we simply enjoyed the sun and wind.

I cut the engine as we reached our destination, jumping to the front of the boat and out, I pulled it up onto shore, tying it to a tree so that it wouldn't go off leaving us stranded. We quickly got everything out of the boat and started setting up camp, I left my girlfriend with the tent and took out the tarp. There were boards nailed to the tree to set up a roof over where we kept the food and mini gas stove. Once that was hanging, I helped finish up the tent and we started a small fire. We grabbed some hotdogs and decided to roast some for lunch. While we were sitting beside the fire, we heard rustling in the bushes behind us. We both turned around quickly and peered into the brush, but whatever made the sound must have gone away quickly since we weren't able to see anything aside from trees and darkness. We didn't think much of it and turned back towards the fire, finishing up our lunch and putting everything away. It was around two pm at this point and my girlfriend wanted to go fishing. Now that the camp was fully set up, I had no problem with that, and we hopped back into the boat. Stinger is a relatively shallow lake and the best way to fish there was to troll, so when we got out further on the lake, I put the motor on low and we began casting out lines. Lady luck was always on my girlfriend's side when we fished together, and that time was no different. To every one fish I caught, my girlfriend would catch three. We kept a few to have supper tonight, but most were tossed back, taking lots of photos, my girlfriend kissing the first as was the ritual.

As the sun began to lower on the horizon, my girlfriend started to get tired and so we decided to call it quits. When we made it back to shore, I tied up the boat, lifted my girlfriend and brought her to the tent, I kissed her and told her she could nap while I cleaned the fish and prepared dinner. She smiled; told me she loved me before settling in. I closed the tent and went back to the boat to collect the fish. I grabbed the filet knife out of my bag and made quick work of the fish. I put the perfect filets onto a plate and made sure to toss the entrails into the lake. It was the best way to keep wild animals like bears away. I cleaned the blood from the board and grabbed my fish batter, I filled a pot with some cooking oil and began properly coating the filets as I waited for the oil to start boiling. Once it did, I tossed in the filets and put some rice on to cook as well. It didn't take long for both to finish, adding a few more logs on the fire and making up the plates of food.

It was seven by this point and I went to wake my girlfriend, slowly stirring her awake with a kiss on the head, I gave our usual, good morning sleepy head, greeting before stepping back out, as I was stretching from being crouched down, I couldn't help but notice a fallen tree off to the side of camp heading inland. I didn't notice it before and upon closer inspection, it looked as though something pushed it over. I tried looking deeper in, but with the sun mostly gone, it was impossible to see anything. I heard movement at the tent and turned around, I made my way over and passed my girlfriend a plate. Enjoying the flaky taste of fresh fish, it had been too long since I had enjoyed this and savored every bite.

Once we finished eating, we tossed our paper plates into the fire and shuffled closer together. I wrapped my arm around my girlfriend's shoulder. We sat like that and listened to the soft sounds of nature as the sun finally vanished for the day, leaving nothing but the small circle of light from the fire and pitch darkness beyond. I kissed her head and suggested we settle in for the night, pouring some water onto the fire, I made sure everything was properly packed up and crawled in after her. We had set a sleeping bag on the ground as cushioning, another on top as a blanket, getting into my pajamas, I crawled in next to my girlfriend and wrapped my arms around her. I wished her a good night and we both slowly drifted off, cuddled in each other's arms. A loud rustling woke me up, I could feel my girlfriend still breathing steadily in her sleep and so checked my watch, it was two in the morning. I looked around the tent, and that is when I heard it again, loud rustling just outside the tent. A bear, I thought to myself and tried to take some deep breaths to calm my heart, but I failed to do so as the rustling got louder. I refused to move. Each passing moment felt like a lifetime. I heard my girlfriend grumble and thought she had awoken, but when I checked, she was still asleep. At this point, the rustling was right outside the tent. Whatever it was, I could hear its breathing, each breath labored and heavy. I held my breath as I heard some brush up against the tent, waiting for it to break in as it stopped. But after what felt like forever, it finally stepped away and I could hear it rummaging through the camp. I watched as something solid hit the tent, making me jump.

The jump caused my girlfriend to stir awake and I quickly put my hand over her mouth to stop her from saying anything. I whispered softly that something was outside and she must have heard it as well, since she stopped moving. It continued making a ruckus for a bit longer before it finally left. I sighed in relief and finally let go of my girlfriend. She turned to me and asked me what that was. I told her I didn't know but most likely a bear. Since they weren't uncommon in these parts of the woods. We laid there in silence and listened in case it came back, but as the sun began to rise, there were no more incidents.

I slowly opened the zipper to the front door once it was bright enough for us to see without issue, popping my head out of the hole. I looked around the camp but didn't see anything amiss aside from our food being tossed all over. I opened the door the rest of the way and crawled out of the tent. Stretching as I took a better look around. The cooler holding all of our food was opened, the lid tossed far to the side. Most of the food was out and tossed all over the place, a lot of the meat we brought like sausages and bacon were gone. The heavy thing that hit the tent before was a pack of hotdogs, left relatively untouched, I checked that the water was fine and gave the okay for my girlfriend to come out. She crawled out shortly after and saw the mess. She helped me collect everything and clean up. We checked everything and luckily a lot that had been tossed aside was still good to use and eat. I put a kettle on to boil and sat down with my girlfriend to discuss what we wanted to do. Bears were in the area, but if we were careful, they weren't a threat. So, we could stay, But if she didn't want to, I was ok with heading back. I heard the kettle go off and got up, making some tea. I passed a mug of it to my girlfriend and waited for her choice.

After some thought we decided to give it one more day and then we would cut the trip a day short. We had traveled so far to do this; it would be a waste to cut the trip so short. I kissed her head and nodded before getting up to grab some wood, leaving her to drink her tea. I did a quick walk around along the edge of the clearing and collected some sticks. When I got to the section where the tree had been knocked over, I noticed that it had been moved from where it was before. I put my hand on it and crouched down to look at the ground. It was soft and muddy, easy to leave prints and what I saw made my blood run cold, instead of bear paws, like I was expecting, I saw a large human shaped foot, bigger than I had ever seen before. The distinct imprint of toes clearly visible in the deep imprint. I shot up and looked around into the forest but didn't see anything aside from the trees. I quickly walked back to where my girlfriend was putting away her cup and I told her that I felt perhaps it was better to go back today. After everything that happened, I didn't want to risk anything happening to her. She asked me what was wrong and so I brought her over to the imprint, telling her about what my grandfather's friend told me about his seeing sasquatch around here a few years back. She laughed asking if I was playing a joke on her. Her reasoning was that sasquatch was always spotted deep in the States, never in northern Ontario. I shook my head, telling her it wasn't a joke. She looked partially confused at first and then slowly nodded, agreeing with me that we should head back.

My girlfriend quickly got to work on packing up all the food and cooking items we brought. While I worked on emptying the tent before taking it down. As I was finishing up on the tent, we both heard rustling off to our right, in the direction of the fallen tree. We both stopped what we were doing and turned towards the sound. It was hard to see deep into the bush, and I thought it was nothing before spotting movement out of the corner of my eye. I turned to look at it and urged my girlfriend to start loading things into the boat. I could hear her behind me, continuing to keep a close eye on where I saw movement. I didn't see anything else moving and slowly stood up, I grabbed the tent bag and took a step back. I felt a hand on my arm and jumped in fear, whirling around, I saw my girlfriend who said the boat was full and ready. I took her hand and started to walk towards the boat when I was stopped by my girlfriend's face.

It had gone completely pale, looking at something behind me. I slowly turned and what I saw, I will never forget. A man, but much taller than any man I had ever seen, covered in thick fur, its face distorted like a cross between a bear and a monkey with long sharp teeth and deep brown eyes. I sucked in a breath and slowly began backing away, pulling my girlfriend along and trying not to make any sudden movements. I quickly checked behind me and noticed we were close to the boat, turning back towards the creature, it had taken a step forward, now in the clearing with us. Luckily it was still only watching as I began untying the boat, my girlfriend climbing in. I put the tent down gently and gave the boat a soft push, it barely budged. I silently cursed and took a deep breath. I silently counted to three, still watching the creature before turning and pushing as hard as I could. The boat slid free of the ground and into the water, I leapt into the boat as I heard the creature start running towards us. I grabbed the paddle and with a few heavy strokes pushed us a good way away from the shoreline. I turned and looked back, the creature stopping at the edge of the water and screeched at us. It sounded like nails on a chalkboard. I began pulling the cord to start the engine. First try nothing, second try, still nothing. I grabbed the small pump on the gas hose and pumped it a few times. I heard a splash off to our left, the creature tried to throw a stick at us but luckily it landed in the water.

The third try finally brought the engine to life. I quickly turned it to full throttle as my girlfriend and I took off down the lake. We sat in silence until we reached the boat launch. I got out and pulled the boat up, checking on my girlfriend who was shaken up, otherwise fine. We quickly got the truck loaded and drove back to town. On our drive we decided to tell everyone we called the trip early because of a bear, who would believe us if we told them we saw bigfoot. We spent the rest of our vacation at the house, not going out for anything aside from trips to the store and the library to rent a couple movies. We went back home not long after and never again brought it up until now. Ever since then we have never gone back to stinger lake, still taking our yearly trips to Nakina, but always staying at the house.

CHAPTER TEN

BACK IN APPROXIMATELY 1984, when I was just a seven-year-old child, I experienced a profoundly intense encounter that remains etched in my memory to this day. It happened quite unexpectedly while I was engrossed in play within the depths of the woods. Little did I know that this innocent adventure would lead me to cross paths with something unimaginable. Startled by my sudden presence, the creature and I found ourselves locked in a chilling stare, mere feet apart, for what felt like an eternity, but was likely only a minute or so. My body was frozen in fear, unable to move or even utter a sound. Then, with a thunderous roar, it broke the spell, jolting me out of my petrified state. Without a second thought, I fled as fast as my legs could carry me, never daring to glance back until I reached the safety of my home, where I struggled to put into words the harrowing encounter that had just unfolded.

What struck me as particularly unique about this encounter was our vantage points. We were situated on a steep incline, with me positioned above and the creature below. As a result, our respective heights were somewhat adjusted, bringing us closer to eye level. Even from my elevated position, looking somewhat downward at the creature, it did nothing to diminish its immense size and intimidating presence.

The memory of that encounter replays in my mind like an unchanging tape, haunting me for over three decades. Even now, every time the recollection resurfaces, it leaves me trembling inside. At that tender age, I had never heard of Bigfoot or any similar creature. What stood before me was simply a monster—a real, terrifying monster. I resided in a small, rural town in Southeastern Wisconsin, a place where the notion of such creatures seemed utterly inconceivable. It was the 80s, a time before the internet and before cable television graced our homes. It wasn't until years later, when cable finally arrived, that I stumbled upon a TV show featuring Bigfoot. As I witnessed the depictions on the screen, I was struck with absolute certainty that what I had encountered all those years ago was exactly the same creature. It defied logic, as my rational mind argued that these beings, if they truly existed, should only reside in vast wilderness areas like the Pacific Northwest or Alaska. I believed that it would be impossible for them to go unnoticed in an area like Wisconsin, devoid of mountains that could provide more inaccessible territories. In an attempt to rationalize my experience, I tried to convince myself that what I saw was a bear. Yet, the face of the creature remained vividly etched in my mind, and deep down, I knew with absolute certainty that there was a 0% chance it was a bear.

One depiction that closely resembles what I saw is a sketch I once came across, which you had posted, featuring two variations of gigantopithecus side by side—one labeled "temperate" and the other labeled "tropical." The temperate depiction bears a striking resemblance to what I encountered. However, I must clarify that many other depictions of gigantopithecus that I have come across do not resemble what I saw. They more closely resemble conventional apes rather than bipedal creatures. The characteristics that resonate with my memory include the hooded nose, the small eyes positioned closely together, the prominent brow ridge, the upright posture, the extensive hair coverage and length, the broad shoulders with a forward-set head giving the appearance of a "no neck," and the long arms reminiscent of primates. Moreover, there is something about the facial expression that evokes a sense of familiarity. However, I must admit that what I witnessed was simply far "uglier" than any depiction I have come across.

As the years have passed, I have often pondered the significance of that encounter. It has fueled my curiosity and ignited a desire to explore the uncharted territories that lie beyond the boundaries of our understanding. While I cannot provide concrete proof or claim to have all the answers, I remain steadfast in my conviction that what I encountered was a creature that defies our conventional knowledge—a being that continues to roam the fringes of our known world, leaving us to wonder what other mysteries lie in wait, concealed by our own skepticism.

CHAPTER ELEVEN

I'VE BEEN GRAPPLING with a dilemma lately, uncertain about whether I should share the incredible experience that has been weighing on my mind. On one hand, there is a strong desire within me to confide in someone, to express the profound encounter that has left me awe-struck. On the other hand, the mere thought of describing what I saw makes me question my own sanity, fearing that I might be perceived as a delusional individual. But I can no longer suppress the need to share my story and seek validation.

Over the years, I've immersed myself in a plethora of shows and documentaries, eagerly absorbing every piece of information related to extraordinary phenomena. However, despite my extensive exposure to these accounts, I have yet to come across a description that aligns with what I witnessed.

To put it frankly, what I saw defies categorization. It was an enigmatic figure, a towering presence resembling a very muscular old man with pronounced physical features. Its prominent brow ridge, large mouth, receding hairline, and the entirety of its body covered in a patchwork of brown and gray hair, some parts even translucent. Its most striking characteristic was its incredible height, standing at approximately 7 feet tall. And that's not all. There was something else, a fleeting glimpse of movement behind cover—a sight that revealed golden blonde hair, almost luminous in its radiance.

It's important to emphasize that this entity bore an uncanny resemblance to a man, not an ape or a gorilla. The clarity with which I saw it cannot be denied. From a mere 30 feet away, without any obstructions hindering my view, I observed it in broad daylight. I witnessed the astonishing moment when it rose to its full height, pivoted gracefully, and executed two one-footed jumps that carried it effortlessly into the depths of the surrounding woods, spanning an impressive distance of 20 feet. One of these leaps even involved launching itself onto and off the side of a standing tree, akin to a skilled parkour runner navigating an obstacle or attempting to clear an imaginary gap.

I can already anticipate the skepticism and confusion my account might elicit. Yes, I've heard the term "dirty apes" used before, and I am familiar with the iconic footage from the '60s or '70s that often comes to mind when discussing these elusive creatures. However, what I encountered bears no resemblance to those representations. It defied the conventional imagery associated with Sasquatch or other similar entities. Instead, what stood before me was an extraordinary, mind-boggling sight—an agile and athletic 7-foot-tall naked figure, covered from head to toe in a thick coat of hair, roaming the woods at the early hour of 5:45 in the morning. It sounds utterly unbelievable, I know, but I swear on my own sanity that this is what I witnessed.

And now, I find myself grappling with the question of whether this encounter falls within the realm of a Sasquatch sighting or if it belongs to an entirely different classification of extraordinary beings. The uncertainty gnaws at me, fueling my desire to seek feedback and validation from those who may possess a deeper understanding of these mysteries.

If you have any insights or guidance to offer, I would be immensely grateful. It is essential for me to navigate through this labyrinth of uncertainty, to find solace in knowing that I am not alone in this extraordinary encounter and that there are others who can shed light on the enigma I have experienced.

CHAPTER TWELVE

IT WAS SEPTEMBER 30, 2013, and I found myself driving along Route 109, halfway between Hoquiam and Ocean Shores in Washington. I had just finished my visit to Hoquiam and was heading back to my home in Ocean Shores when an unexpected encounter would forever etch itself into my memory.

As I continued along the road, a deer suddenly darted across, heading south, about an eighth of a mile ahead of me. Being familiar with the behavior of these creatures, I knew that where there was one deer, there was often another close behind. I instinctively slowed down, exercising caution. However, what appeared next left me completely dumbfounded.

Instead of a second deer, an entirely different figure emerged from the edge of the road. This figure, a male being, sprinted across the road with astonishing speed, covering the distance in just three strides. I was taken aback, my mind racing to comprehend what I was witnessing. I brought my vehicle to a complete stop, utterly shocked by the surreal sight before me.

This enigmatic being reached the top of the roadside berm and turned to face me. In that moment, our eyes locked, and a rush of unsettling emotions coursed through me. His grin was unmistakably menacing, leaving me with an undeniable sense of threat. Without further hesitation, he pivoted back around and vanished into the dense brush that lined the roadside.

I had just encountered a Sasquatch, up close and personal. The encounter was so intimate that I could have reached out and touched him, as my car window was rolled down, placing me no more than 20 feet away. His facial features were remarkably human-like, except for the absence of a chin and a pronounced brow ridge. His nose, though human in shape, possessed a slightly European rather than African appearance. Piercing black eyes met my gaze, while his skin and hair exhibited shades of gray. The remnants of teeth he revealed were akin to those of a human, albeit in a severely deteriorated condition. It was clear that oral hygiene was not a priority for him.

Observing his movements provided further insight into his uniqueness. When he ran, his palms faced downward, unlike our upright thumbs-up position. And when he stood upright, his palms were oriented backward, in contrast to the forward-facing thumbs of a human. Additionally, his arms appeared slightly longer than those of a typical human, though not excessively so—merely half a hand's length beyond what one might expect. As the encounter unfolded during midday, with the sun casting its rays from the south, I could discern the shape of his head through the hair. Although the hair rose significantly, giving the impression of a pointed head, the underlying structure was undeniably human. Roughly estimating his height, I would venture to say he stood between 7 to 8 feet tall. Unfortunately, the encounter transpired too swiftly for me to capture photographic evidence. It was a fleeting moment, but one that would forever remain vivid in my mind.

Furthermore, there were additional peculiarities that caught my attention. As previously mentioned, his hands turned inward more than a human's, and his arms exhibited a slight elongation. The face, nose, and teeth resembled those of a human, while the absence of a chin further distinguished his appearance. These details served to further cement the profound uniqueness of this remarkable being.

Since that fateful day, I have replayed the encounter countless times in my mind, attempting to reconcile the disbelief and awe that gripped me. It was a remarkable experience, one that defied conventional explanations and expanded my understanding of the world around me.

Thank you for allowing me to share.

CHAPTER THIRTEEN

LET me take you back to May 21, 2011, a day that will forever be etched in my memory. It was on this day that I had a confirmed sighting, an encounter that shook me to my core. But before I delve into the details of that momentous event, I must mention the strange occurrences that have been unfolding in this area since 2010, setting the stage for what was to come.

As I recount this experience, please bear with me as my emotions are still raw and my recollection vivid. Every moment of that encounter remains etched in my mind, as if it happened just yesterday. I remember the uncertainty that filled me, the fear mingled with curiosity, as I grappled with the anticipation of what this mysterious creature would do next. It stood a mere 50 yards away from me, observing my every move. I watched intently as it swiftly maneuvered behind some thick brush near a colossal boulder on the hill, its gaze fixed upon me.

Allow me to paint a picture of what I witnessed. The creature stood tall, measuring between 6 to 7 feet in height. Its head had an ovalish shape, framed by reddish to dark brown fur. I vividly recall the sunlight glinting off its broad shoulders, which were as substantial as those of a linebacker donning full gear. Its eyes, amber-brown in color, stared straight into my soul, unyielding and penetrating. The creature possessed a flat face, and its long, matted hair exuded an air of wildness. It felt as though those immense eyes were peering through me, leaving me paralyzed in fear until the surge of adrenaline finally spurred me into action.

Without a moment's hesitation, I ran. I hurled myself down the hill, approximately 8 feet above the road, desperate to reach the safety of my car. I called out to my friend, who was with me by the river, urging them to join me immediately. "Get into the car now," I pleaded, my voice trembling with urgency. We needed to leave, to escape the presence that had shaken us to our very core. I didn't stop until I reached the sanctuary of my home, far away from the haunting depths of those woods. It was supposed to be a day of leisure, swimming, and fishing along the tranquil waters of the Applegate River. Yet, our time there was cut short, lasting no more than an hour. The proximity of the encounter to my home, a mere 60 miles away, rendered the trip seemingly wasteful in terms of time and gas. The adrenaline coursing through my veins propelled me to speed back home, my foot heavy on the accelerator.

You may wonder why I am so certain that this encounter was no ordinary encounter with a bear or a cougar. Allow me to clarify. A bear would have swiftly vanished into the depths of the woods before I even registered its presence, as they possess a keen awareness of their surroundings. Similarly, a mountain lion would have likely chosen a different fate for me, making it impossible for me to share this account. No, what I witnessed that day was something entirely different. It was a creature that defied the natural order, for it stood upright on two legs. Growing up amidst the wilderness and forests of the Pacific Northwest, I have encountered countless creatures that inhabit our planet. Yet, this being was like nothing I had ever seen before, except in the grainy videos capturing elusive sightings. It resembled Patty, the infamous figure captured on film, forever etched in the annals of Bigfoot lore. The encounter left me unsettled, unsure if it meant harm. But to me, in that moment, it exuded an undeniable sense of threat.

It is important to note that there have been many unspoken sightings in the Red Buttes Wilderness, an expansive region stretching from the Oregon/California border to Highway 96 in Siskyou County. This area encompasses Saied Valley, Happy Camp, Indian Creek Road, Oregon Caves National Monument, and countless other locations. I stumbled upon a report shared by a hippy farmer from Talkemla, who revealed a deeply ingrained understanding of the Bigfoot phenomenon. He and his companions, from their earliest days, had been warned about the presence of these enigmatic creatures in the area. According to him, they are highly territorial and known to be aggressive. Venturing into this domain means subjecting oneself to the possibility, or rather the danger, of encountering one of these elusive beings.

So, as I share my story with you, I do so not just to recount my personal encounter, but also to shed light on the broader tapestry of sightings and unspoken experiences that have woven themselves into the fabric of this region. We find ourselves at the threshold of an ancient mystery, one that demands our attention and exploration. It is my hope that by sharing my account, I can contribute to the collective knowledge surrounding these elusive creatures and perhaps unravel a fragment of the enigma that has haunted these lands for generations.

CHAPTER FOURTEEN

FOUR YEARS AGO, in late August 2019, my family and I made the decision to go camping on our property which happens to border federal and BLM land.

Our property is beautiful but the BLM land has a splendor we all love. It's a nature reserve, teeming with wildlife. It's not uncommon to encounter deer, turkey, foxes, and a variety of other indigenous animals, who have grown so accustomed to human presence that they willingly approach for hand-feeding. The area boasts a strict no-hunting policy, allowing these creatures to flourish undisturbed. Among its notable features are the labyrinthine caves and babbling creeks that crisscross the landscape. In fact, the creek bordering our property holds historical significance, having been named by none other than Squire Boone and frequented by the Boone family. Further-more, abandoned mills, remnants of a bygone era, silently narrate their stories, with some even having been constructed by Abraham Lincoln's father. It is within this rich tapestry of natural wonders and American history that our camping adventure unfolded.

As we set up camp that evening, an unusual occurrence caught our attention. We noticed rocks rolling on the ground at various points during the night. Initially, I worried that someone might be lurking in the woods, deliberately throwing stones. However, given the remote and rural nature of our community, such an event would have been highly unlikely.

Adding to our perplexity was the presence of a haunting sound, reverberating through the night. It resembled a mix between a woman's scream and a wolf's howl, far deeper and louder than the familiar yelps of foxes we were accustomed to hearing.

As the hour grew late, my children grew weary and decided to retire to their tent. My eldest son insisted on using his own dome camping tent, a decision that made me feel uneasy, despite our seemingly safe surroundings. To alleviate my concerns, I requested that he position his tent within direct view of our family tent's window, allowing me to keep a watchful eye on him.

Exhausted, I entered my own tent after extinguishing the fire, seeking solace in its warmth while awaiting the arrival of dawn. The time was approximately 2 a.m.

Suddenly, a peculiar sound emanated from outside the tent, originating from the depths of the surrounding woods. I discerned a cracking noise accompanied by heavy footsteps trampling through the grass. The sequence went, "WHOOOSH thump WHOOOSH thump WHOOOOSH THUMP," prompting a chuckle to escape my lips. I assumed it was a deer or raccoons, their arrival coinciding with our retreat to slumber. However, my amusement was short-lived, for the sound was distinctly bipedal. Moreover, an unpleasant odor wafted into the air—an amalgamation of wet dog and skunk, reminiscent of the pungency one encounters in an elephant pen at the zoo. Suddenly, my tent began to jolt as if being repeatedly bumped from the outside. The creature continued its relentless advance, heading directly toward my son's tent. Without warning, the unimaginable occurred—my son's entire tent lifted off the ground, suspended in the air as if weightless. It shook violently, while my son screamed in terror, desperately pleading for it to stop. It's important to note that my other son, who was 14 at the time, had fallen ill and retired early due to him not feeling well. It was inconceivable that this massive entity could be my son, considering the tent was elevated several feet above the ground.

Fearful for my son's life I shouted loudly for it to go away.

In response to my outcry, the creature abruptly released the tent, causing it to crash back to the ground. It swiftly retraced its steps, running with astonishing speed toward my tent, which once again became the target of its forceful bumps. Then, with a resounding "WHOOSH thump" and the unmistakable sound of branches breaking, it vanished into the depths of the woods.

My son immediately sought refuge in my tent, and together, we phoned my husband, who was returning home from his night shift job.

Fast forward to the next year, mid-October 2020. My son and daughter were outside our home when an overpowering stench enveloped them. Even with both garage doors wide open, the putrid odor permeated the air. Curiosity piqued, my son ventured out to investigate the source of the foul smell. To our astonishment, an enormous creature, draped in dark fur with its eyes illuminated by the porch lights, stood in the middle of our yard—merely ten feet away from the very spot where the tent incident had unfolded four years prior.

In a moment of realization, my other son approached me and declared that the description of this creature matched precisely what he and his friend had encountered near our creek. It had been hunched over at the water's edge, but as they drew closer, it swiftly rose onto two legs and briskly retreated into the depths of the woods.

As someone who typically requires concrete evidence before embracing extraordinary claims, I must confess that I have now become a believer. This journey has transformed me, unveiling a realm of mystery and wonder that lies just beyond the veil of our everyday existence.

CHAPTER FIFTEEN

WHAT I'M about to detail took place in the early 1970s. I have refrained from sharing it often and have told others who write or talk about this sort of thing. I wanted to share with you in the event you want to put it in your book.

————

We had parked the truck and decided to take a break from our hunting expedition. Placing our lunch on the hood of the vehicle, we stood around, occasionally pacing, as we enjoyed our meal. The road leading to the ramp was newly constructed, about 25 feet wide, and flanked by cleared timber spanning approximately 30 to 40 feet on each side. From the ramp, the road stretched straight ahead for a good 400 yards.

The day was perfect for hunting, with the sun shining brightly and clear skies above. The air was filled with the melodious songs of birds, adding to the serenity of the moment. As we savored our meal and basked in the beauty of our surroundings, an unpleasant odor suddenly assailed our senses. It was a putrid stench akin to that of an outhouse. We scanned the area, trying to locate the source, but nothing unusual came into view.

However, the stench grew increasingly intense, prompting us to gaze down the road. To our astonishment, we spotted a dark figure, human-like in shape but far too large to be a man, traversing the clearing about 200 to 250 yards away from us. The creature emerged from the woods along the river, moving deliberately with long strides. What struck us most was the way it held its forearms parallel to the ground, as if carrying something, although we couldn't discern any object in its grasp. The witness suggested that due to the creature's midsection being covered in long hair, it might have concealed a small animal, held close to its body and blending with its fur color.

Remarkably, the creature never acknowledged our presence and swiftly crossed the cleared area and roadbed. It took mere seconds for it to traverse the entire opening. Its stride left a lasting impression on us, as each step covered an impressive distance of over eight feet, all without any signs of running. In just around 12 steps, the creature disappeared into the depths of the woods.

Feeling a sense of unease, my father retrieved his shotgun from the truck's cab, loaded it, and placed it on the hood. He kept a watchful eye on the woods while we finished our lunch, but we didn't catch sight of the creature again. Later that afternoon, we returned the boat to the river and continued hunting until darkness fell, encountering no further incidents.

As for the creature's description, it stood at a towering height of over eight feet, possibly even reaching nine. Its body was covered in shaggy and patchy hair, predominantly rusty-red with black streaks dispersed throughout. The hair wasn't sleek but rather had a rough texture. Notably, the hair on its legs, back, sides, and midsection appeared longer than that on its upper shoulders and head. Unfortunately, we never got a full view of its face. The creature's head seemed to rest directly on its shoulders, lacking a distinct neck, resulting in a shape reminiscent of a "dinner bell," with the shoulder muscles sloping up to form the flared lower part of the "bell." In a way, the positioning of the head on the shoulders resembled that of a large gorilla.

Its chest and shoulders were massive, exuding strength and power. We noticed that the upper arms, from shoulder to elbow, seemed noticeably shorter than the lower arms extending from the elbow to the hand. The waist, while not exceptionally narrow, appeared more shaggy and adorned with longer hair. There was no discernible evidence to determine the creature's gender, but both of us believed it to be male.

CHAPTER SIXTEEN

IN SEPTEMBER OF 2012, I decided to take a three-day vacation from Northern Nevada to the Southern Coast of Oregon. As a photographer for my website, I wanted to capture some stunning scenic shots before the weather turned cold and dreary for the rest of the year.

Accompanied by my fiance, we embarked on a hike about six to eight miles above Brookings, Oregon, in Curry County. Our chosen path led us through a densely wooded area, following the loop trail located approximately a quarter mile past the renowned Natural Bridges viewpoint.

Initially, our hike proceeded without any notable incidents, although the diminishing daylight prompted a sense of urgency to hasten our return, despite no logical reason to do so. It was an inexplicable feeling, as if the hairs on the back of my neck stood on end. I struggled to articulate the discomfort that washed over me. Along the trail, we didn't encounter any fellow hikers during our ascent or descent.

It was when we paused after hearing loud snaps echoing through the forest, resembling the sound of branches breaking, that our unease heightened. Initially, we couldn't spot anything amiss. Resolving to continue walking, we suddenly noticed bushes about twenty yards ahead swaying back and forth. Sensing something was off, we stopped once more, only to be assaulted by a repugnant stench reminiscent of rotting garbage festering under the scorching sun.

By then, my initial nervousness had escalated, compounded by the encroaching fog and fading light. The misty forest became veiled in a light rain. Struggling up a steep section of the trail, I exerted all my effort to reach its end.

As we neared the final ascent, a compulsion led me to glance behind me, despite not fully understanding why. It felt as if I were being watched, although I chastised myself for entertaining such notions. To my astonishment, I glimpsed a head rising above the tree branches, its body concealed by the dense vegetation. The head was adorned with dark reddish-brown fur and positioned at an impossible height above the ground. If this figure was a man, he must have stood close to eight feet tall. I blinked repeatedly, questioning my own sanity, hoping it was a mere figment of my imagination.

Yet, the creature I beheld didn't vanish into thin air. Instead, it regarded me with a curious gaze for a few fleeting seconds before disappearing from sight behind a tree. Gripping my fiance's hand tightly, too frightened to disclose what I had witnessed, fearing he might venture in search of it, I hurried back to our vehicle as swiftly as possible. I assure you, I am not delusional. This was no optical illusion caused by light or fog. Something immense, with an ape-like face, observed me intently.

The memory of that encounter remains etched in my mind forever. Strangely, the forest fell eerily silent a few minutes prior to the incident. The crickets ceased their chirping, the birds muted their melodies, and a profound stillness enveloped everything. We attributed it to the onset of the light rainfall, but it felt as if nature itself held its breath in that moment.

CHAPTER SEVENTEEN

THIS IS a true story from my past, an experience that has stayed with me for over 20 years. As someone who loves backpacking and has explored remote areas in the western states, encountering various wildlife, including grizzly bears, I had never encountered anything as strange as what happened on this particular occasion.

It was late summer 1989, a Friday evening after work. I decided to venture out alone, accompanied by my dogs. My destination was White Rock Lake in Tahoe National Forest, a place I had never been to before. The challenge was finding the lake since the roads were unmarked. According to the topo map, I could reach it via a 4-wheel drive road.

I found myself driving slowly on rough, rocky dirt roads, trying to figure out my location. The roads seemed to fade away or intersect with other 4-wheel drive paths, leaving me disoriented. I was in the middle of nowhere, with no lakes, significant creeks, or clear destinations in sight for miles.

Deciding to wait until daylight to avoid further confusion in the darkness, I pulled my 4-wheel drive pickup off the road, although I probably didn't need to since I hadn't seen anyone or anything. I parked a few yards away from the rocky road, hidden by the surrounding trees. I grabbed my sleeping bag and laid it out in front of my truck, settling down with my dogs under the starry night sky.

Sometime in the early morning, around 3 or 4 a.m., while it was still pitch black, I woke up to the sound of something walking towards me on the road. It was a heavy, steady footfall, clearly bipedal in nature. At first, I assumed it might be another backpacker, given the rhythm of the steps. But then I questioned why someone would be out here on this road in the middle of the night, without light, surrounded by miles of dense forest. Although I knew it wasn't a bear (I had encountered many bears in the wild), I couldn't identify what it could be. Nonetheless, I still thought a backpacker was the most reasonable explanation.

As the sound grew closer, I pondered whether I should say something, but I didn't want to startle anyone unnecessarily. I convinced myself that the passerby would simply continue on without noticing me. However, my growing nervousness was unusual, as there aren't many things in the wilderness that make me feel that way. Strangely, my dogs remained silent and motionless, which added to the suspense. Typically, they would have at least barked as a warning. This heavy bipedal entity continued approaching, getting closer to the spot where I had parked my truck off the road. I lay there, holding my breath. I didn't know what to expect and hoped it would pass by without even realizing I was there. The darkness obscured my vision completely.

As it drew nearer, I could sense its size, as the rhythm of its footsteps indicated a significant presence. In my nervousness, I remained utterly silent. At that moment, a thought of encountering a sasquatch didn't cross my mind. I had never given much thought to such things, especially in the Sierras. But that was about to change. The entity reached the point where my truck was parked off the road... and suddenly, silence. It stopped. Although I couldn't see it in the darkness, it stood only a few yards away from where I lay in my sleeping bag.

I'm not sure if I made a sound or if one of my dogs did, but something triggered a reaction from it. The entity emitted the most horrifying, piercing scream imaginable—a scream that defies description. It had lungs like nothing I had ever encountered before. Then, still screaming, it turned around and ran back down the road in the darkness at an astonishing speed. It continued to scream, the sound echoing through the forest without ceasing. I could hear the screams fading in the distance.

I lay there in complete shock, unable to believe what had just transpired. Eventually, I snapped out of it and quickly gathered my belongings, tossing them into my truck. My dogs were equally disturbed by the experience. I assumed the entity had moved far away by then, so before leaving the area, I drove down the road with my brights on, attempting to find any footprints or signs of something unusual. My adrenaline was pumping. Although I didn't actually step out of the truck, I opened the door and peered down, hoping to spot footprints or any clue about what I had encountered. The road was too rocky to show any prints. I then let my dogs out, hoping they might pick up a scent (although I didn't know what I would do if they did), but strangely, they immediately jumped back into the truck. This was out of character for them. I tried once more, but they insisted on staying inside. Realizing they were as unnerved as I was, I knew it was time to get out of there. I drove several miles back toward the main road, my adrenaline still surging.

Before this experience, I hadn't given much thought to sasquatches, but now I'm definitely a believer. People try to explain it away, but I know what I heard. I didn't see anything, nor did I detect any unusual odor, but it was so close that I could feel its presence. And when it screamed, it was so close that I'm surprised I didn't feel the spit from its mouth. Nothing in those forests could scream like that or run that fast, especially nothing walking upright. I don't dwell on the subject of sasquatch, nor have I made it my mission to search for them, but I know they exist. My experience is still vivid in my mind. Whether or not others believe it is irrelevant to me. I'm not sharing this account to convince anyone; I'm simply sharing an experience I had one night in the Sierras near Truckee.

CHAPTER EIGHTEEN

INTERESTING HISTORICAL ACCOUNT sent in from a reader.

———

Elkanah Walker, born on August 7, 1805, was an American pioneer settler who played a significant role in the early development of the Oregon Country, encompassing present-day Oregon and Washington states. He grew up on a farm near North Yarmouth, Maine, being the sixth child of Jeremiah and Jane Walker. Elkanah's thirst for knowledge led him to attend the Bangor Theological Seminary.

Elkanah and his family embarked on a journey to the Oregon Country, joining a group of missionaries who were also seeking to spread their teachings in the region. From August 1838 to June 1848, Elkanah Walker, along with his colleague Cushing Eells and their wives, established and resided at the Tshimakain Mission. This mission, supported by the American Board of Commissioners for Foreign Missions, aimed to study the local language and introduce the Protestant faith to the Spokane People, a Native American tribe residing in the area.

During their time at the Tshimakain Mission, Elkanah Walker and his companions immersed themselves in the local culture and language, working diligently to build relationships with the Spokane People. Their mission involved not only religious teachings but also education and community development. They sought to improve the lives of the Spokane People through their efforts, providing education and healthcare services alongside spreading their Protestant beliefs.

Through their dedication and perseverance, Elkanah Walker and Cushing Eells left a lasting impact on the Spokane People and the wider Oregon Country. They played a crucial role in bridging cultural gaps, promoting understanding, and contributing to the social and spiritual growth of the region. Elkanah Walker's legacy as a pioneer settler and missionary is remembered as a significant chapter in the early history of the Oregon Country.

In his diary he had an interesting section something they natives feared called, The Men Stealers.

Elkanah wrote in diary the following:

"Bear with me if I trouble you with a little of their superstitions. They believe in a race of giants, which inhabit a certain mountain off to the west of us. This mountain is covered with perpetual snow. They (the creatures) inhabit the snow peaks. They hunt and do all their work at night. They are men stealers.

They come to the people's lodges at night when the people are asleep and take them and put them under their skins and to their place of abode without even waking. Their track is a foot and a half long. They steal salmon from Indian nets and eat them raw as the bears do. If the people are awake, they always know when they are coming very near by their strong smell that is most intolerable. It is not uncommon for them to come in the night and give three whistles and then the stones will begin to hit their houses."

Reverend Walker's mission was situated around twenty-five miles northwest of what is now Spokane, Washington. In his diary entry, he described a snow-capped peak to the west, which could have referred to several mountains in the Cascade Range. It is possible that he was observing mountains like Mt. Baker, Mt. Rainier, Mt. Adams, or even Mount St. Helens. Alternatively, he might have been referring to Mt. Hood, located on the Oregon side of the Columbia River. The exact mountain he was describing remains uncertain, as the region was surrounded by majestic peaks, each with its own distinct beauty.

CHAPTER NINETEEN

BIGFOOT WAS NEVER something I gave much thought to, especially growing up in Louisiana. Sure, I had heard stories about it as a kid, but I always considered them to be nothing more than tales. Little did I know that my perspective was about to change on that fateful spring day.

Craving some peace and quiet away from the hustle and bustle of daily life, I decided to go for a solitary walk. Nature has always been my solace, a place where I could find serenity. I made my way down to the Red River, a spot I often frequented during my strolls. As I walked, I consciously tuned my senses, focusing on the sounds and sights around me. I took pleasure in the simple act of listening.

When I arrived at the edge of the bridge overlooking the river, something caught my eye. There, squatting by the water's edge, was a figure. Initially, my thoughts raced to the possibility of encountering a homeless person or a local enjoying the outdoors. However, as I observed more closely, I noticed that this individual was covered in hair from head to toe. Confusion washed over me. Why would someone be donning a Bigfoot costume in such a secluded area? My eyes darted around, half-expecting to see hidden cameras or mischievous teenagers orchestrating a prank. But there was no one else in sight, no evidence of a hoax.

My attention turned back to the mysterious figure, and as I continued to watch, details began to emerge. It was engrossed in breaking open mussels or clams, whatever it could find in the river. I couldn't help but wonder why someone would eat them raw from such a polluted and trash-laden waterway. That's when it hit me like a thunderbolt: this was no ordinary human. The realization sunk in, and a shiver ran down my spine.

The creature continued its primitive feast, completely oblivious to my presence. It never once turned to face me, and I stood frozen, transfixed by the encounter. In that moment, I made a decision to quietly retreat and rush back home to retrieve my phone. I desperately wanted to capture this astonishing sight on camera, but by the time I returned to the bridge, darkness had enveloped the surroundings, and the creature was gone without a trace.

What struck me most about the creature was its appearance. Covered in a dense coat of brown hair or fur, it remained squatting the entire time, displaying an impressive feat of balance and stability. I, on the other hand, struggled to hold a squat position for more than a few seconds. Its hands, though resembling human hands in shape, possessed a darker color and a texture reminiscent of gorillas or apes. The creature's height was difficult to ascertain accurately, but it appeared to be on the younger side, perhaps standing around 6 or 7 feet tall. To determine its true size, I would need someone to assist me in measuring.

As I made my way back home that evening, a whirlwind of thoughts and emotions consumed me. The encounter had shattered my skepticism and thrust me into a world of unknown possibilities. Bigfoot, a creature once dismissed as mere folklore, had become an enigma that demanded further exploration and understanding.

CHAPTER TWENTY

IN 2011, my family and I went on a hunt near the Grand Canyon. We set up camp close to where our family had a strange encounter before.

On Friday night, around 9 pm, my sister and I walked down the road from camp and made some noises, like howling and whooping, hoping to get a response. We tried for about 30 minutes but didn't hear anything back, so we returned to camp.

When we got back, my sister took my daughter and nephew into the camp trailer to put them to bed. Just as they went inside, things started to get exciting. My brother and I were sitting by the campfire, talking, when we heard a loud crash, like a large branch breaking off a tree, or something stepping on a big branch. It was so loud that we both noticed it. We tried to act casual and just listened for any more sounds while continuing our conversation.

For the next 30 minutes or so, we heard something circling our camp. There were two separate things, and they weren't being quiet. They were making a lot of noise, breaking branches and rustling in the trees. One of them paced back and forth behind the camp trailer, while the other moved from the northwest side of the camp towards the east. Sometimes we heard what sounded like a smaller tree being shaken, or heavy footsteps in the tall grass. We could tell there were two of them because we could hear both at the same time doing different things.

Then they started throwing rocks and sticks. The first thing we heard was a stick hitting a tarp we had set up for shade near the trailer. After that, there was a continuous barrage of small rocks and sticks being thrown around the campsite. The biggest rock that was thrown landed between us and the camp trailer with a thud that scared us both. At that point, we decided to go into the trailer for more cover. Inside, my sister and nephew were still awake, and they said they could hear everything we had heard from inside. My sister mentioned hearing footsteps behind the trailer the whole time, and she even heard a loud, heavy sigh at one point. She also heard branches breaking and either rocks or twigs being thrown at the trailer. My nephew confirmed her account, and we all tried to go to sleep.

As we lay in the darkness, we heard a loud metallic thud outside the trailer. There was a metal box with food on a small table, and it sounded like something had either knocked on the box or thrown something hard at it. We eventually fell asleep, except for my brother, who couldn't sleep. He continued to hear things being thrown at the trailer for a while. He did eventually fall asleep but was woken up in the early morning by the sound of something being dragged across the canvas roof of the trailer above his head.

The next day was uneventful as we didn't try making any more calls. My nephew had gotten sick from being so nervous the night before. It rained that night, and another hunting group had set up camp nearby.

On Sunday night, my sister and I went down the road again to make some calls, this time on the opposite side. We repeated our attempts from Friday, but once again, there was no response. We went back to camp and sat around the fire for about 30 minutes without anything happening, and then we went to bed.

During the night, something shook the camper trailer violently at least six times. It felt like someone was grabbing the sides and twisting it forcefully from side to side. It wasn't the wind because the trailer didn't sway in one direction; it was more like someone was deliberately shaking it. All three of us adults felt it throughout the night. My brother also heard a low growl around midnight that lasted about 10 seconds. He described it as a subtle but strong sound, and he could feel the vibrations it produced. It felt like it was slightly shaking him. The next morning, we packed up and headed home.

During the weekend, we checked the camp for any signs or footprints. The ground was covered with thick layers of oak leaves and pine needles. The only things we found were the small sticks and rocks, about 3-4 inches in size, that were used to pelt our trailer.

CHAPTER TWENTY-ONE

MY ENCOUNTER TOOK place in 2021. I've hesitated to share my story for almost two years because the other person who witnessed it doesn't want to be involved or have her name associated with it.

Around 11 am, my friend and I left to go geocaching. (Geocaching is a hobby where you find hidden objects based on GPS coordinates.) We went to a rather popular trail because this is where people will leave caches to find.

The trail in question wass an abandoned railway with overgrown sections, muddy spots, and various surroundings like fields, ponds, streams, trees, roads, homes, and forests.

While on the trail, we passed a church and a graveyard. Inside the graveyard, we found a geocache hidden in a bush. Afterward, we walked across a field of tall grass to return to the trail. We noticed a path of matted down grass, possibly made by deer or other geocachers heading back to the trail from the graveyard.

On the other side of the grassy area, there was a line of trees with a stream beyond it, and then more trees with the rail trail just beyond that. We realized we had to jump across the stream, but it seemed too wide for us. However, we noticed footprints in the mud, indicating someone had made the jump before us. We assumed it was another geocacher.

We followed the stream for a few minutes until we found a narrower spot where we could jump across. Continuing along the rail trail, we found a few more geocaches. Suddenly, a group of turkeys ran out from the bushes on the right side and disappeared into the left side.

I quickly took some photos of the turkeys with my iPhone and asked my friend if she saw them too. As I looked up the trail, I saw a tall figure step out from where the turkeys had emerged. It walked the same path as the turkeys and then stopped, turning its torso to face me directly.

At that moment, I realized it wasn't a person. It stood about 7-8 feet tall, covered in uneven salt and pepper hair that appeared dark grey and black. Its face was flat, resembling a monkey's face with dark, hairless skin around the eyes, mouth, and nose. I couldn't recall specific facial features as my attention shifted to its left arm, which was bulky and covered in hair. It held a motionless turkey under its arm, as if carrying a football. Before I could make eye contact again, it swiftly moved into the trees.

Later, my friend mentioned that the creature made eye contact with her, wrinkled its nose, and showed its teeth. She didn't provide many additional details about its appearance, and she seemed reluctant to discuss it further. The encounter was completely silent, with no grunts or heavy breathing.

After it disappeared, I realized I could have taken a clear photo since I was around 50-75 feet away from it. However, I was too shocked to remember that my phone was set to the camera app. The distance estimation was based on the geocache app, which showed the location of the next cache near where the creature and turkeys had appeared. The app's accuracy could vary due to poor cellular connection at the time.

Without discussing it, we decided to end our day and returned to our car. I've tried talking to my friend about the sighting, but she refuses to discuss it. She made it clear that if I choose to share my story,

I should use pseudonyms and exclude her from any mention because she doesn't want anyone knowing what she did or didn't see.

Thank you for allowing me to share.

CHAPTER TWENTY-TWO

BACK IN 1973, when I was just11 years old, my family and I lived east of Knoxville, Tennessee. It was a pretty sparsely populated area, and not much exciting stuff happened there. However, one day my younger brother and his friends came rushing to us, claiming they had seen a bear peeking into the Brad's house. Well, you can imagine how intrigued us older kids were by that news. We immediately hopped on our bikes and pedaled down the old highway towards the Brad's house, hoping to catch a glimpse of the bear ourselves.

As we were cycling along the road, something big and dark suddenly crossed our path and disappeared into the woods. One of my friends shouted that it wasn't a bear, but actually a man. I wasn't quite sure what it was, but yeah, it was definitely walking on two legs and had a uniform color. We reached the point where we believed it had entered the woods. This was our special trail that led to our fallen tree fort, which we proudly called "The "Hideout". The trail twisted and turned, taking us down into what I guess you could call a canyon or drainage area.

There were lots of trees and vegetation, and there were no houses or people around for quite a distance. I dropped my bike and led the way down the trail, eager to find out where the man was headed and whether he would disturb our fort. We ran down the trail, and as we approached the final bend, I abruptly stopped and glanced down to see something monstrous instead of a man. It had come to a halt near a log bridge that spanned a small dry creek bed. Right at that spot, the trails split, with one going up the draw and the other crossing the log bridge to continue on the opposite side. Our fort was located a bit farther down the trail. So, upon seeing this thing, my first thought was, "This isn't real." I couldn't quite make out what it was until it turned its body and looked up at me. By this time, the other kids had caught up and were piling up behind me, as I had stopped abruptly.

The creature stared at me with a completely expressionless face— no emotions whatsoever. It was bizarre. I turned around and urgently yelled at everyone to scramble back up the trail as fast as they could. We all bolted out of the trailhead, but I struggled to grab my bike and mount it in the rush. Eventually, I gave up and tossed it aside, sprinting all the way back home. The rest of the kids managed to reach our house, some running, some still on their bikes. My friend Sam, who had also seen the creature, asked me what it was. The other kids hadn't seen it, but they were just as frightened as Sam and me. Sam and I told them it was a woods monster, but when I tried to tell my mom the same thing, she dismissed our story.

The things that stuck in my memory were the creature's lack of emotion, which struck me as strange. Any animal or person would surely react in some way to a bunch of kids charging toward them in the woods, right? It had a pointed head with a patch of blonde hair on the left side, but apart from that, I can't recall many other details. I have no idea how big it actually was, what color its skin was, or even the color of its eyes, which I assume were black since I don't remember seeing any white in them. I estimate that it was about forty to fifty yards away from me, down the trail.

When my dad came home, I tried telling him the whole story, but it didn't really stick with him either. I had to convince him to walk down the road with me to retrieve my bike. After that incident, we never ventured back into the woods. However, a few weeks later, something else happened. We had all bought new pocket knives and were sitting on a ledge, overlooking the canyon/drainage area, whittling sticks and still talking about whether the woods monster was still lurking around. Unfortunately, my pocket knife slipped out of my hand and flew over the ledge, landing amidst the trees and bushes below. We peered over the edge and spotted my new knife lying on the ground. Three of us mustered the courage to make our way down and retrieve it while the others stood watch. Once again, we had to navigate a series of switchbacks to reach the bottom. As we were heading back up the trail, we suddenly heard rustling noises from above, right where we needed to go. Instantly, we all panicked and began running down the main trail that led to the beach. We had never gone all the way to the beach before. After a long sprint, we emerged onto the shoreline and started heading south toward the houses that I knew were there. Finally, we reached the first house, frantically knocked on the door, and a lady answered. We asked to use her phone, and I called my mom to come pick us up.

That encounter with the woods monster and the subsequent knife incident were unforgettable for all of us. Even though our accounts were dismissed by our parents, we couldn't shake the fear and curiosity that lingered in our minds.

CHAPTER TWENTY-THREE

SO, I'm not really sure about the exact order of things that happened, but let me know if you think this is weird or not. I never realized what one of these things were until I started listening to your podcast a few years ago. I emailed you a while back, but I didn't share all of my experiences that happened at my childhood home where my mom still lives.

So, I grew up in Marion, SC. It's a tiny town about an hour away from Myrtle Beach. Population's around 6 thousand, and it's spread out. Mom's still out there in the country. Back then, we had two houses on our right, and one across the road from us, opposite a few fields. Country life, you know? To the left and behind our place, there were just fields for miles. Depending on the season, it'd be corn, soybeans, or tobacco. I got two older sisters, and we all lived in this small home with a barn-like thing we called the boat shed. Dad kept his boats, lawnmower, and stuff like that there. In our backyard, we had this big oak tree, and this massive magnolia tree in the front. Funny thing is, mom actually grew up on that land and moved back after she got married and had us.

We used to have these "prowler" issues, as my parents would say. Banging on windows, things going missing from the boat shed, and these "people" peeking into our windows. Now, let me tell you about one time. I was probably around 10 years old, and I had this major fear of the dark – whole different story why – and my big sis asked if I could spend a night in her room. My other sis and I shared bunk beds in another room, and we were super tight, like best buds. Me and the older sis, we had our moments, you know? She could be real mean, but sometimes she'd surprise me with some kindness. Should've been suspicious, really. So, I thought it was cool she was asking me to crash in her room, even though I was kinda scared of her.

Anyway, her room was like pitch black, only light was this red glow from her digital clock on the dresser. So, there we are, in our PJs, and she's telling me to get into bed. This bed's shoved in a corner, so you can only get in from one side. I crawl in, heart already racing 'cause I'm thinking, "What's she up to?" She's being weirdly nice, saying not to be scared, that she'll hold my hand till I fall asleep. I'm thinking she's planning something, like smothering me or something, LOL. So, we're lying there, it's a decently comfy bed, and she kills the light. I'm lying there, feeling better 'cause I can see a bit from the light coming through the blinds. She's like, "It's all good, I'm right here." I'm like, "Fine, whatever." I'm not sure why she's acting so chill, but it's late, and my eyes are getting used to the dark and the tiny bit of light.

I start drifting off, not sure how long I was out, but suddenly, I hear tapping. Even as I type this now, I'm feeling exactly how I felt that night, like 40 years later! I'm just looking around with my eyes, frozen with fear. I don't know why I'm so scared, 'cause I don't know what the sound is. I move my arm under the covers to feel if my sister's there, and yep, she's there, fast asleep. The tapping's coming from the window and it's getting louder and louder. I shift my eyes over, not moving my head, and I see this HUGE dark figure blocking most of the window. I'm holding my breath, feet freezing, realizing that's fear, right? I'm petrified. I think these "prowlers" are trying to break in. The blinds are kinda slanted down, so lying there, I can see a bit of what-ever it is. All I can make out is that it's black and has these super white teeth. A big ol' mouthful of 'em, and I can hear it breathing, all raspy and gurgly.

I grab my sister's arm, whisper-shout, "Someone's at the window."

She's like, "What?" I say, "Someone's trying to get in!" Trying not to move, talking real low. She shouts, "What?" I scream, "Someone's trying to get in!" She looks, sees the figure, and bolts out of the room, screaming for Dad. I slide out of bed, don't look back 'til I hit the floor, then crawl outta there faster than lightning. "Dad, Dad, someone's trying to get in the window! Hurry!" Now, Mom and Dad are asleep, but Dad jumps up when we scream, grabs his .38 revolver – yeah, he had that thing for dealing with these "prowlers" – and dashes out the front door in his underwear. Mom calls the neighbors, they grab their guns too and go help Dad. Mom's convinced they're gonna accidentally shoot each other, but that's Dad. He comes back in a bit, saying he heard 'em running through the tobacco field, saw a dark figure breaking the stalks, but couldn't see details. And just like that, we're supposed to go back to bed like it's all normal. Yeah, right. I'm in the living room, sis goes back to bed, parents too.

I'm glued to the TV the whole dang night, totally freaked. I can still see it now, like I'm there. Can still hear it. Do I know what that thing was? Nope. But listening to your episodes where people talk about hooded folks or mysterious figures, it all comes rushing back. So, about a year ago, I went back to Mom's. Listened to some more of your guests' stories, talked to Mom – Dad's gone, passed away six years back – but Mom's still holding strong at 84, got my nephew with her, so she's not alone. She's got a load of stories from that house, which I'll share someday. Went back to that window where that "person" was ages ago, measured it up. No bricks or flower beds under there, just the hedges that were always there. The window's bottom is at 5 feet, and that thing took up the whole dang window!

So, I'm guessing it was like 7 and a half, maybe 8 feet tall, unless whoever it was had a ladder or something. Me and Mom just stood there, totally amazed. How did we just think that was a regular person? It hit me like a ton of bricks! Told a few close friends, got the "You're crazy" look and a grin, so I let it be. But I can't. The more I think about all the wild stuff that happened out there, something was going on, man.

CHAPTER TWENTY-FOUR

ONE REALLY COLD day in Oklahoma, something totally bizarre happened that I can't forget. You know those days when everything's covered in snow and it's super quiet outside? Well, this was one of those days. The streets were empty, no cars, no people, just this thick layer of snow everywhere.

I was like fifteen and working at this fast-food place about a mile from where all this weird stuff went down. My dad called and said our car was stuck in the driveway because of the snow, so I had to walk home. The snow on the ground was so bright, like reflecting the sunlight.

So, I'm walking, and I see this thing moving on my left. I turn my head and there's this figure playing around in the snow. At first, I thought it was a kid wearing a dark snowsuit or something, but then I got a better look. This thing was covered in long, dark hair or fur, head to toe. And it wasn't a kid, it was like five feet tall and maybe around 160 pounds.

I couldn't believe what I was seeing. This creature was just there, fooling around with the snow, bending over and tossing it up in the air, like it was having fun. But honestly, instead of being excited, I got really scared. I mean, I was pretty far from any houses, and there was nobody else around. It was just me and this strange thing.

I was only about thirty or thirty-five yards away from it, and I had a long way to go before it wouldn't be able to see me. I thought about running, but then I figured if I did, it might start chasing me. I remember reading that animals can do that.

So, I stayed put, just watching it. The longer I looked, the more I realized this wasn't something normal. It was like nothing I'd ever seen before, something out of a movie or something. I kept staring at it, and then I managed to look away and started walking, then running, as fast as I could until I felt like I was really far from there.

Thinking back to that day, it still gives me goosebumps. It was so strange and scary at the same time. I can't help wondering what that thing was, where it came from, and if anyone else has seen anything like it. It's like a mystery that nobody can figure out, and it's stuck in my mind like a puzzle that I'll never solve.

CHAPTER TWENTY-FIVE

HEY, I've got a couple of wild stories that happened out in the mountains of New Mexico, and I can't help but share them. So, here goes – my grandparents used to run this summer camp, nestled about 40 miles east of Albuquerque. Every summer, I'd head out there and basically live the camp life for a while.

Now, picture this – the camp sprawled over this pretty vast piece of land, about 150 acres to be precise, and it cozied right up against the Cibola National Forest. Fast forward to 1992, and I'm 12 years old, just a kid with an adventurous spirit. One day, I'm tagging along with my grandfather, and we're headed to this "power house" to fire up the generator – you know, because we made our own power with a combo of solar, wind, and a backup generator. So, while he's busy tinkering away, I do what I do best – wander off, playing around with the camp dogs. Well, okay, technically they're my grandparents' dogs, but you get what I mean.

Anyway, there I am, having a grand old time with sticks and just doing boy stuff down in a ravine that runs alongside the back of this power house. The sun's on its way down, casting its warm, orangey glow on everything. It's that time of day where it's still kind of light, but you can tell dusk is just around the corner. I'm lost in my own little world when I realize my canine buddies aren't around anymore. That's when I decide to glance up the hillside from where I am, and bam – that's when things get real interesting.

Imagine this – there's this auburn-hued creature moseying across this clearing up the hill. Now, here's the kicker – I can't see its feet, just about knees or thighs up. The sun's playing peek-a-boo behind the hill's crest, back-lighting the scene and making it tough to make out every little detail. But one thing's clear – it's got a human-ish shape, and it's completely covered in hair. It's like nothing I've ever seen before. Smooth as silk, it glides across the clearing in just about three steps. And the head, oh man, that's a whole other story. It's cone-shaped, crowned with these tufts of hair flowing off the back. Now, it's important to note that from my vantage point, I can't see every little thing, like its feet or the finer facial features, but man, the memory of that sighting is etched into my brain.

Now, let me tell you, I'm frozen in place. Petrified is an understatement. My brain's racing, my heart's pounding, and I can't even move a muscle. It's like time stood still. I only see it for a few seconds, but those moments feel like an eternity. It's not until my dogs come back, wagging their tails and tongues hanging out, that I finally manage to snap out of my paralyzed state. At that point, my fear starts to ebb away a bit, 'cause hey, my furry companions are here, right? But truth be told, I couldn't tell if they saw what I saw or if it even fazed them.

Now, I'm back up at the power house, and I've got to tell my grand-father about this. So, I spill the beans, expecting him to be just as wide-eyed as I am. But nope, he's this rational dude, a nuclear physicist no less, and he nonchalantly suggests it was probably a bear. But hold on a sec, I know what bears look like. We had our fair share of black bears in those parts, and this thing I saw? Not a bear. Not by a long shot. The shape, the movement, the color – it all screamed Sasquatch, even though my brain couldn't wrap itself around the reality of it.

Time moves on, as it tends to do, and by the time 2001 rolls around, I've spent countless days hiking and camping on that property. I'm the king of the outdoors, comfortable in the woods like a second home. So, I decide to take on the role of a Big Brother to a ten-year-old kid through a program at my church. We're camping one fine day, just roasting marshmallows by the campfire, when the kid's freaked out. He's seen these glowing red eyes across the woods from our tent. I figure it's just a critter, and I go out to check, but there's nothing there. We get back in the tent, but the night's not done with its surprises.

There's this ruckus, this rustling, as if something's building a nest or maybe even a shelter close by. The kid's petrified, and I'm doing my best to calm him down. I keep stepping out, looking around with my flashlight, and every time I do, the noise stops. It's eerie, this weird silence that follows every time I investigate. This back-and-forth goes on for about an hour, until I feel like maybe there's someone out there, messing with us. The thought of a creepy person lurking around gets me more on edge than any wild animal would.

In the end, I lose patience, and I burst out of the tent, screaming at whatever might be out there to scram. But guess what? There's nothing. Not a trace. It's like whatever it was, it vanished into thin air. We decide to pack up and head back to the house, and as I'm going through the woods the next morning, I stumble upon this bizarre tree structure, not too far from our tent. It's huge, and it's got these claw marks, these long, thin finger marks all around it. It's like nothing I've seen before, and it sets my mind racing.

So, here I am, years later, replaying these stories in my head. Back then, I didn't think much of it – just chalked it up to weird woodland stuff. But now, as I listen to stories about Sasquatch encounters, the pieces start to fall into place. Those red eyes, the strange structure, the eerie commotion – it's all starting to align. And you know what? Maybe I did come face to face with the elusive creature. Or maybe it's just my imagination running wild. Either way, these experiences, well, they're etched into my memory like some kind of strange, otherworldly campfire tale.

CHAPTER TWENTY-SIX

BACK IN THE DAY, nestled in the rustic heart of York County, Pennsylvania, I had a childhood that was steeped in the beauty of nature and the mysteries of the world around me. Our little piece of heaven was situated near the Susquehanna River, a slice of paradise tucked between the quaint locales of New Bridgeville and Greenbranch. You see, my upbringing was anything but ordinary, for I found myself in the midst of a tale that would make even the most skeptical minds raise an eyebrow.

It was during the fall, a season of vibrant colors and crisp air that invited you to explore the great outdoors. The exact month escapes me, but I remember the warmth in the air, a pleasant reminder that winter hadn't yet tightened its grip. On that fateful day, my two older cousins and I were on a childhood adventure, embracing the freedom of youthful innocence as we roamed the yard and the enchanting woods that bridged our neighboring properties.

Let me give you a glimpse into our world – our home was a little off the beaten path, around four to five miles from the main road. A narrow dirt road, barely wide enough for a single car, meandered through the undulating hills, accompanied by the soothing presence of the Susquehanna River. My mom and I occupied a cozy piece of land, while the wooded expanse between our abode and my uncle's place, my cousin's father, served as a magical pathway connecting our lives. Those woods were our secret realm, a place where our imaginations ran wild as we ventured back and forth, opting for the scenic route over the dusty road. Beyond our land, more woods and the ever-peaceful farm stretched as far as the eye could see.

As the sun dipped lower on the horizon, casting a golden hue over the landscape, the day's adventures began to wind down, and the call for dinner brought us home. Yet, amidst the laughter and shared stories of our day, I realized that something was amiss – I had forgotten a prized possession, some cherished toy or trinket, back by our lawn shed. My mission was clear, and with a sense of purpose, I headed out to retrieve my missing treasure.

The setting sun painted the sky with shades of orange and pink as I made my way to the shed. A familiar urgency overtook me, and I felt the need to relieve myself, a customary country ritual that required no explanation. However, as I went about this ordinary task, a wave of unease washed over me, an inexplicable sensation that set my heart racing and my muscles freezing in place. It was as though time had come to a standstill, leaving me suspended in a moment that defied all reason.

With every fiber of my being, I felt as if I were being watched, scrutinized by an unseen presence that sent a chill down my spine. Frozen in my tracks, I struggled to comprehend the sensation, my breath coming in slow, deliberate puffs as I strained to pierce the veil of uncertainty that had enveloped me. As I gazed up, I was met with an image that would forever be etched into the tapestry of my memory – a colossal, brownish-red figure, covered in a shaggy coat of fur, gracefully traversing the woods along the edge of the cornfield. It was a sight that defied logic, a being of immense proportions that seemed to belong to another realm entirely.

Fear gripped me like a vice, and though I longed to scream, my voice remained trapped within, stifled by a potent mixture of awe and terror. Before me was a creature of gargantuan proportions, a silent sentinel that exuded an air of majestic mystery. Its body was cloaked in a rugged coat of hair, the strands measuring three to four inches in length, while its elongated arms dangled effortlessly at its sides. Two round, pug-like eyes stared intently at me, captivating and unwavering, as if peering into the depths of my very soul.

The creature's approach was deliberate, a purposeful stride that betrayed an air of quiet confidence. Remarkably, not a single sound accompanied its movement, as if it glided across the earth's canvas with ethereal grace. As my eyes remained fixated on this enigmatic visitor, I couldn't help but note its unusual features – the eyes, round and inquisitive, seemed to harbor a wisdom beyond human comprehension. The jaw was partly open, revealing teeth that gleamed like polished ivory, while the creature's head held an air of curiosity that matched my own.

In the stillness of that fleeting moment, a silent exchange seemed to transpire, a wordless conversation between two souls connected by an inexplicable bond. Time itself seemed to hold its breath as we locked gazes, each seeking to understand the other's presence in this cosmic encounter. And then, as if prompted by an unseen force, the creature emitted a peculiar sound, a gentle huff that resonated through the air. Its head tilted back, those unblinking eyes never leaving mine, while its mouth revealed the gleam of perfectly aligned teeth.

Now, as I reflect upon that surreal experience from the vantage point of adulthood, I recognize the calm that emanated from the creature's demeanor. It bore no sign of hostility or aggression; rather, it exuded an aura of tranquility, as if it sensed that I posed no threat to its realm. Our silent communion continued, a meeting of minds unbound by language, until the world beyond our gaze interjected.

A distant voice shattered the enchantment, a voice I recognized as my mother's urgently calling my name from the front door. The creature, too, appeared startled by the intrusion, swiftly pivoting on its heel and retreating with a grace that defied its colossal form. In a matter of strides, it vanished from sight, leaving behind a sense of wonder and a myriad of questions that would linger for years to come.

As I sprinted back to the haven of my mother's embrace, I found myself grappling for words to convey the inexplicable encounter I had just witnessed. "I SAW A MONSTER!" I blurted out, my breathless utterances met with a mix of concern and skepticism. My mother, ever the voice of reason, dismissed my account as a trick of the imagination, attributing the sighting to the whims of a child's mind.

Weeks turned into months, and the memory of that extraordinary day remained etched in my consciousness. Despite the disbelieving dismissals and the rational explanations, I clung to the truth of my encounter, steadfast in my conviction that I had indeed locked eyes with a creature that defied all rational explanation. Over the years, the memory became a cherished secret, a testament to the mysteries that lie hidden within the fabric of our world.

Now, as a seasoned adult, I find myself recounting this tale with a wistful smile, fully aware of the incredulity it might evoke. Yet, as I listen to stories of Sasquatch and the enigmatic creatures that roam our world's forgotten corners, I can't help but chuckle to myself. If only these storytellers knew the truth that I hold within – a truth that transcends doubt and resonates with the echoes of that unforgettable encounter.

As the years have passed, the memory has only grown more vivid, a beacon of inexplicable wonder that beckons me to the wild places of our world. And though I may never again stand face to face with the enigmatic giant that graced my life that autumn day, the memory serves as a testament to the mysteries that continue to weave their threads through the tapestry of our existence. So, let the skeptics scoff and the doubters dismiss – for I, a humble dweller of York County, have glimpsed the extraordinary, and it is a truth that no rational explanation can ever diminish.

CHAPTER TWENTY-SEVEN

LIVING HERE IN EAST TENNESSEE, close to the border with Kentucky, has given me some experiences that I still struggle to explain. It's a quiet place, nestled amidst the hills and woods, where my family and I have made a home. Some strange occurrences have left their mark on our lives, and I've often wondered about the mysteries that surround us.

One memory that stands out is when my oldest son recounted an eerie encounter. He had been in the deer blind, that little shelter we set up for hunting, when an inexplicable feeling compelled him to glance out the window. What he saw sent a shiver down his spine – a towering figure with auburn-colored hair, traversing the hayfield above the blind. It was like nothing he had ever seen before, a big, big man covered in hair, disappearing into the distance. That incident left us all questioning the boundaries of our understanding.

Then there's the curious case of the missing eggs. Eggs, you might think, should be a constant in a household like ours, yet they seemed to vanish without a trace. It's almost as if someone, or something, was helping itself to our egg supply, leaving us baffled and wondering. It's a little unsettling, I won't lie, but it's also a mystery we've come to accept as part of our rural life.

One evening, my sons were feeding the chickens a bit later than usual. We have these movable chicken coops that allow us to avoid the hassle of shoveling manure. These sturdy structures sit atop the grass, and on this particular day, they were positioned near a wooded area at the far end of our field. That's when it happened – a bone-chilling scream erupted from the woods, a chilling blend of growl and screech. It was a sound that seemed to pierce the night, sending my sons sprinting back to the safety of our cabin. The source of the scream remained a mystery, its echo leaving us all unnerved.

Our family's journey also led us to building a post and beam straw-bale house, a labor of love that consumed our days and nights. I often camped out on-site in a tent, ensuring I was there to greet the sunrise and oversee the construction. It was during one of those nights, in the quiet darkness of July 2013, that I was awakened at 3 AM by an unexplainable impulse. My tent became a cocoon of stillness before it was shattered by a series of screams – loud, human-like screams, repeated five times in quick succession. What was truly astonishing was how rapidly the source of the screams traversed the hillside. The distance it covered in mere seconds left me bewildered, thinking that perhaps someone on a vehicle was responsible. Yet, it moved too fast for a mere human. The ridgeline, the same one my son had seen the enigmatic figure on, seemed to serve as a conduit for this perplexing phenomenon.

The unsettling encounters didn't stop there. During the summer of 2018, as the warm days began to wane, I found myself in a moment of eerie stillness. From the loft window of our temporary cabin, I heard a howl that seemed to defy explanation – it started low, like a deep rumble, before rising in pitch and ending with a coyote-like yip. It echoed through the holler, creating an atmosphere of both intrigue and trepidation. Even my son, in the loft across from me, has his own stories to tell – of fingernails rapping on his window, perched high above the ground. To this day, he keeps a blanket draped over his window, a simple defense against the unknown.

Then came the day I was picking blackberries near the edge of the woods, close to that grove of PawPaw trees. It started innocently enough, with small pebbles being tossed my way. Trying to remain brave, I attempted to keep picking, my heart pounding with each rock that struck the ground near me. In a moment of courage mixed with desperation, I decided to sing aloud, an attempt to quell the rising fear. The tension in the air was palpable, a feeling of being watched and assessed by something unseen. As I filled my bowl with blackberries, I couldn't shake the discomfort that clung to me.

Then, there were the trees. Oh, those massive trees that tumbled down as if pushed by an unseen force. It happened not once, but multiple times – four gigantic trees crashing down while I was out on the farm. The sheer power required to bring those giants to the ground left me awestruck and bewildered, my mind racing to comprehend the inexplicable.

There was also that peculiar night, when I spotted lights in the woods. Our compost heap, nestled beside the apple orchard at the top of the hill, seemed to be at the center of this enigma. My son, perhaps emboldened by a blend of curiosity and naivety, had wolf-whistled into the night. In response, an echoing wolf whistle emerged from the darkness, leaving us both unnerved. Later, as I gazed uphill, I noticed a peculiar phenomenon – a light, a single beam that seemed to stretch from the forest floor to the underside of the leaves. Was it a person with a flashlight? Or was it something else, something far beyond the realm of understanding?

As I reflect on these encounters, I am reminded of the thin veil that separates our ordinary lives from the extraordinary. In a world filled with bright lights and bustling cities, I find solace in the mysteries that unfold under the cover of night, deep within the woods and fields of East Tennessee. It's a reminder that even in our modern age, there are forces and beings that defy explanation, leaving us humbled and intrigued by the uncharted realms that lie just beyond our reach.

CHAPTER TWENTY-EIGHT

GROWING up in a small town out in western Ohio, I was fortunate enough to have grandparents who owned a charming horse farm. Being the eldest grandchild, I had a special bond with my grandpa, and that bond led me on some unforgettable camping adventures from a young age. It all started when I was around 4 years old, tagging along with my grandparents on their camping trips. By the time I was 6, I had already embarked on my first trail ride. Those were the days when we would pack up and head to the great outdoors, exploring places like Hocking Hills, Salt Fork, and Tar Hollow State Park.

Now, let me take you back to a time when the simplicity of life and the wonders of nature filled my days. We may not have had all the modern conveniences at our campsites – no electric, no running water, and no sewer connections. Our campsites were primitive, offering only pit toilets and baths in the creek that meandered alongside the campground. And as if that wasn't enough, my grandpa was adamant about not running the generator for AC, even during the sweltering summer months. Imagine my plight – my bed was perched above the front seats of the RV, a spot that turned into a furnace during those scorching nights. So, if the forecast promised a dry night, my ingenious solution was to sweep out the horse trailer, stack bales of hay, drape them with a tarp, and create a makeshift, cooler sleeping spot right there.

The years from around 1986 to 1994 hold a collection of peculiar memories, events that I used to brush off as odd occurrences with logical explanations. But then, something happened that made me reconsider everything – the moment I first heard the Ohio howl played for me. That eerie sound triggered a memory that was tucked away in the corners of my mind, something I had experienced firsthand.

The setting for one of these curious happenings was the horse camp at Tar Hollow, nestled on the opposite side of the State Park from the main camping and lake area. My routine before bed involved tuning into the one local radio station that came in reliably, just to catch the overnight weather report. Armed with the knowledge of a rain-free night, I would set up my sleeping arrangements for the evening. However, around 1 a.m., my peaceful slumber was interrupted by a strange, yet oddly familiar, sound – it was like a tornado siren, but without the usual pattern. Low to high, then silence for a few minutes, repeating this unsettling sequence about four times over a span of ten minutes. The odd part? The direction from which the sound seemed to originate wasn't where the nearest town was situated. Curiosity got the better of me, and I woke my grandparents up, trying to figure out if there was an emergency. They dismissed it, claiming I must have dreamt it, and sent me back to sleep.

The memories get tangled up between various camping sites, forming a puzzle of experiences that I now recognize as part of a larger, enigmatic tapestry. One such instance took place within the campground at Tar Hollow, where the campsites were arranged in three concentric circles. The biggest circle was situated in the middle, boasting spacious sites for larger rigs. To the south lay a decent-sized circle, while the northern end held a small circle tucked into a heavily wooded area. It was in this small circle that I had an encounter that would forever linger in my mind.

One eerie night, I was roused from my sleep by a sound that resembled a mule's bray. These creatures can make quite an array of odd noises, and given that there was a guy with a mule who occasionally camped nearby, I didn't think much of it. The sound lasted only 2 to 3 seconds, a blend of a scream and a mule's call, emanating from the direction of the small circle. Morning came, and I mentioned this to my grandpa, suggesting that the mule guy had arrived late at night. Our usual morning routine led us through the campground, greeting fellow campers and soaking in the ambiance of the great outdoors. As we wandered back to the small circle, we found no trace of anyone camping there, nor any mules. The eerie memory left me pondering the strange occurrence, especially given the backdrop of a larger narrative that had been circulating around the campfire.

Another camper, a fellow rider who frequented our outings, shared a chilling story that further deepened the sense of mystery. He recounted an incident during one of his solitary rides, accompanied only by his loyal dog. Riding along a familiar trail that we often traversed, he entered a valley that stretched about a mile and a half. There was a smaller valley branching off from this one, ending in swampy terrain and private property. As he rode, he was suddenly struck by a putrid odor, unlike anything he had ever smelled before. His dog darted toward the swampy offshoot, and he heard a commotion as something crashed through the underbrush. The dog returned, covered in a slimy substance that matched the nauseating scent. His tale, however, was met with skepticism, as back then, the concept of Bigfoot was more punchline than possibility. Despite the jabs from fellow campers, he never rode alone again, and the trail that once held routine familiarity was now a path of wary glances and rapid gallops.

Then there was the peculiar incident that transpired on Rattlesnake Ridge, a spot earned its name due to the timber rattlesnakes that frequented the area. The loggers had left a pile of logs and brush near the trail, a spot that served as a haven for these slithery creatures. Our horses, usually prone to a leisurely pace, were suddenly agitated, their nervousness compounded by a putrid stench that hung in the air. It was a smell so foul that it sent us packing after just a few minutes – a rapid retreat from a place where we'd normally rest and recharge. The horses' eagerness to leave struck me as odd, especially given the sweltering heat of the day. The experience led to half-joking comments about Bigfoot's involvement, a topic that had once been a punchline but was now a seed of intrigue.

Our escapades often included a dose of adult beverages, a pleasure that became synonymous with our trail rides. During one memorable outing, a bottle of Wild Turkey made its way into our supplies. By around 1 p.m., one of our female riders had imbibed a bit too much, rendering her unable to ride. Ever the responsible teenager, I volunteered to escort her back to camp. While the rest of the group continued their adventure, we headed back, hoping the fresh air would help her sober up. Guiding her horse at a slow pace, we embarked on the journey back to camp, tackling the familiar trails. But this trip would hold a twist of its own, one that added yet another layer to the mystique.

Our leisurely ride was abruptly interrupted by an overpowering stench that seemed to permeate the air. It was a smell that defied description, causing both of us to wrinkle our noses in disgust. As if the odor weren't enough, our horses were suddenly on edge, hastening their pace as they climbed the hills. Normally, I would rein in my horse during such ascents, but their urgency overruled my control. By the time we reached the crest, the horses were heaving, and a sense of unease settled over the surroundings. The source of the odor remained a mystery, as we couldn't find anything amiss in the vicinity. Ultimately, we made it back to camp without any further disturbances, but the incident left an indelible mark on my memory.

Perhaps the most spine-tingling encounter, however, unfolded within the confines of my sleeping quarters – the RV trailer. It all began with an odd rustling sound, like someone gingerly treading through the creek located about 30 yards behind the trailer. Now, the creek was no walk in the park, its bed composed of flat sandstone that could rival a skating rink. Yet, there it was – step, pause, step, pause – the distinct cadence of footsteps echoing through the night. Just as I puzzled over this phenomenon, another peculiar sound joined the nocturnal symphony – the clacking of rocks, arranged in groups of three. Clack-clack-clack, followed by a pause of two or three minutes, only to repeat the eerie pattern five or six times. As I tried to make sense of it all, the puzzle pieces slipped into place when I heard our horses growing restless and nickering.

The sound of our horses, which were tethered between the trailer and the creek, filled the night air. It wasn't an unusual occurrence on its own, but coupled with the otherworldly sounds from the creek, a sense of foreboding crept over me. I peered into the darkness, straining to discern any movement or shape in the night. My gaze followed the horses' line of sight, their focus directed toward a particular spot. Yet, despite my efforts, I couldn't spot anything unusual. I shrugged it off, chalking it up to a curious deer or some other animal wandering through the woods. Exhausted and wary, I tried to settle back into slumber, hoping that the mysterious disturbance was nothing more than a fleeting anomaly.

These fragments of my past, woven together, create a patchwork of enigmatic experiences that defy simple explanations. They transport me back to a time when the mysteries of the natural world sparked my curiosity and left me contemplating the unknown. As I recall these memories now, I'm reminded that the world is a vast and intricate tapestry, and sometimes, within the ordinary fabric of life, there are threads of wonder and inexplicable phenomena waiting to be unraveled.

CHAPTER TWENTY-NINE

IN THE WINTER OF 1989, when I was a teenager, I had a sighting on the reservation. I was 15 at the time and saw a tall, hairy man rapidly crossing the road during a snowstorm. He was huge, and the whole thing happened so fast that it was hard to get a good view. I reported it to the tribal government, and they took my statement. I was always curious about what I saw, and that sighting has led me to work for the tribal government in Oklahoma now.

Over the last ten years with the tribal government, I was the one assigned to investigate any reports of a large creature on the reservation. Occasionally a report would come in and I would investigate it, but for the most part the reports of a hairy creature stopped. About a year ago, I began taking in more reports from people who were seeing a large figure they described as a Sasquatch, with demonic eyes. They believed these sightings were a bad sign or warning. Recently, one of my co-workers said his mother saw something near their house, which is in an area with lots of trees. The description was almost identical to what I saw as a teenager. He said that the large figure is "hanging around" near their home. She doesn't live on the reservation but just outside of town.

I had mentioned to my boss that I saw something like that when I was a teen. He sent me to spend a night or two just south of the reservation in the wilderness to investigate since I had a previous encounter. I went to the nearest wooded area that had camping, found a spot, and set up my tent. A creek was nearby as well. There were also large areas of evergreen trees nearby where any large animal could easily hide.

I made it to the campsite early in the afternoon and set up. I also had a few trail cams that looked like rocks, so I spread them around the area in hopes of catching something on video.

It got dark quickly, and I decided to go to sleep early since I'd most likely be up in the middle of the night. I had only been asleep for about 2 hours when I heard something hit the side of my jeep, like a rock. I dismissed it, but then I heard it again.

I came out of the tent and looked around the area with my flashlight. On the passenger side of the jeep, the side that was facing away from my tent, I found a few dents in the door. I knew they weren't there before. I looked on the ground and saw a bunch of rocks. It looked like someone had been throwing rocks at my jeep. Unfortunately, the trail cams weren't facing that way. When I returned to my tent, I noticed that the front of the ten had been slashed. It looked like it was slashed by a large claw.

I slept lightly and through the night I could hear a type of grunting which was followed by a bizarre yell and other sounds. I woke up around dawn and decided to go and check the trail cams and see what had happened while I slept. I grabbed my bear spray, flashlight, and my rifle and headed into the woods.

Unfortunately, the trail cams had not been tripped so there were no recordings of what was making the yells and screams in the night. I noticed markings on the tree trunks that looked like claw marks, like the marks that were inflicted on my tent. Some of them were fresh and I do not remember seeing these on my preliminary walk through the afternoon before.

As I continued to look around, I noticed there were no sounds of birds and small animals. There were several strange shaped and bent small trees, almost twisted in two. I know I did not see them the day before either. I felt in my gut I should go back to camp, but I was curious, and I kept going. It only took about ten minutes before I started to hear a low-pitched growl. I reached in my pocket for the bear spray, to just be safe. I never saw any evidence of a black bear or of Sasquatch and decided to check along the creek.

The creek wasn't too far from where I had camped the night before. There were not a lot of trees along the creek bed. I thought I might have an easier time looking for any tracks or other evidence that would indicate what was out here. When I got to the creek, I walked down the edge near the water. There were a few dead fish on the banks. It looked like something pulled them out of the water and ate them fresh, then just left the bones. I walked a little further and then I started to smell a very foul and rancid odor, like something was rotting and then a little worse. I thought there might be partially consumed fish or other animals around, but I was unable to find anything or the source of the odor.

I continued to walk down the creek and kept my eyes open for any signs or activities of bears. There were not any, but I did stumble upon another pile of half consumed fish. I looked around and closer to the water, where the ground was still soft. I found a series of large footprints. The prints led from the water and up to the pile of rotting fish. At best guess, the prints were made by a creature who was walking upright. The print was about 17 or 18 inches long and about 6 inches wide. There was a well-defined heel and what appeared to be four toes. The top of the prints was a bit smudge due to the mud, but it appeared to be a bipedal animal. I had my camera with me and took several photos, one which included my foot for a size comparison. I was unable to find any more evidence along the creek, so I returned to my camp.

Seeing as how my tent had been ripped open the night before, I decided to pack it up and head back into the office.

CHAPTER THIRTY

I WORKED on a farm in Western Tennessee and on the weekends, I worked in town at a second job. I live just outside of Ridgely. Since I worked 7 days a week, I never had a problem sleeping, until this one night in October of 1999. I just couldn't sleep.

It was around 1:00 AM. I decided to get up and go into the kitchen and get a glass of water. I stood at the kitchen sink, and I started to stare out the window. It was dark in the back - we didn't have any exterior lights at that time. The area surrounding my house is mainly wooded and my house was situated below a sizable mountain. Inside, there were a few small kitchen lights that were plugged into the outlets near the floor for safety. The weather was good that week. There was no rain or wind that night.

Out in the backyard, I noticed three pairs of red eyes walking in single file. They were about 20 yards away and in the woods at the back of the yard. I grew up here and had hunted my entire life. I knew all the animals that were local to the area. I had seen all types of animals and eyes walking around in my yard at night before, but not like this. Something felt different this time.

These eyes were different from other animals. They were up higher, around 7 feet from the ground. That ruled out any local wildlife I could think of. The eyes walking through the woods were intense and were glowing a red color. They were the same red as a "Coke Cola" bottle-cap. I noticed that these eyes stayed at the same height - there was no bounce in their steps. Whatever was walking around was most likely heavy and had a very smooth stride. Even though it was pitch-black outside, I could only see a few moving branches in the yard. I didn't see any figures or silhouettes. I did not hear any noises or vocal-izations.

Directly behind my house, there were about four miles of wilder-ness. It was mostly government land, and I was never sure what they did with it. It just remained untouched and stayed that way, almost like it was a buffer zone between the houses and the facility. I wasn't sure what I saw walking around back there. I originally thought that it was a Sasquatch or some other unknown creature. I had heard for years about people seeing things on the government land and we joked that they were doing some sort of hybrid experiments. I never told anyone that I saw something there that night. It was a small town, and I didn't want word to get around and have people start to think that I was seeing things, or I was delusional.

The next morning after the "bottle-cap" incident, I woke up early and walked over to the spot where the eyes vanished deeper into the woods. I looked around and I found a fresh tree branch that looked like it was snapped off from the tree. I looked up and about 9 feet up you could see where the branch used to be. It appeared like something huge had just twisted it and snapped it off. It was large and about 4 to 5 inches in diameter. I didn't check for tracks because of the ground cover. There were a lot of fallen leaves and twigs on the ground already and it would take too long to look for any type of tracks. While I was walking around, I did stumble across an area that had a peculiar smell. I could tell that it was barely lingering on. It smelled like maybe there was a group of rabid skunks that were there and then were frightened, sprayed the trees, and then disappeared.

I walked around for a little bit more and I tried to climb up to where I saw the eyes disappear. It had started to get too difficult for me to climb to where I lost sight of the eyes, even though whatever I saw out here had moved easily across the land and through the trees the night before. I think one thing that kept me from getting to sleep was the neighbor's dog. It had started barking around 11:30 PM and continued for an hour.

About a week before this happened, I woke up in the middle of the night by strange noises outside. My neighbor's dog was barking that night too. It sounded what I imagined a tree being hit with a baseball bat or pipe would sound like. There was a pattern to it too. Three knocks, silence, then three more knocks. That kept going for about half an hour. There was silence for a little bit, and I started to go back to sleep, but then there was a huge sound of metal being smashed. This went on until about 3 AM.

The only other person who heard all the banging was my sister who was visiting with her two children. The kids slept through it, but the next morning my sister asked what all the ruckus was about the night before. I have not heard of any other Sasquatch reports like that.

CHAPTER THIRTY-ONE

I WAS ten years old when my mother met the man who would become my stepfather. We lived in Illinois, and he lived in Colorado. They met online in one of those old chat rooms from the nineties when the internet first started becoming a thing. Though they were together for more than a year when my siblings and I finally met him and when my mother finally met him in person, it wasn't until we were all packed up and moving to Colorado to live with him that I would meet him face to face. His name is Stan, and he was a nice guy. I tried to be stubborn and hold onto my anger over my mother moving us so far away from my dad and the only home we had ever known but Stan was a good guy and my siblings, and I couldn't help but warm up to him. Stan had a cabin in the middle of nowhere and while my siblings and I felt very out of place there, having grown up our whole lives in Chicago, we quickly acclimated to the solitude and peace the forest that surrounded us brought. I have four siblings. I have one younger sister and three older brothers. We had to drive a few miles to get onto the main road in the tiny town the cabin and forest were in, to get the bus to school. We had no neighbors, but we all had so much fun, and Stan taught us everything he knew about living in the woods. By the time we had been there a year it was like we had lived there our whole lives. One of the main things he taught us was how to detect and protect ourselves, if necessary, from wild animals. There were a lot of predators in those woods, but we hardly ever saw any of them and when we did, they would stay away from us if we stayed away from them. It was a really great time in our lives.

One night, after we had been there for a little over a year, my mom and Stan went out on a date. They were going to be gone all afternoon and wouldn't be home until after it got dark outside. We weren't nervous or anything and when they left my siblings and I decided to go play manhunt in the woods. We all had walkie talkies and it was something we did often. We weren't afraid to be in the woods in the dark, but it was summertime and therefore we had plenty of time before the sun went down. We all went and played the game and had a good time. My little sister always tagged along with me because I was the closest to her in age and honestly, I was the nicest of all of us boys to her. She looked up to me, I guess. As we were looking for a good hiding spot, my sister stopped suddenly in her tracks and told me she felt funny. She said she thought our brothers had already found us and that we should hide somewhere else. When I asked her why she thought that she said that she felt like we were being watched and had heard a funny noise. I stopped to listen for a minute and the same feelings of being watched overtook me. It was overwhelming and for some reason I felt a strong sense of fear and dread as well that seemed to have come out of nowhere. I also heard what sounded like someone walking, because there was rustling in the leaves somewhere nearby. I didn't see anyone though and there were no animals around either. The forest didn't go quiet, but it went very still. It was eerie suddenly and I couldn't put my finger on why. My little sister started to cry and said she wanted to go home. I radioed my brothers, and they came and me up with us. I offered to bring her home and stay with her, but it seems the feelings and emotions she and I had been feeling were contagious and all my brothers felt it too. We just wanted to get out of the woods.

We talked about it amongst ourselves as we walked and decided it was because only a day earlier Stan had told us some stories about a local legend, and something he saw with his own eyes a few times in those same woods, about a wild man. That's what he called it anyway. He said it was a gigantic ape-like creature, but it wasn't an ape at all but a man. He claimed it was primitive and had come from long ago, when the area started to be more populated, and some of the human beings went to join the new settlers and some chose to remain in the woods, living off the land and remaining "wild." It was quite a story and it sounded so ridiculous and obviously made up, none of us took it very seriously. We were suddenly starting to rethink our initial assessment of those tales. However, Stan was also a prankster and we all had that in the back of our minds. That's when we heard the first growl. It was low and guttural, and it didn't sound like any of the animals we had all become so familiar with. We looked around but didn't see anything. We started walking faster. We heard another growl and what sounded like something was banging on the trees around us. My oldest brother screamed that the wild man was out there, and he and my other two brothers took off like lightning through the woods, leaving me and my sister out there to fend for ourselves. My little sister screamed and started crying hysterically so I picked her up and started to run after them. I took one more look around as I did so and that's when I saw the hairy creature.

It was at least ten feet tall. It looked like the incredible hulk in a gorilla suit, but it also had the face of a man, but not quite. It really did sort of look like modern depictions of cavemen. I ran with all my might and almost caught up with my brothers as the beast chased us through the woods. We were all screaming and terrified and the faster we ran it seemed the faster it became, and it gained on us very quickly and easily. We all made it to the cabin at around the same time, but my brothers got in the door first and they locked me out! I was pounding on the door and screaming for them to let us in, but they wouldn't. They said the wild man would come in with us and me and our little sister should go hide somewhere else. I almost couldn't believe it. To make a long story short I grabbed her and ran to the open garage and put her in the old car Stan had in there that he had been working on as a hobby with one of my older brothers. I then proceeded to run as fast as I could to the door to close it, just as it was closed almost all the way, I heard a loud growl and saw the wild man's feet. It slammed into and banged on the metal garage door. I crawled into the car in the front seat and got down on the floor. I told my sister in the back to do the same. Five minutes later we didn't hear anything anymore and I got out of the car to be able to listen better. The door to the house that was connected to the garage swung open suddenly and my brothers told me and my sister to get inside. For the next hour I yelled and screamed at them, crying the whole time, wondering how they could just lock us out and leave us to the mercy of that creature the way they had. They made no apologies though and eventually we all settled down. It was eight o'clock before we knew it and the sun had gone down. We all decided to stay in our mom and Stan's room with all the lights off until they got home. Our little sister fell asleep on their bed while the four of us just sat there quietly. None of us wanted to say it but we were all scared that thing would come back and get us somehow if we made any noise. We knew it was lurking out there somewhere, just waiting for the right moment to strike.

I went to the window to look outside and see if I could see the headlights to my mom's car coming up the hill that led to our driveway. I kid you not, the second I put my face to the window, I was greeted with a hideous face staring back at me. I was looking in the eyes of the wild man. I screamed and immediately started to cry. My brothers all looked and saw it too. For it to be even with the window the way it was it had to have been eleven feet or more. It took up the entire window too. It was massive and it was mad. It wanted to get us. We thought we had gotten away but now there was nothing but a piece of glass separating it from us. We all ran to stand against the door, which was as far away from the window that we could get without leaving the room. The beast put its first right through the window as if it were nothing and it seemed like it didn't faze it one little bit. It roared and the stench coming from it was overwhelming. We could do nothing but stand there and scream, even as we heard a loud crashing sound coming from the kitchen, which was the room right behind the door we were standing up against. There was more than one! It took a moment for that to really register. We didn't know what to do and the one at the window was trying to climb in. It was vicious and its face was twisted in rage and determination. It wanted to get to us, and nothing was going to stop it. We heard loud banging and all sorts of random noises coming from the kitchen and we knew another one was out there and that it had smashed the glass of the back door. Suddenly and without warning, the noises in the kitchen stopped and the one in front of us trying to get through the window stopped what it was doing as well. It looked like it was listening and finally and for the first time, its attention was drawn away from us by something. It took off running like a bat out of hell and when my older brother went to the window, he said he saw three of them, all of them as big or bigger than the one trying to get into the bedroom, running faster than he ever saw anything run in his life, back into the woods. I heard my mother scream for us.

We all ran to her. We came barreling out the front door and me and my little sister tried jumping into her arms. We were terrified and traumatized. All my mother and Stan saw though was the dents in the closed garage door. We were all yelling and talking over one another, but Stan seemed to pick up what we were saying immediately. "The wild man?" he said, "you saw him?" We all said that we did, and he ordered all of us kids and my mother inside the house immediately. They saw the mess and my mother was about to throw a fit because she thought that we had broken all the glass and made the mess. Stan understood and told us all to go to our rooms. He and my mother fought for hours about the fact that he had never told her about the creature. She knew how dangerous it was and how it could have ended very tragically. Eventually life went back to normal, but it was never the same again. We had a lot of long-term effects and eventually myself and two of my brothers were diagnosed with post-traumatic stress disorder because of what we had been through. We were hardly ever left alone in the cabin anymore and when we were, it was only when it was necessary, and we were left with a gun. We all had to learn how to use several different types of firearms too. I never saw the creatures again, but I know now that they were what everyone refers to as bigfoot. They weren't friendly and they weren't full of peace, love, and rainbows. They were dangerous predators who surely would have killed every single one of us had the car not scared them off that night. I think they followed us home and remembered where we lived. They were cold and calculated and I'll never forget the anger, the rage in that thing's eyes as it stared us down trying to get to us through the bedroom window. We invaded their territory, and they got revenge by invading ours.

I've often wondered if what Stan told us about where they came from and what they are is true. The eyes were cold, but they looked very human, despite the hatred in them. We didn't play in the woods much after that and we all moved as far away from there as we could without abandoning our mother and Stan, as soon as we were old enough to go out on our own. This tale should serve as a warning for anyone who has any fantasies in their head about what bigfoot is and how they behave. It could be the difference between life and death, whether you heed this message. Thanks for letting me share it.

CHAPTER THIRTY-TWO

IN THE SUMMER OF 2001, I was working in Monarch, Montana as an animal control officer. The department kept getting complaints forwarded to us about a dumpster near the edge of town being tampered with. Residents were finding garbage taken out of dumpsters and then thrown on the ground.

After several weeks of reports, I decided the only way to find out what was doing this was to go out at 3 AM to see if I could catch the 'culprits' in action. I thought I would find either humans or raccoons going through the trash dumpsters. I went to the area in question, turned off the truck and headlights and rolled my window down. I was within five feet of the dumpster. I was there about 30 minutes before any activity happened.

While sitting in my truck, I saw the large silhouette of a human-shaped figure. I waited for a bit and the figure started to open the dumpster and began to throw trash around and on the ground. I quickly turned on the headlights so I could catch him in action. As soon as I turned the headlights on, I saw an extremely tall figure completely covered in hair and going through the dumpster.

The figure was about seven feet tall and was covered in dark, brownish-black hair. The hair was shaggy too and I noticed the hair was thinner on the arms. The arms hung low and seemed like they started basically at the base of the head. They hung down past its knees. I really didn't see much of a neck, but it had broad shoulders and a large oval-shaped head. I could see the eyes. They were totally black. It had hair on its face, but not around its eyes or mouth. As soon as my headlights hit the figure, it looked at me like it was scared.

Right away it started moving off. It didn't run but walked real fast in a weird jumping-skipping strut. Not like a person would run. I think I saw it for about thirty seconds before I got my truck in reverse and got out of there. While I was backing up, I did notice this really bad odor. It was like a wet dog smell mixed with rotten eggs, sulfur, and sewer overflow. It's one of those smells you just can't ever forget. I watched as the creature disappeared into the shadows and I just couldn't believe it. I had seen Bigfoot in the recycling bin.

A few weeks later, in August, my sister and I were driving down State Rd 89, just past Monarch. It was early evening. The sky was starting to get darker than it normally should have been, and I knew there was a storm approaching. It was still enough light to see without headlights. Just after I passed a golf course, the road took a turn into a heavily wooded section. There was something on the road that caught my eyes.

Crossing in front of me, about thirty yards away, were four figures walking across the road. They were walking single file, heading east from one densest part of the woods to the other side where it was also very dense. My sister and I both gasped at the same time. I recognized that tall, hairy figure from that night a few weeks ago. It was Bigfoot again.

The first one in the line was the largest and was about eight feet tall. It was covered in the same dark brownish-black hair as the one I saw near the dumpster. Behind him was a slightly smaller figure, which I assumed to be a female. Then there was a smaller creature. It was about six feet tall. I assumed that to be a younger Bigfoot. There was also a fourth creature following. The smallest one was between four to five feet tall. They were all holding hands and walking single file. They didn't seem to be in that much of a hurry. They all had long legs and they all had long strides, so I know they could have moved faster if they wanted to. I think they were going slower so the smaller one at the back could keep up. The family of Bigfoots walking past us didn't seem to care that we were close and in my truck. I rolled down the windows to hear if there were any sounds or vocalizations. There were no unusual noises or sounds, no grunting or talking. Even the birds were silent in the trees as the Bigfoot family passed through. They simply walked past us and back into the woods. Since there was a huge storm on the horizon, I thought they might be trying to get somewhere and take shelter. I knew there were a few wild caves that way and I thought they might be heading there.

I wanted to wait to see if there were any more Bigfoots who were hurrying and looking for shelter, but the storm was almost here, and my sister really wanted to get home before it hit. On the way back to Monarch, I told my sister about the reports we had been getting about someone breaking into trash bins and about the creature I saw that night.

CHAPTER THIRTY-THREE

ALRIGHT, let me share this wild story that happened not too far from where I live, up in the Hastings Highlands area, near Lake St. Peter, Ontario. I've been camping at the same park there for about 30 years, and let me tell you, I've seen my fair share of moose, bears, deer, wolves, birds – you name it. But what I'm about to tell you, it ain't any of those usual suspects.

So, there's this spot locals call the "dump," where folks go to chuck their garbage and stuff. It's also the place where tourists and campers sneak in to try and catch a glimpse of black bears. It's so common that you'll find loads of vehicles there, with people watching these bears. Well, one evening, I decided to take my buddy along, he's from Toronto and never seen a bear before. We set up and waited, 'cause usually when there's incoming traffic, it spooks the bears, and then you wait for 'em to reappear – takes about half an hour on a busy night.

Now, this particular night, the dump had set a few fires to manage the garbage piles. So, I told my buddy the chances of spotting any bears were rare 'cause they're wary of fire. After waiting for about half an hour, I told him it wasn't our night and he was a bit disappointed, but he understood. And right then, when we were starting to pack it in, we saw this huge log fly through the air from one corner of the lot, followed by raccoons and critters scampering out like crazy. We're both looking at each other like, "What the heck?" Then comes this incredibly loud, bone-chilling scream or growl that just sent shivers down our spines.

Now, through all the smoke and the light from the fires, we notice the outline of a person there. We're thinking, "Is that a ranger or a worker?" We kinda shrugged it off, but then we turned on our head-lights. As soon as we did, this thing jumped down into a hole full of garbage, and we could still see its head sticking out.

Mind you, this hole is like 10 feet deep. We were scared out of our wits, so we start the vehicle and inch forward a bit. Just then, this thing screams again, turns towards us, and hurls this massive appliance right at us. It jumps out of the hole and starts challenging us. We're both terrified, can't believe what's happening. It's easily 10 feet tall, massive, and grunting at us. We decide to hightail it out of there, but as we're leaving, we see it in the rearview mirror until it fades away.

So, we reach the entrance, stop, and get out – even though my buddy's against it 'cause he's scared out of his wits. I light up a cigarette and try to wrap my head around it all. And then, out of nowhere, BAM! A rock smashes into my windshield. (Yeah, I've still got that windshield, can show it to you.) And then comes this terri-fying scream. We could hear this thing approaching, all the cracking and thumping getting closer. We freak out and bolt out of there.

I drop my buddy off back at the campsite, get him settled down, and we agree to keep it to ourselves. Still scared but super intrigued, I tell my dad. He's up for it and wants to check it out. I'm freaked, but I take him along since the dump is just a quick two-minute drive from the campsite. We drive back, pull in, and just as we're reaching the end of the winding road that leads to the dump, this huge creature sprints across the road. It's like 50 feet wide, and it cleared it in just a few strides – that's enough for my dad. He saw it, and we turn right around and head out.

Oh, but here's the kicker. Later that night, we all hear the dogs from the post office/general store going absolutely berserk. Their barking and commotion could be heard all the way from our campground. We thought maybe wolves were attacking the dogs, but then, at the end of all that noise, we hear that unmistakable scream. It spooked everyone, and while it wasn't super loud due to the distance, it was unique enough to send chills down everyone's spine. The next morning, the campground owner tells us that five dogs had been attacked, and guess what – they were missing! Broken chains, signs of a struggle, but no dogs.

Okay, so that's the long story. Sorry for rambling, but I've never done this before. I've got all the nitty-gritty details and a lot more to tell about this Sasquatch encounter, but this area, right around where those Halliburton tunnels are, from that other caller you had? Yeah, that's where it happened. I've been coming here for three decades, and I truly believe that this whole Algonquin to Toronto stretch of woods is a squatch hotspot. I mean, it's so densely forested, like that other caller said, you can't just stroll through it – you can't even see through it. I'm telling you, these creatures are out here, and they're out here in numbers.

CHAPTER THIRTY-FOUR

HEY, I'm from New Hampshire, and after reading some books, including yours, and hearing about other people's encounters, I finally feel brave enough to share my own experiences. Seriously, what I've seen is just mind-boggling.

Okay, so my first run-in happened back in 6th grade – I'm in college now, just so you know. At that time, I was really into playing travel football around the Northeast, which meant early mornings and some travel. I've grown up in New Hampshire, so I've seen my fair share of regular Northeast animals like deer, black bears, and foxes. I mean, it's nothing out of the ordinary. Now, this particular morning, I was getting ready to head to a tournament in Massachusetts, which meant an early start – like 4:30 or 5 in the morning. As I was eating my cereal, I noticed something odd through my sliding glass door. See, I've got a view into my neighbor's backyard through some trees, and when the leaves have fallen off, you can easily see his place from my dining room table.

So, there I am, munching on cereal, when I spot this decently sized deer in my neighbor's yard. Now, we've got some pretty good-sized deer here in NH, so it's not a shock to see one. I glance back at my cereal bowl, and out of the corner of my eye, I catch a blur of movement. Before I know it, I'm looking up, and that deer is down on the ground, with this massive, bulky figure crouched over it. It's like this giant dude, as if one of the world's strongest men threw on a ghillie suit and decided to take down a deer. The sheer size of him was mind-blowing.

I stared at him for a few seconds – not too long – and then he looks up from the deer, just like I had glanced up from my cereal, and locks eyes with me. Now, the view wasn't crystal clear because of the trees and branches, but one thing was for sure: he knew exactly where I was. And I had a gut feeling that the distance between us could be covered real quick. If he decided to make a move, that glass door wasn't going to do much to stop him. We held this gaze for what felt like forever, but was probably just a few moments. Then, he reaches down with his massive arms, picks up that deer like it's a piece of paper, and looks right at me. I'm no expert on deer or humans, but considering how hefty that deer was and how much it must've weighed, I find it pretty darn hard to believe that even the toughest strongmen could lift it up so effortlessly, just tuck it under their arm, and walk away.

So, I'm tracking this guy's movements with my eyes, and when he stands up, I realize he's incredibly tall. I mean, he's not just the thickest and widest "human" I've ever seen – he's also the tallest, by a long shot. And here he is, right in my state, in my neighbor's backyard. It doesn't make any sense – nothing about that creature added up. The speed, the strength, the size – none of it made sense.

Now, onto my second encounter. This one happened a few years later when I went camping up North with an ex-girlfriend. We were up in a state park way up in northern NH. We arrived pretty late at night, and the campground was quite rugged – the kind that experienced campers like. To be honest, we didn't really care about that; we just wanted some alone time, you know, typical stupid teenager stuff. So, we set up our tent late, and I gotta say, things didn't feel quite right to me. I mean, I knew there were other people around, but it felt like they were keeping an eye on us.

We get the tent set up, do our thing for a while, and then I had to hit the bathroom. There's this outhouse with showers a few hundred feet from our site, so I grab my little flashlight and head over. As I'm walking, I notice there's not another soul around us. That feeling of being watched was getting to me, but I tried to brush it off. Then, I hear some snapping sounds to my left, up on this little hill. I turn to look, and peeking out from behind this boulder on the hill is this massive figure. I could only see part of its head and shoulder, and they were both incredibly thick. This thing pops out for a split second and then disappears behind the boulder again. I didn't hear it leave immediately, but trust me, I wasn't about to go up there and find out.

To be honest, I was shocked I didn't wet myself right then and there. I did what I needed to do and then hightailed it back to our campsite. I never told my ex about it 'cause she was super jumpy about anything supernatural. But let me tell you, that incident left me on edge for the rest of that camping trip.

CHAPTER THIRTY-FIVE

LET me take you back to my junior year of high school in 2012. Picture this – Morgan County, Ohio, an old gas road snaking through Wayne National Forest. It was one of those evenings in mid to late April, that hint of spring in the air. I was out there on a mission – Turkey scouting was the game. You see, the turkeys roosted in that neck of the woods, and I had heard their calls many times. So there I was, on the cusp of darkness, trying to communicate with the turkeys using a couple of hoot owl sounds. But there was silence. Not even a peep.

I paused for a moment, just sitting there, and then I heard it – shuffling down the trail a little ways ahead. My initial thought was that I'd startled a deer or maybe a couple of raccoons. These woods were known for their critters, after all.

Determined to get some action, I took a few steps down the trail, maybe a couple of hundred feet or so. I had a plan – I wanted to hoot again, see if I could get a turkey gobble in response. That would have been a solid confirmation that a Tom would be roosting near that tree come morning.

But then it hit me – a putrid, gut-wrenching stench. It was a smell that had me thinking of death, like a rotting carcass. I followed my nose and went over a hill, half-expecting to come across a dead deer. It wasn't deer season at that point, but there had been some issues with what they called blue tongue or something similar. It made me think that maybe a deer had succumbed to it.

So, I peered over the hill, scanning the area. But there was nothing there. Well, not exactly nothing. Movement caught my eye – there was a large oak tree, and behind it was a head. A big head, mind you – blackish brown and staring right at me.

Now, here's where it gets wild. My first thought, believe it or not, was "gorilla." Before you dismiss that, let me explain. You might recall the Zanesville exotic animal massacre. Over 50 exotic animals were set free by their owner, who tragically ended his own life. The local authorities had to take down these animals – think bears, lions, cheetahs, tigers, even wolves. So, the idea of a rogue gorilla wasn't entirely outlandish in my mind. I mean, this was just a couple of miles from my house, and a mere 49 minutes from Zanesville, Ohio.

Curiosity got the best of me, so I took a cautious step closer. As I did, the creature – let's call it that for now – pulled itself partly from behind the tree. What I saw then was staggering – it was crouching, yet still towering over me. I'd estimate it stood somewhere between 6 feet 6 inches and 7 feet tall. A true giant in the animal kingdom.

Then, in an instant, it changed the game. The creature burst into a sprint, coming right at me. Adrenaline surged through me, and my instincts kicked in. I braced myself, lowered my shoulder, and dropped my head. With a guttural yell that I won't repeat here, I prepared for impact. I locked eyes with the creature when it was maybe 15 feet away – a moment frozen in time.

But fate had other plans. At the last possible moment, the creature seemed to veer off, pivoting in a different direction. Maybe my scream had startled it, or perhaps it simply changed its mind. I didn't wait around to find out. My heart pounding, I turned and bolted, racing back the way I came.

When I got home, I shared my heart-pounding experience with my stepdad. His response? Laughter. He'd hunted those woods for years and had never seen or heard anything remotely like what I described. But I knew what I saw, and the memory stuck with me.

I've ventured back into those woods since that day, searching for a trace of the enigmatic creature. Yet, like a phantom, it seemed to have vanished without a trace. Perhaps these creatures are like bears, capable of roaming several miles. Maybe it wasn't from the immediate area and had just wandered into that patch of forest.

Whatever it was, one thing's for certain – that encounter was etched into my memory. The Ohio woods hold mysteries beyond what we can fathom, and to this day, I can't shake the image of that towering, crouching figure, a true enigma of the wild.

CHAPTER THIRTY-SIX

LET me take you back to the summer of 1980, a time when I was just a 10-year-old kid exploring the wilds of Trinity County, California. My dad was living in a quaint little town called Hayfork, nestled amidst the rugged landscape of tall trees, shrubs, and open land. He had a cozy haven on a 10-acre patch a few miles up the mountain, at the end of a dead-end road. It was a time before smartphones and video games, and I was excited to be spending the summer there with my dad, his girlfriend, her two kids, and my brother – a mix of teenagers and me, the young explorer.

The cabin my dad had built became our haven. It was a rugged structure with planked floors, a grand wood stove, and a split log sofa that must have seemed like the pinnacle of comfort in those days. The summer heat had us kids raring for adventure, and we decided a sleepover outside would be the perfect way to experience the wilderness. Gathering our gear, we set ourselves up under the starry night sky. It was a seemingly innocent idea, until the eerie hour of midnight when my resolve wavered. Suddenly, the idea of sleeping outdoors lost its charm, and I decided I'd rather head back to the cabin.

The neighbor boy – my newfound friend – offered to walk me part of the way home. The moon cast a soft glow, painting the road with its light as we meandered down their driveway, flanked by tall, imposing trees. Eventually, he pointed me toward the gate in the distance – our cabin was just a stone's throw beyond that point. My unease began to grow as I contemplated that final stretch, but I didn't want to appear scared.

As he disappeared into his own driveway, I began my solitary walk to the cabin. The plan was simple: reach the gate and then sprint like my life depended on it, straight to the safety of the cabin. The latch clicked shut behind me, and as I turned around, my heart skipped a beat. Roughly 100 feet away, something caught my attention – a figure, a presence, moving through the clearing. My mind raced, desperately trying to make sense of what my eyes were taking in. It was a figure that resembled a man, I told myself, running alongside a dog-like, wolfish creature. Fear surged through me, freezing me in place.

Nearby, a massive manzanita bush seemed to beckon me, offering me cover. I crouched down and hid, watching, waiting. Time seemed to stretch, each moment an eternity as the figure continued its dash toward the thicket of trees. Finally, it was gone from my line of sight. The adrenaline coursing through my veins propelled me forward, and I sprinted to the cabin, my heart pounding in my chest. I collapsed onto the rustic split log sofa, my head sinking into a well-worn, dirty pillow. It might have been uncomfortable, but it was a sanctuary – a haven. Beneath me, I could hear the faint sounds of rodents scurrying beneath the floorboards, but I felt safer than I had ever felt before.

Inexplicably, I chose to keep my harrowing experience to myself. Looking back, I can't quite understand why. Maybe I wasn't even sure what I had seen. The memory lay dormant for years, a secret locked away. It wasn't until recently, much later in life, that I started to openly share my encounter. And that's where your podcast came into play – discovering it was like finding a key that unlocked a door I had long forgotten.

The creature that had dashed through my vision left me bewildered. It didn't fit neatly into any box. The best way I can describe it is as a lean, tall being – maybe a Bigfoot, maybe not. The moonlight offered enough illumination for me to make out its general form, and it's an image I can still summon when I close my eyes. The thing that puzzled me even more was the dog-like creature beside it. I've wracked my brain trying to come up with an explanation, but the pieces just don't fit neatly together.

The gate was a portal between worlds, between safety and the unknown. The creature's movements were otherworldly, a blend of grace and peculiarity. It moved differently – legs that seemed to navigate uneven terrain, arms that scooped in an almost rhythmic motion. The details might have been shrouded by moonlight, but the impression it left on me was indelible. I can't say with certainty that I came face to face with a Bigfoot that night, but I can say with absolute certainty that it wasn't an ordinary man walking a dog. The mysteries of that summer night remain, a vivid memory etched into the fabric of my past.

CHAPTER THIRTY-SEVEN

IT WAS the late spring of 1985 and El Paso, TX was the backdrop for a bewildering encounter that etched itself into the memories of myself, my brother, and two close friends. The stage was set with a dramatic late afternoon thunderstorm that lingered longer than usual, unleashing a deluge of rainwater that transformed the neighborhood's stormwater retention basin into a sight to behold. This reservoir, typically mundane, was now a glistening expanse, a testament to the storm's power.

As evening descended, my brother and I embarked on a bike ride to our friend Jimmy's place, with a pit stop at Tom's house en route. The camaraderie was palpable as we pedaled through the neighborhood. Our destination was set – another friend's house – but fate had other plans for us. Drawn by curiosity, we found ourselves at the basin's edge, awe-struck by the sheer volume of water that had accumulated there. It was a scene none of us had witnessed before, and the allure of this unusual sight compelled us to pause and take it in.

The clock had struck ten, casting the surroundings in an inky darkness. The feeble glow of a distant streetlight barely managed to cast a pale aura on the basin's waterline. As we stood by the street curb, gazing across the waterlogged expanse, a peculiar sight arrested our attention. A figure materialized on the far side of the basin, partially illuminated by the faint porch lights of the nearby houses. Our initial assumption was that it was a person – after all, what else could it be?

With intrigue tinged with a hint of jest, one of my friends dared to call out to the enigmatic figure, "We see you over there!" But there was no response. The figure remained stationary, its unsettling swaying movements casting a mystifying air over the situation. Like a pendulum, it shifted left and right, up and down. Our attempts to make sense of this odd behavior only deepened the puzzle.

Playfully, my friend Jimmy added a hint of bravado to the mix, shouting, "We're coming over there to kick your ass!" This proclamation, seemingly innocuous, spurred the figure into action. It began to move, a dance of sorts, a pas de deux with itself, tracing a curious pattern along the water's edge. It swayed, it shifted, and it defied explanation. Our collective bewilderment grew.

Then, as if caught in a bewildering illusion, our gaze momentarily wavered. And in that fleeting lapse, the figure vanished. Panic surged through us, and our focus shifted to the right side of the basin, the direction from which the figure had vanished. Dark shadows seemed to weave a tapestry of mystery, and our flashlights, feeble beacons of light, struggled to pierce the shroud.

Suddenly, a sound – the gentle, rhythmic shush of water being displaced – drew our attention to the heart of the basin. Instinctively, I swung my flashlight downward, casting a dim illumination on a series of delicate ripples, a serenade of liquid motion moving toward me. It was as if the water itself held a secret, whispering tales of the enigma that approached.

My gaze followed the course of the ripples, tracing their path upward until they converged on a sight that would forever be etched into my mind's eye. Before me stood a figure – an embodiment of the inexplicable. My flashlight's beam first danced upon its chest and two arms, shrouded in a coat of light brown hair. The chest itself was a lighter hue, akin to a sun-kissed tan. As I lifted my gaze, the figure's head emerged from the darkness, and in that pivotal moment, our flashlight beams converged.

Two beams of light met the figure's gaze, and the world seemed to hold its breath. Eye shine, an unearthly green-gold brilliance, stared back at us, an unspoken testament to the unknown. Time stood still, the world reduced to that surreal tableau – two beams of light and a pair of mesmerizing eyes. And then, in a heartbeat, adrenaline surged through my veins, propelling me onto my bike, my senses aflame with primal urgency.

My brother, my friends – we were a swift-moving tide, racing back to Jimmy's house as though the very essence of the unknown pursued us. Bikes clattered, heartbeats thundered, and we sought refuge within the safety of Jimmy's garage, the door sliding shut behind us. There, beneath the dim glow of a single bulb, we regaled Jimmy's mother with our astonishing tale. Our words tumbled out in a frenzied rush, fueled by the sheer bewilderment of what we had witnessed.

Her calm demeanor and understanding gaze soothed our frenetic nerves, though her reaction was far from the panic we felt. She listened, her motherly wisdom serving as a balm for our shared experience. As we recounted our encounter, our voices echoed the enigma that had unfolded under the cover of night.

Hours slipped by as we hashed and rehashed the details, dissecting every nuance and attempting to unravel the mysteries of that fateful evening. The events that had unfolded defied explanation, remaining lodged within our collective consciousness, a puzzle without a solution.

Though time has moved on and years have passed, the memory of that encounter remains as vivid as the day it transpired. The memory of the swaying figure, the mesmerizing eye shine, and the inexplicable dance between light and shadow continues to linger, etched into the annals of our shared history. And while the years may have dulled the edge of uncertainty, the essence of that encounter remains – an enduring enigma, a chapter in the chronicles of the unexplained.

CHAPTER THIRTY-EIGHT

SO, back in 2018, during my construction project days, I had this wild experience that I just can't forget. Now, you gotta know, I come from Wyoming, a place where the Bighorn Mountains were like a second home to me. Nature and the great outdoors were in my blood. But after moving to Missouri and getting into the construction gig, I found myself traveling all over the state for my work. That's when things took a seriously unexpected turn.

It was a typical morning, around 5:30 AM, and I was hitting the road with one of my crew members. We were headed to a job site about 3.5 hours away. The sun was barely up, and the world was just starting to wake. As we were driving along, something out of the ordinary caught my eye. It was this big, dark figure that sort of stepped out from the trees onto the road. My first thought? Bear, of course. But this bear was different. It was standing on two legs, which is pretty weird for a bear. I started easing off the gas to get a better look.

As I got closer, I realized this wasn't your usual bear behavior. It was moving, well, kind of gracefully. Like it was gliding across the road. I mean, bears don't move like that, right? And the steps it was taking, they were huge. In just two steps, it crossed the entire two-lane highway. I was gobsmacked, to say the least. But then things got even weirder. As I passed by, it stood up taller, turning toward my car. I caught a glimpse of its head, and that's when I knew something was really off. It definitely wasn't a bear. My gut was telling me, "Bigfoot."

I know it sounds crazy, but that was honestly what crossed my mind. Bigfoot, the legendary creature people talk about. I couldn't believe it. I had to turn around, to see if I could spot it again. I was itching to get a better look. So, we doubled back. But guess what? By the time we got back to where I saw it, it had vanished. Just like that. Vanished into thin air.

Now, here's where it gets even more bizarre. While we were parked there, scratching our heads, another car came zipping up the road from the opposite direction. They slammed on their brakes, came to a screeching halt, and then sped away like they were fleeing from something. I kid you not, it was like a scene from a thriller movie. That moment right there, it sent shivers down my spine.

And you know what made it even eerier? The whole area got deathly quiet during that sighting. No birds chirping, no rustling leaves, nothing. It was like nature itself was holding its breath. I can't even begin to describe how unsettling that silence was. I mean, I've been in intense situations before, being a former marine and all that, but this was a whole different kind of unnerving.

So, we hit the road again, heading to our destination, but my mind was just racing. What had I just seen? A creature that was walking on two legs, with a head that wasn't like any bear I'd ever seen. I kept replaying the whole thing in my head, trying to make sense of it. But honestly, to this day, I still can't explain it. It's one of those things that sticks with you, you know? A bizarre encounter that makes you question what's really out there in the woods.

CHAPTER THIRTY-NINE

I RAISED my kids in the same cabin in the mountains that I grew up in. It's an old miner's cabin in the middle of nowhere and completely secluded from everything and everyone. It's located in Colorado, and it takes anywhere from forty-five minutes to an hour just to get down the mountain and back to any semblance of civilization. The closest big city is two hours away and the tiny town at the bottom of the mountain is another forty-five minutes to an hour once you are down that mountain. I bring all of this up just to enforce how secluded our home really was, but we wouldn't have had it any other way. Growing up, and my kids have always said they've felt the same way, it was like living in a fairytale. The moose, bears and other wildlife were our only neighbors and my kids played together in those woods and all over our gorgeous property without any fear, just as me and my siblings had done. My encounter with the strange and possibly paranormal didn't happen until all my kids were older and moved out of the house except one. My daughter had moved back in with me. My wife, her mother, had passed away suddenly a couple years before and I had a bad accident one night when it snowed on the mountain, and I was caught in it trying to get up the mountain. I was driving much too fast and ended up driving off a cliff. Luckily, I got away with only two torn rotator cuffs and a broken hip. It took me a long time to convalesce from those injuries and my daughter Jaime was the only one of my kids who wasn't married yet. She didn't have as many responsibilities as her older siblings and so she moved back into the cabin to help take care of me. It was a very long and painful recovery process but by the time the end of Spring rolled around I was feeling a lot better and a lot like my old self again. My daughter had been a Godsend and I don't know what I would have done without her. One night she and I were sitting in the living room, each of us reading a book, when there was a loud banging sound that made us both jump.

It sounded like it was coming from the side of the cabin. My immediate thought was that someone was trying to break in but immediately that didn't make sense because if it were someone trying to burgle us, they would have been trying to get in through the front door or one of the windows. The banging was coming from the side of the house and neither one of us could understand it at all. I went into my bedroom and grabbed two guns. I handed one to my daughter and told her the minute she saw someone coming through the door or one of the windows to just start shooting. The whole cabin was shaking and while I briefly considered that maybe it was a confused moose that was ramming the side of the cabin, that also didn't make much sense once I put some thought behind it. Whatever was banging on the side and slamming into it, had hands. I don't know how we both knew that, but we did, and we were sure that it couldn't have been an animal. However, the banging had so much force behind it we were also sure that it wasn't a human being either. I honestly thought the logs were going to come rolling into the house, that's how bad and violent it was. There were other noises too, that gave away the fact that it couldn't have been a human being. The growling and heavy breathing weren't noises humans typically made. Whatever it was sounded extremely angry though and it also seemed intent on getting inside of the house. We turned off all the lights and just waited. We stayed like that for almost an hour before it stopped, and we didn't hear or feel anything anymore. I ran to the window and peeked out, but I didn't see anything out there. We were both very scared but as a father, I tried to downplay my fear and the situation itself, to try and make my daughter not only feel better, but much more comfortable. She was terrified and I hated to see her feeling like that in her own home.

I calmed her down after about twenty minutes of reassuring her that it had to have just been a confused moose and eventually, we both went to bed. A week passed without any other strange or scary incidents, and I felt like I was finally ready to get out of the house. I had been cooped up all winter and aside from staying on the property, I hadn't been outside that whole time. I hadn't been able to do any of the things I loved all of which involved being in the woods. I wanted to start off slow so I asked Jaime if she would accompany me on a walk. We had always gone for walks and while her siblings and my wife would accompany us sometimes, it was something Jaime and I enjoyed doing, just the two of us, since she was very small. We had a trail that we called our own and she immediately agreed to go with me. I had to take it slow and to get to the head of the trail we had to drive down the mountain just a little bit. I let her drive and we parked off to the side, where there was a space for someone to park but I think that was for emergencies or something, back when the mines were open and running for the miners who lived all over the mountain in the cabins, and not for leisure activities. However, we figured it didn't matter much because ours was the only cabin still standing and even if someone did call the authorities and complain, their fastest arrival time would have been two hours. We didn't plan on being out there for that long anyway. I took my time and Jaime stayed right next to me the whole time. Jaime had a backpack with her with bear spray and a blow horn in it. I had taught my kids to respect the wildlife out in that forest and on that mountain from the time they could walk. We've been on many walks and hikes out there where we ran into a mountain lion or hungry bear and all we would have to do to get them to quickly run away and leave us alone was to sound the blow horn. They would be so terrified they would leave us alone very quickly. I was proud of her for remembering because I hadn't thought of it. I've often wondered if that's what saved our lives that day. I won't ever know for sure, but I have a suspicion that it just might be.

We walked for an hour and were just about to turn back when my hip really started hurting me. I had to stop for a few minutes and take a break. I could see Jaime was worried about me, but I reassured her I was okay. The truth of the matter was that, while I was in pain, a very strange and unusual feeling was coming over me as well. I felt scared but there was no apparent reason for the fear I was feeling. The hairs on the back of my neck stood up suddenly and I noticed that it seemed like there was no noise anymore throughout the entire forest. Just as I thought about how quiet and eerie the usually very inviting and comfortable woods were, my daughter spoke up and told me she was experiencing all those same things. I told her not to be silly, that everything was just fine and that we would make our way back to the car in just a minute. It was going to be dusk soon and no matter how safe we always felt out there we both knew that being out there in the middle of the forest on the mountains in the dark was simply inviting trouble or an animal attack. I saw something moving out of the corner of my eye. I didn't look right away because I didn't want Jaime to follow my gaze. I somehow just instinctively knew that something was watching us from over to the right side of me. I casually glanced over there and sure enough I saw something. I couldn't make out exactly what I was looking at because it was far enough away that all I could make out was that something was there. The shape of it didn't look familiar as it was far too tall and wide to have been a human being but for those same reasons it couldn't have been an animal either. I was even more frightened at that point and so I decided to play through the pain so to speak and told her we needed to start walking back to the car and that we needed to do it quickly.

She didn't ask any questions and we were on our way. We had only been walking for five minutes or so when I looked down and saw about a hundred shell casings. They were all over the ground and scattered in all different directions. It occurred to me and the first thought that popped into my mind was that someone else had been out there, and that they had been forced to defend themselves against something using one hundred rounds of ammunition. I couldn't even fathom the creature that it would take that much ammunition to stop an attack from. I could tell Jaime was thinking the same things as I was but before either of us could say a word, we smelled the most horrible, rotten smell we had ever come across. It made our noses burn and our eyes water. I knew that whatever I had seen watching us when we were taking that short break was still out there, that it was still watching and now following us and that it had been whatever the person had been shooting at. I told her to move quickly, and she did. Suddenly a giant rock whizzed past Jaime's head. She turned around and at first, she was giggling because she thought I was playing some sort of joke on her. She had been in front of me and when she turned to look at me, she realized immediately that it hadn't been me who threw the large, softball sized rock at her. I had two torn rotator cuffs and though they were healing, I couldn't throw a pebble with either arm. I saw the figure step out from behind some trees about a yard away from where me and my daughter were standing. It had black hair all over its body, was eleven feet tall and half as wide or more and it looked evil. It just seemed malevolent somehow and I heard the words in my head "get out of here and don't come back" but I can't be sure if the creature was communicating with me or if I just had enough common sense to know we needed to hustle. I told her to keep walking and not to look anywhere but at the ground. It looked like a giant, black ape and it was pissed. We had encroached upon its territory.

As we walked, we heard growling sounds, extremely loud ones and I knew the creature was right behind us. We heard it crashing through the woods and those same softball sized rocks were whizzing past both of our heads as we got out of there as fast as we could. The more we walked the closer the growling and breathing sounds got to us and I knew we were going to be attacked. I knew it was about to make its move, we were moving too quickly for it not to attack us, and that it was about to do it soon. I told Jaime to stop and hand me the blow horn and when she did, I squeezed it and it blared through the woods. I did that four or five times and it seemed like it backed the creature off. I didn't see it anymore and neither one of us heard it. It wasn't until we got to the car that we heard a very loud and ferocious sounding howl/growl that echoed through the woods and made my blood run cold. As we got into the car, I took one quick look back and saw the creature standing there, arms crossed over its chest, staring at us with hatred in its eyes. We drove home. Once we got to the cabin, we locked all the doors and windows and slept in the living room that night, with one of us on each couch. We haven't had another issue or encounter with whatever that ape-like creature was in the woods, and it's been eleven years. However, we are much more careful when we go on walks now, and Jaime always makes sure she isn't out there at night under any circumstances. I walk with my grandkids now and my kids and Jaime and I have both told them the story of what happened to us out there. It took months for us to put two and two together that the creature in the woods was more than likely the same one that had been trying to bust through the logs to get to us inside of the cabin the night before.

I didn't know what to make of all of it at first but Jaime and I, after doing some extensive research online, are more than satisfied that what we encountered that day and the creature trying to break into the cabin, was bigfoot. I know many people believe that bigfoot is peaceful and just wants to be left alone, with some of them even going so far as to believe they are spiritual beings from other dimensions. While all of that may be well, good, and true in their experiences, in mine and Jaime's we knew we were going to be killed. I wholeheartedly believe if I hadn't thought to blow that airhorn that day that would have been the end of us. While it didn't completely get rid of the bigfoot creature, it did slow it down and make it hesitate enough that we were able to make it back to our car and get the hell out of there.

CHAPTER FORTY

BACK IN THE mid-90s I was out in Rosedale, Illinois, just minding my own business, picking up creek stones for my wife's flower bed. You know how it is, just going about your day, not expecting anything out of the ordinary.

This stretch of Rosedale Valley is about 2 to 3 miles long. There's this road, Coon Creek Road, that winds through it, with a creek on one side. And then, on the other side, there's this open field that stretches up to the hillside. Both sides of the valley are these thick woods, and the terrain can get pretty steep.

I had been down there by the creek, tossing those stones up by the road. I must've walked about a mile and a half down that creek, and I was on my way back to the van. And that's when things got weird. It's like all of a sudden, my senses were on high alert, and the hair on the back of my neck stood up. Have you ever had that feeling, like something's not quite right?

Anyway, I stopped in my tracks, just looking around, trying to figure out what set off my instincts. And then, I saw it – this massive, dark thing on the hillside across the field. At first, I thought it might be a tree stump or something, but there was something off about it. It was

159

this dark brown to dusty gray color, and it was swaying from side to side, real slow.

I couldn't take my eyes off it, like I was in a trance or something. And then, out of nowhere, it stood up. I mean, picture this – this tall figure, like 7 to 8 feet, covered in hair, just standing there. And the weirdest part? The more we stared at each other, the more that swaying got intense. It was like some kind of standoff, and I was locked in this silent conversation with whatever this thing was.

But you know how it goes, right? Reality finally snapped back, and I was booking it back to the van. Adrenaline pumping, heart racing, the whole nine yards. And as I was sprinting, I could see this creature, whatever it was, starting to make its way up that steep hillside. Now, that's no easy feat, my friend. But it was like it knew I was spooked and was just showing off.

The crazy part is, as it was climbing, it turned around and looked back at me one more time. Like it wanted to make sure I was getting a good view of its disappearing act. I mean, can you imagine? It's the kind of thing that makes you question reality, you know?

I've shared this story with folks, and I've gotten my fair share of reactions – some laughs, some raised eyebrows. But let me tell you, when you lock eyes with something that's way out of the ordinary, it sticks with you. And that swaying, hair-covered mystery on that hillside? Well, it's a memory that's gonna stay with me for a long, long time.

CHAPTER FORTY-ONE

IN 2022 I had an encounter with what I think was a bigfoot on the Buffalo River in Arkansas. I'm out there hiking the bluff trail, or as they call it, the goat trail. I'm all about capturing some awesome photos and just enjoying the great outdoors. Now, I'm not one to usually chat about this kinda stuff, but there's always been this inkling in me that there's more to the wilderness than meets the eye.

So, I park my truck at the steel creek campgrounds, a spot I know from a previous adventure with my son. The trail follows the river, crossing it a bunch of times. Armed with my trusty camera, I set off early in the morning, around 7:45 or 8. I cross a couple of creeks, take some snapshots of the water and those towering bluffs. All seems well and peaceful.

Then things start getting eerie. I'm about a mile into the hike, and I've just finished my second creek crossing. Now, I'm walking into an area with tall grass and trees, and that's when I hear it – this deep, guttural sigh or grunt. My heart's going haywire, and then it happens – this massive creature stands up right in front of me.

I can't see it clearly, just catch a glimpse of the back of its head and this absolutely colossal hand brushing a tree branch aside as if it's no big deal. The trees around it are swaying and creaking as it moves away, and all I can do is stand there, feeling like I'm stuck in some surreal dream.

Honestly, I'm frozen solid, except for the fact that I didn't end up wetting myself, which I can only credit to my pre-hike bathroom break. But let me tell you, my legs might as well have been glued to the ground. It's like time's suspended, and there I am, watching this scene that defies all logic.

Eventually, I manage to shake off the shock. I figure, "Okay, pal, you can either freak out and flee like a headless chicken, or you can keep your cool and just continue what you came here to do." So, I choose the latter, but I decide I'm gonna make as much noise as humanly possible. I start chattering away to myself, just so that whatever that was knows I'm still very much present.

I proceed to the bluff, snap some pics, and try my best to act nonchalant, even though my mind is racing a mile a minute. A few hours later, I'm heading back to the same spot, and then I hear it – this massive crash that sounds like a tree being ripped apart. I turn my gaze, and I see the trees shaking, but it's not heading toward me, it's like they're swaying in the direction that creature had gone.

Instinctively, I whip out my phone to capture the moment, hit record, and – you guessed it – everything suddenly stops. No more trees moving, nothing! It's as if whatever it was sensed the camera and thought, "Nah, I'm outta here." By this point, I'm practically shouting every thought that pops into my head, cause I'm rattled, to say the least. Armed with nothing but my voice, I dash back to my truck like there's no tomorrow.

I can say that I wasn't really terrified in the sense that I'll never go back out to the woods alone. In fact I've been back over a dozen times since and haven't seen or heard a thing, but one day I'm sure I'll run into it again.

CHAPTER FORTY-TWO

WHEN I WAS 13 years old, I had this incredible adventure with my dad and one of his friends in northern Arizona. We decided to go on a horseback ride in an area that was off the beaten path and not frequented by many people. It was an untouched part of nature, full of mystery and excitement.

Our main goal that day was to hunt down some pesky porcupines that had been causing trouble in the area. Armed with our trusty 30/30 Winchester rifles, we were ready to take care of business. As we rode along, we had already managed to shoot a few porcupines that were hanging out in the trees. They were usually pretty high up, so it took some precise aim to hit them.

But then, as we made our way up a ridge, something caught my eye in the distance. I squinted and noticed a massive cottonwood tree down in the valley. And guess what? There was something perched up there that I initially thought was a porcupine. I excitedly pointed it out to the adults, saying, "Hey, look, there's a porcupine!"

But as I continued to observe it, I quickly realized it was much too big to be a porcupine. My curiosity grew, and I became convinced that it wasn't any ordinary creature. It was like nothing I had ever seen before in my young life.

This mysterious being stood tall and proud, towering above the ground. Its sheer size astonished me. It must have been about as tall as I am now, standing at 6'4". Its whole body was covered in a dense, dark brown fur that glistened under the sunlight. From the distance we were at, I could make out the individual strands of hair, and they seemed surprisingly long and coarse. It gave the creature an intimidating presence, as if it were the guardian of the wilderness itself.

As I continued to watch, mesmerized, the creature seemed to sense our presence. With incredible agility, it leaped down from the tree, landing gracefully on its hind feet. The sight was awe-inspiring. It then started to move towards us, its body swaying with each step. Its gait was unlike anything I had ever seen, both human-like and yet strangely otherworldly. Its long, muscular arms swung back and forth with a grace that seemed almost hypnotic.

The creature closed the distance between us, covering about 40 feet in what felt like a few heartbeats. It moved with a calculated confidence, each movement deliberate and purposeful. As it reached a nearby line of thick brush, it turned to face us, its piercing gaze locking onto ours. I could feel the intensity of its presence, as if it were peering deep into our souls.

Then, in a surprising display of agility, the creature squatted down, disappearing into the protective embrace of the brush. Even though it was no longer visible, I couldn't shake the feeling that it was still observing us from its hidden vantage point.

I turned to the adults, my excitement brimming, and suggested that we take a shot at the creature. But they hesitated, their expressions filled with a mix of fear and uncertainty. They whispered worriedly about the possibility of the creature's mother being nearby, and we ultimately decided it was best to err on the side of caution.

With heavy hearts, we turned our horses around and made our way back to the truck. Our original plan to explore the area further had to be abandoned in light of this extraordinary encounter. The atmosphere was thick with both wonder and a tinge of fear as we rode back, our minds racing with questions and our hearts pounding with the memory of what we had witnessed.

To this day, that encounter remains etched in my mind. The details of that creature, its imposing stature, the flowing dark brown fur, and the enigmatic way it moved—everything about it continues to fascinate me. It was a moment of pure connection with nature's secrets, a reminder that our world is still filled with wonders yet to be fully understood.

CHAPTER FORTY-THREE

I WAS dead set on reaching the summit of Mt. Elbert, the highest peak in Colorado. I had already tried twice before, but both times I had to turn back due to bad weather. Determined as ever, I decided to go solo this time around. It was late June of 2009 and I set out from the trailhead early in the morning all by myself.

The weather that day was surprisingly perfect and warm for the season. It seemed like there hadn't been much snow during the winter because even at the summit, there was very little snow left. I reached the top at around 1:45 pm, basking in the accomplishment. The view was breathtaking, and I took some pictures with my trusty digital camera to capture the moment.

However, it wasn't until later, around 3:30 pm and at an altitude of approximately 11,500 feet, that something truly extraordinary happened. I was making my way down, feeling exhausted from the long hike. The trail I was on wasn't very popular due to its steepness and ruggedness, so I hadn't encountered a single person all day. As I traversed through the only level portion of the trail, a high mountain plateau that lasted for about 300 yards, I heard a strange sound—a mix between a scream and a growl, with a surprisingly high pitch. The sound seemed to carry for miles, sending shivers down my spine.

I immediately froze in my tracks, my hand instinctively reaching for the holster of my pistol. I scanned the area, trying to locate the source of the sound, but the mountainous terrain made it difficult to pinpoint. I first looked to my right, into the dense pine forest, but I couldn't spot anything unusual. Slowly, I did a full 360-degree scan, and that's when I saw it—a Bigfoot, standing about 7 to 7 1/2 feet tall, approximately 50 yards away from me. I was wearing army camo, and for a few seconds, I could tell the creature was trying to figure me out. I was both terrified and amazed, so I couldn't bring myself to move.

Suddenly, the Bigfoot turned around and took off with incredible speed and long strides. It ran in a way that resembled a human's movement, albeit with a slightly hunched upper back and a more powerful gait. Its fur or hair appeared to be a mix of black and brown, thick and matted in certain areas. I lost sight of it after about 10 seconds of its rapid retreat. At that point, my heart was pounding so hard that I thought it might burst out of my chest. The sound of my own heartbeat echoed in my ears. Without hesitation, I pulled out my pistol and cautiously continued down the trail, filled with adrenaline. I constantly looked over my shoulder, scanning my surroundings, not taking any chances.

It wasn't until I reached the cabin I had rented that I realized my camera had been in my backpack the whole time. I hadn't even thought about capturing the incredible sighting on film. But that didn't matter to me in the end. I knew what I had seen, and no one could ever take that away from me.

To this day, the memory of that encounter is etched deeply in my mind. It was a surreal experience, one that I will always carry with me, reminding me of the mysteries that lie within the unexplored corners of our world.

CHAPTER FORTY-FOUR

THERE WAS a time when I was obsessed with all things Bigfoot. I read everything I could, watched all that was available. But I needed more. I thought the only way I could get enough was to visit the remote wilderness of British Columbia. And in 2009, I did just that. I decided to take a vacation by myself and try to find a real Bigfoot - all by myself. The towering mountains, dense forests, and untouched landscapes were breathtaking. If nothing else came from this trip, I'd always have that. I knew that this trip held the potential for extraordinary discoveries.

Motivated by a deep curiosity. a desire for evidence, and the fact that no one wanted to go with me, I went on this trip alone. Solo. By myself. I knew it would be just me and Bigfoot. When I arrived in British Columbia, I rented a SUV with GPS, grabbed a few maps, a couple of cameras, and essential survival gear. I was ready to unmask the truth about Bigfoot.

I drove out to the cabin I rented for two weeks and unloaded the supplies I would need. I settled into the cabin, unpacked, and got the maps out. I spread them across the kitchen table and began to figure out what my first move would be. Equipped with the latest in essential Bigfoot gear, I prepared for my trek into the wilderness. I had a detailed map that marked areas known for Bigfoot sightings. My trusty camera, loaded with fresh batteries and an ample supply of memory cards, was ready to capture any evidence I might encounter. Additionally, I packed survival equipment, and my cell phone with backup batteries. Before setting off, I let a few close friends know where I was and where I was going. I allowed them to track me through my phone and the GPS that I had enabled. The isolation and vastness of the surroundings were both invigorating and humbling, reminding me how wild and untamed nature could be.

It wasn't long before I stumbled upon a remarkable find. It was in a secluded area of the forest where I came across a patch of undisturbed forest floor. As I carefully examined the ground, I discovered a series of large, distinct footprints mashed in the soft earth. The footprints were of a remarkable size and shape, unlike any I had ever seen before.

The footprints were huge! Each print measured approximately 18 inches in length, around 8 inches wide. The deep imprints indicated significant weight and pressure, further adding to the impression that they were not of any ordinary creature. The toes were well-defined, with an arch that hinted at a powerful being. The sheer distinctiveness of the footprints left little room for doubt - I had found evidence of Bigfoot.

As I stood there, staring at the footprints, I found I was speechless. This was the evidence I had been looking for - proof that the legend of Bigfoot, like most things, might indeed have a basis in reality. The sheer size and clarity of the footprints got me excited, and I was even more crazed with the idea of finding Bigfoot.

I started to track the trail left by the creature's footprints. I followed the imprints, noting their depth, spacing, and direction. The trail led me through thick undergrowth, across babbling streams, and over rocky outcrops. This was like the most intense workout I had ever done, but I knew the rewards would outweigh all the exertion.

I kept hiking along the trail, photographing and documenting each footprint carefully. I measured the size and shape of every print, ensuring accurate records of their distinct characteristics. Careful examination of the depth provided additional insight into the weight and pressure exerted by the creature that had left the imprints. I noted the time of day when I found them along with anything along the trail - extra leaves, broken branches, and crushed grass. I thought everything was valuable. I would rather have too much info than not enough. As I continued to follow the trail, patterns and direction of movement began to emerge. The footprints seemed to be heading in a specific direction, with a consistent stride length that indicated a purposeful and deliberate gait. I felt like Bigfoot was on a mission and I was hot on the trail.

Along the path, I found various other animal tracks, from deer to bears. Careful analysis and comparison allowed me to rule out these tracks as potential sources of the creature's footprints. The distinctive characteristics of the footprints made them unique and different from those of other known animals in the area.

As I continued my investigation, so many different emotions washed through me. On one hand, the awe-inspiring nature of the footprints filled me with a sense of excitement and wonder. The possibility of being in the presence of Bigfoot was a surreal experience. Yet there always was a lingering skepticism in the back of my mind. I began to wonder if I would discover the real truth, once and for all?

I carefully considered alternative explanations for the footprints. I thought about the possibility of hoaxes or misidentifications. I needed to remain objective and analytical, keeping an impartial perspective. I really had to make sure there were no potential biases. Despite my best efforts to remain skeptical, the sheer consistency and distinctiveness of the footprints made it increasingly difficult to dismiss them as misinterpretations.

During my expedition in the Canadian wilderness, I had several unexpected encounters with the local wildlife. I continued on my journey, going further into the wilderness. Each day I went into the untamed territory, and I would come in contact with several varieties of animals - deer, squirrels, and birds. Seeing all these creatures live together and in harmony made me realize that this was a diverse ecosystem and that each creature lived together in this delicate balance of nature.

After several days, I saw no new signs of Bigfoot, so I decided to stay in my hideaway cabin and look over the evidence I documented. I analyzed the stride length and gait exhibited by the tracks. By measuring the distance between each print and observing their alignment, I could figure out patterns that indicated a consistent movement. The length of the stride, which was significantly larger than that of any known animal in the region, suggested to me the presence of a creature that was huge and had an exceptional gait. I began to wonder if Bigfoot lived a nomadic lifestyle or if he lived in a certain area. Did he have to travel for food? Was he a hunter or a gatherer?

I only had two days left on my trip, so I thought I would sit down and reflect, write down my notes while they were fresh in my mind. During my time in the wilderness, I witnessed unexplained sounds and movements along with strange calls that echoed through the forest. Several times, late at night, the silence was broken by crashes and rustling in the underbrush. I would look after these experiences, but I never saw a Bigfoot or a tall moving shadow in the trees. I knew there was a possibility of a close encounter with Bigfoot, but he never manifested.

The evidence I had discovered, combined with the unexplained sounds and crashes, only seem to fuel my imagination. The idea that I could come face-to-face with this creature frightened me, to be honest. The solitude and remoteness of the surroundings amplified the danger, leaving me in a constant state of alertness and readiness for whatever might lie ahead.

Like all good things, my time away from the real world was coming to an end. My expedition in the wilderness was over. I felt a sense of accomplishment and excitement for having witnessed the remarkable footprints left by Bigfoot during my trip. The pages of my notebook were filled with sketched depictions of the footprints, accompanied by detailed measurements and notes. Each page served as a record of the evidence I had gathered. I knew this was not my last trip and I would continue to search for Bigfoot. Although this trip was over, the memories of those footprints and the thought of the next trip stayed with me, driving me deeper into the land and world of Bigfoot.

CHAPTER FORTY-FIVE

IN A TIME when men had nothing better to do than explore every godforsaken corner of the earth and then tell loud stories about it, it so happened that a man named Jackson Townsend attempted to cross the Rocky Mountains. Said J.T. is a relative of mine and left us a diary that, after many detours, was finally inherited by me.

Being an avid explorer myself and loving hiking and traveling, I have always read his entries with excitement and curiosity. And finally, as I got older, I let those inspire me. This enabled me to cross several countries off my bucket list at the tender age of twenty.

Like him, I also wanted to cross the Rocky Mountains, which I finally did in July a few years ago. In fact, I was sitting in my tent reading his guidebook on this venture when I had my strange encounter.

In his diary at the time, he wrote:

"I saw the footprints of a gigantic being. It had huge toes and long toenails. The ball of the foot was as wide as my hand, and the foot was almost twice as long as my forearm."

The story made me smile. He often spoke of strange finds during his hikes through the Rockies in his journal. And, of course, I didn't believe a word he had written.

When I finished reading, I turned off the light and lay down to sleep. It was a warm night, and I wasn't afraid of the animals living on the high ground. I snuggled down in my thin sleeping bag and stared through the top canvas of my tent, behind which I could see the starry sky. Many people underestimate the beauty of nights in the wild nature. I just can't understand it.

I was about to close my eyes when I heard the crunch of falling rocks. At first, I thought it might be rubble kicked off by some mountain goats. So, I closed my eyes again and tried to fall asleep when stone crunched against stone again, and small pebbles rolled against my thin tent wall. I wasn't hurt or anything.

It was just enough to make me open my eyes again and sit up so I could see behind me and behind my tent where the rocks had landed.

In addition to the stars, there was also the moon in the sky, which allowed me to see my surroundings a bit. Behind me was a relatively steep stone wall against which I had pitched my tent to protect against sudden rain and wind. At the foot of this wall were gigantic boulders and rocks, which I had to climb the following day to continue my journey. On these, I could see the outline of a figure that I didn't recognize at first. I wondered if it was a human sitting on a rock or if the figure was just incredibly gigantic.

The longer I stared at the strange figure, the less certain I was of what I saw. But then the black shadow began to move, to straighten up, unfolding to its full height.

My heart was in my mouth, and I managed not to twitch a muscle in my body of fear. The creature was massive. What if the stories told by my ancestor were true, and there was a gigantic creature that lived in the Rockies and was now disturbed by my presence? Would the alien beast kill me now? Punish me for entering its territory without being asked?

I watched with wide eyes as the creature came closer and closer. With every step, I could see more of it. Long, strong legs covered with thick fur. The arms were also muscular and covered with a thick coat. I couldn't tell from the shoulders whether it was the same fur or whether it had long hair. I didn't even recognize the face in the darkness until it slowly crouched before me. It was only two strides from me and hunkered down with a heavy panting, its vast hands supporting its massive upper body, and the figure cocked its head curiously so that the moonlight gathered in its eyes.

So, we stared at each other, motionless; I panicked, and it was curious. Slowly it came a little closer and seemed to sniff the air before it snorted disapprovingly and shook its head slightly. Was it anger? Would it now tear my tent and drag me out of it?

My lungs were already starting to burn. I held my breath for so long, believing any casual movement could startle the animal. As I tried to breathe as quietly as possible, I heard the creature in front of me do the same. And so, we breathed together. Slowly, carefully. It was a strange thing, this sharing of a breathing rhythm. But the figure didn't seem bothered by it.

Suddenly, without warning, it straightened up and stalked away. It didn't look around. Didn't even seem to notice me anymore. I watched with my mouth open as it slowly disappeared into the darkness and didn't look back once.

I flopped onto my back, panting, and made a quick effort to calm down. I didn't even notice how quickly the time passed, and when the first birds chirped in the distance and the sun was already visible at the top of the hill, I got up and quickly packed my backpack. I just wanted to get out of the place. What if the creature changed its mind and returned to do something to me?

Tired and torn, I climbed the hill and saw the already snow-covered part of the Rocky Mountains looming ahead of me.

As the dark gray slowly gave way to white snow, I stopped.

I saw a trail in front of me. Not that of an animal or even a human. Something much larger had taken the path ahead of me, leaving footprints yards long and wide. Such as my ancestor had described in his travel journal.

CHAPTER FORTY-SIX

BACK IN THE summer of 1991, I was a cadet at the US Air Force Academy in Colorado Springs, Colorado. I had only been at the Academy for a few weeks and was in the final stages of basic training when something strange occurred.

Now, the Academy itself is situated at the foothills of the Colorado Rocky Mountains. Basically, if I stepped out of the Cadet area, I would find myself standing amidst the mountains. There was an abundance of brush, trees, and various natural elements that could conceal just about anyone or anything you could imagine.

One particular night, around 9 PM, my roommate and I were lying in bed, engaged in conversation about our upcoming "camp out" in Jacks Valley. This was an area adjacent to the Academy where we often conducted field training. As we were talking, we suddenly heard a blood-curdling scream, as if a woman were screaming at the top of her lungs. It was absolutely horrifying to hear. What struck me as most intriguing was that just prior to the piercing noise, we could hear other cadets in their rooms talking and joking, creating a lively atmosphere.

The campus was winding down for the night, and everyone was preparing for the following day. I distinctly remember the ambient noise level being quite high. However, the moment that scream reverberated through the air, an eerie silence fell upon us. It was as if someone had muted the world around us. I turned to my roommate and asked if he had heard what I and everyone else had just heard. (I know, it seems like a dumb question!)

He looked at me and casually remarked, "Oh yeah, that's the local bigfoot." I couldn't believe my ears, but of course, I had heard it too. He went on to recount a story his friend had shared about encountering a big, hairy "human" drinking by a nearby lake. Apparently, when his friend noticed the creature observing him, it stood up, turned away, and disappeared into the forest.

Needless to say, the following week in Jack's Valley was quite nerve-wracking for me. I found myself more worried about venturing out alone to the latrine at night than I was about navigating the challenging Assault Course. The possibility of encountering that mysterious creature, locally referred to as bigfoot, haunted my thoughts and made every dark corner seem more ominous.

CHAPTER FORTY-SEVEN

IN MARCH OF 1988, I found myself in Alaska as the Team Commander of a Special Forces "A" Team. Our mission? Strategic Reconnaissance training. We were a team of 11 experienced soldiers, each with a significant background in Special Forces operations. Armed with rucksacks and equipped with cross-country skis, we trudged through the deep snow, making our way through a densely wooded area.

As we approached a section where the woods became too dense for our skis, I made the decision to venture ahead on snowshoes, accompanied by two other soldiers, in order to scout the path. It was during this exploration that we stumbled upon something that immediately caught our attention. Tracks. Tracks belonging to a two-legged creature, cutting through the woods at a perpendicular angle to our own course. Now, human tracks were an extremely rare sight in those parts of Alaska. But what made these tracks truly unique was the length of the stride and the absence of crushed snow around the holes, both on the entry and exit sides.

Intrigued, we stopped to investigate. As we removed our snowshoes, our feet sank deeply into the snow, plunging about 2 feet above the knee. Every step we took in the deep snow left behind a crushed

area on the entry side of the hole, followed by a subsequent disturbance when we pulled our foot out to take the next step. Additionally,
our feet left drag marks in the snow, no matter how hard we tried to
lift them without touching the surrounding surface. The best we could
manage was a stride between steps of around 1 1/2 feet. But the tracks
we were examining displayed a stride of over 5 feet between steps,
with no signs of disturbed snow on either the entry or exit side. It was
baffling.

We paused to ponder the possibilities, engaging in a discussion
about what could have created these tracks. With our collective experience in tracking humans and animals alike, we attempted to come up
with a plausible explanation for the phenomenon before us. However,
only one explanation seemed to align with all the evidence, even
though it defied reason. Based on our extensive knowledge, we made
an educated estimate regarding the height and weight of the creature
responsible for the tracks. We concluded that it was a two-legged
being, towering around 9 feet tall and weighing approximately 500 to
600 pounds.

Yes, that was our best guess. Filled with curiosity, I made the decision to temporarily set aside our training mission and follow the tracks
further into the woods. Equipped with snowshoes, we trailed those
mysterious footprints for about an hour, until we heard it. From somewhere ahead of us, echoing through the distance, came the most spine-
chilling sound any of us had ever experienced. In an instant, all other
noises in the woods ceased, and the silence was deafening. It was a
silence we were all too familiar with, akin to the moments just before
launching an ambush, when the entire forest holds its breath, aware
that imminent death is about to strike. The sound itself was a hybrid of
a howl and a roar.

Overwhelmed by the unnerving atmosphere, my Team Sergeant,
the most senior and experienced member of our group, halted our
progress. He looked at me and said, "Sir, speaking on behalf of myself
and the rest of the team, we really don't want to find out what lies at
the end of these tracks (expletives deleted)."

To be honest, this surprised me. These men, with their years of
service in Special Forces, had never shown fear towards anything,

whether it had two legs or four. I understood their trepidation, and I agreed to resume our original mission. Furthermore, there was a unanimous decision among us not to discuss this incident with anyone upon our return. Keep in mind that we were on a training mission and didn't have live ammunition. Any potential confrontation with the creature responsible for those tracks would have posed a great deal of danger. Our curiosity about the origin of the tracks was outweighed by the realization that we would be utterly outmatched. Most importantly, we simply didn't want to know what was lurking at the end of those tracks.

Tracks in the snow are far easier to ignore and deny than actually encountering the being that created them. We, my soldiers and I, were truly frightened by what we had heard and seen, and the soldiers, for the first time, didn't want to know. The tracks we followed traversed the crests of ridge lines and low-lying areas as much as possible. Whenever the tracks crossed a ridge line, it happened in a saddle where it would remain hidden from view. What struck us as peculiar was that while the tracks depicted someone far too large to be human, the entity, whoever or whatever it was, moved through the woods with the exact tactics and evasion techniques we employed during escape and evasion scenarios.

It was as if this creature possessed an intimate knowledge of the land, maneuvering skillfully to bypass clearings well before they came into view. It made a conscious effort to remain unseen. Reflecting back on that incident countless times, I've often wondered what might have happened had we continued to follow those tracks. There are arguments for both sides of the issue, pros and cons. Personally, there are certain things that cannot be denied, and ever since that day, I have developed an incredibly deep respect for Sasquatch.

CHAPTER FORTY-EIGHT

THIS STORY I'm about to share happened around 15 and a half years ago, and it's something I've never talked to anyone about. Not even my wife, whom I've been married to for almost 18 years. She's a skeptical person and hard to convince of anything. She knows that I believe Bigfoot exists because I've mentioned it before, but I'm pretty sure she would think I was crazy if I ever told her this story.

I was out deer hunting in the beautiful Wasatch Mountains, about 4 and a half to 5 miles east of Pineview Reservoir in the Cache National Forest. I arrived at the magpie campground around 10:00 am. As far as I could tell, I was the only one there at the campground, although it extended further east than where I was. I parked at the westernmost parking lot and crossed the bridge over the south fork of the Ogden River. After crossing the river, there was a trail that went east, running parallel to the river. I followed the trail until it branched off, leading south through a small canyon.

The day was absolutely beautiful, and I was thoroughly enjoying the sounds and scenery around me. As I made my way through the canyon, about halfway in, I made a conscious effort to be as quiet as possible. I didn't want to alert anything to my presence. The trail continued up the canyon for some distance (I can't recall exactly how far) until it turned west. Just after the turn, the surroundings opened up a bit, and there were steep slopes on either side. It was at this point, not long after I made the turn, that I heard something strange. It was a noise I had never heard before. It was a low grunting, growling sort of noise, but what struck me was the sheer volume of it. The sound seemed to reverberate, and I could almost feel it. It's hard to put into words, but it was something like "huuuuuuurrrrruuu." The sound had a low pitch, and it dropped even lower towards the end.

I immediately stopped in my tracks and scanned the slope to my right, where the sound had originated. The sound repeated, but I couldn't pinpoint the exact location. I stood there, listening intently. The noise would repeat with pauses of maybe a minute or two in between. I couldn't figure out what could be making such a sound. A moose crossed my mind as a possibility, but I wasn't too keen on encountering a moose, so I remained on guard as I continued towards the sound. As I proceeded further up the trail, I heard the noise again. This time, my eyes were able to lock onto the source. About a hundred feet up the steep slope to my right, and roughly 350 to 400 feet ahead of me, there was a dense patch of trees and brush. The sound was coming from that spot. I felt somewhat relieved at least knowing where it was coming from. I figured if I made some noise, maybe it would leave.

So I started stepping on branches and kicking small rocks, hoping it would scare away whatever was up there. I continued up the trail, expecting to catch a glimpse of it soon, but it remained hidden. I reached a point directly beneath the sound, about a hundred feet below the thickly covered area. I stopped at a tree and sat on a thick branch. I was pretty sure that whatever was up there knew I was right below it. Then the sounds became more agitated. I strained my eyes, trying to see into the dense cover using my binoculars, but I couldn't make out anything. Along with the noise, I noticed some tree branches in the thick area shaking about 9 or 10 feet above the ground. I thought to myself, "Okay, here it comes." But it still wouldn't come out. A sense of unease started to creep over me. I just knew I was being watched, and whatever was watching me didn't want me there. The noise intensified even more. I couldn't believe the lung capacity this thing had.

The volume was immense. Then, to my dismay, two rocks, about the size of basketballs, rolled out from the thick cover and started heading down towards me.

That was the last straw for me. I quickly got up and immediately started heading back the way I came. I didn't run or make any sudden movements to avoid causing a disturbance. I walked out as calmly and swiftly as I could, but I kept checking behind me to make sure I wasn't being followed. I could still hear the noise until I rounded the bend in the trail. Once I got around the corner, my anxiety and fear began to subside, and I started feeling alright again. It was evident that whatever I had heard wanted me to leave, and I was more than happy to oblige.

I've hunted and fished alone for many years, and I've always felt comfortable in those situations. But I had never heard anything like what I experienced that day. The sheer magnitude of the noise and the unsettling feeling of being observed left a lasting impression on me.

CHAPTER FORTY-NINE

I NEVER REALLY CONSIDERED MYSELF a Bigfoot enthusiast or anything like that. I mean, who really believes in that stuff, right? But let me tell you, everything changed for me one unforgettable day.

It was the late summer of 1991, in this small town called East Canton, up in Northeast Ohio. I can't tell you the exact date, because honestly, it didn't seem important back then. All I know is that it happened sometime during that month. See, I grew up in East Canton, and I knew those forests around town like the back of my hand. Spent so much time hiking with my dad and friends, exploring every nook and cranny.

Anyway, that day was just not going well for me. I had this massive argument with my girlfriend, and I just had to get away for a while, you know? So, I decided to escape into the woods for the night. Now, camping alone wasn't really my thing at the time. I had just gotten my hands on a used Ford Tempo, and that car had changed my life. Suddenly, I was more into malls and meaningless stuff like that. Thank goodness I didn't give in to that urge. Instead, I packed up some basic camping gear and headed out for a night of solitude.

I knew exactly where I was going. There was this perfect spot about two miles away from my parents' house. It was like an endless stretch of woods with these old abandoned coal mines hidden within. And above those caves, you had these beautiful pine trees that somehow managed to grow and create this stunning setting.

Now, I didn't bring much with me. Just a blanket to lay on, which turned out to be a mistake. I also had a machete for chopping firewood and, of course, my trusty flashlight for the nighttime adventures. I always liked to travel light, but sometimes I regretted it. Like when it got really cold, and I wished I had brought a thicker blanket or a sleeping bag.

So, my buddies Tommy and Brad came along with me to help set up camp. Not that there was much to set up, to be honest. I think they just wanted to hang out. We started by clearing the pine needles and making a safe space for a fire. We were always careful about that because we had permission from the landowner to hike and camp there whenever we wanted.

As the sun began to set, Tommy and Brad had to leave since they had work early the next morning. And honestly, I was glad for some alone time. Don't get me wrong, I enjoyed their company, but I needed to be by myself to sort things out in my head.

The fire was crackling nicely, and it was a good thing because August nights in Ohio can get pretty cold. So, fire meant warmth, and I was starting to find some peace in that solitude. You know, the wilderness has this way of enveloping you, helping you escape from everyday problems. Well, not this night.

Now, I should mention that back then, I wore these thick glasses like the bottom of soda bottles. I had perfect vision with them, but they were a bit of an insecurity for me. So, I carefully placed them near my blanket. If you've ever worn glasses and relied on them to see clearly, you'll understand why.

Suddenly, I heard some twigs snap nearby. I won't lie, when you're alone in the deep, dark woods and you hear something like that, it gives you a good scare. But deep down, I knew it was probably just some small critter, like a rabbit or squirrel. Nothing I hadn't heard before, you know?

I was feeling pretty comfortable, and exhaustion took over. I fell asleep faster than I expected. But then, at 3 AM, I abruptly woke up with this intense feeling of unease. It wasn't a nightmare or anything, but it was like I had been rudely yanked out of my sleep. Everything seemed normal at first glance, but that weird sense was there. And let me tell you, I had felt that peculiar sensation before. I'm not exaggerating, and I hope there are others who can relate to what I'm about to describe. It was this overwhelming feeling of being watched, like on a whole other level. Not just a general chill or alertness, but an intense awareness that tingled behind my ears. It was like hyper-sensitivity, you know, like having a Spidey-sense. I mean, I'm no Spider-Man, but that's probably what it would feel like when trouble was looming.

Now, as anyone who wears glasses can understand, the first thing I did was fumble around to find them and put them on. Dead silence. Not a cricket chirping, not a tree frog singing, just complete and utter silence. But I brushed it off as a bad dream or something. At that point, I hadn't heard anything strange or figured out why I had been abruptly awakened.

But then I noticed how freezing cold it was. I was shivering, and the fire had dwindled down to a few dying embers. So, I leaned over and started blowing on the coals, trying to revive the flames. And that's when it happened. I heard the most bone-chilling scream, or should I say shrill, that I've ever heard to this day. It was something beyond natural. I can't even begin to describe it accurately in words, unless you hear it for yourself. Trust me, it was absolutely terrifying and unsettling. The kind of sound that sends shivers down your spine and cuts through every nerve in your body. The pitch and volume of that scream were just off the charts. Even if I were deaf, I would have felt it.

Let me tell you, in that moment, my first thought was, "You've got to be kidding me." Because I had never heard anything like it in my entire life. It reminded me of those apes you see in those old National Geographic documentaries, but way louder. And this was Ohio, not Africa. And it wasn't just a one-time thing either. That screaming went on, in about 5-10 second intervals, coming from both ends of the camp. It was like a back-and-forth exchange of shrills and rustling.

Now, I was already shocked by the screaming, but then I saw something moving across the land. Fear gripped me like never before. There was this huge creature, standing on two legs, thumping its way about twenty to thirty feet away from me, right through my campsite. I say "thumping" because, you see, I was sleeping on top of those caves, which acted like a natural floor. So every step this thing took, I could feel it. It didn't swing its arms around like a gorilla, but it had similar features from what I could make out. I can tell you one thing for sure, though—it was no man.

Since it was a moonlit night, I could see that the creature was massive and covered in hair. The top of its head reminded me of a gorilla, and most of its body was covered in hair, with a few exceptions, kind of like an orangutan. The hair looked black, but there could have been other colors mixed in. You know, all dark hair looks black at night, and you don't notice the subtle shades until you observe it closely.

I only saw it from the side, so I couldn't make out its eyes. I wish I had, though. I can't give you an exact height either, because it was running on a ledge, and I couldn't see below its calves. All I can say is that it was massive. I'm trying my best to describe what I saw, but the thing didn't exactly pose for me, you know? All I know is that it was colossal, and it scared the living daylights out of me. At that point, I had no choice but to believe that the seemingly ridiculous myth of Bigfoot was real. Either that or I was losing my mind.

And you know what? I could still hear that screaming from the rear of the camp. That made me think there were two or more of those creatures. One thing I should mention is that I didn't catch a whiff of any foul smell that people often associate with encounters like this. Maybe it was because the air was still and windless that night?

Instinctively, my only thought was to get out of there, no matter what it was. It was as if that creature was telling me, "You're not welcome here," in its own way. And I took that warning seriously. I obviously picked the worst possible spot to sleep.

Now, my dad always taught me not to run from wild animals because they can sense fear. But in that moment, I grabbed my flashlight and left everything else behind. I walked away, no, practically ran away, as fast as I could. When I was about twenty feet away from the campsite, the continuous screaming finally stopped. The silence that followed was somewhat comforting, to a certain extent. I no longer felt like I was in immediate danger, and I didn't hear anything pursuing me. As soon as I cleared the woods and reached the road, I ran. I ran all the way to my parents' home, which felt like the longest and toughest sprint of my life. My chest hurt from all the heavy breathing.

I urgently pounded on my parents' locked door (I didn't live there anymore), and my mom rushed to open it. Naturally, it took me a while to catch my breath, but eventually, I managed to explain everything that had just happened. And when my dad came home from work, I told him too. Now, keep in mind, I was just a nineteen-year-old kid back then. But my parents were good, they listened to me. I'm not sure if they fully believed me, but they agreed that something traumatic must have happened to me to put me in such a disturbed state. My dad had been hunting for Morel mushrooms for decades, and he had never encountered anything like what I had experienced.

So, that's my story, the night I came face-to-face with something that defied all logic and reason. And believe me, it's not something I'll ever forget.

CHAPTER FIFTY

I GREW up in the eighties and in the area where I lived there were a lot of legends about bigfoot and cryptids like them. I always believed in the legends but not because I had ever encountered one myself but because many people I knew and am related to have their own encounters and told me all about it. I was fascinated and wanted nothing more than to have my own encounter with bigfoot. I finally got my wish when I turned twenty-five, but it was nothing like I imagined it would be and I think that's because of how heavily I had romanticized the experiences I had heard from the people around me. My encounter with bigfoot was terrifying and it left me with many more questions than answers, many of which I still haven't found answers for to this day. It was 1995 and I had just purchased several acres of land I planned to use for nothing but camping. There were two barns on the property but other than that it was all very much overgrown and obviously hadn't been used or landscaped in a very long time. I honestly didn't mind though and took to clearing it all out as much as I possibly could. In between the two barns looked like a nice bit of land to have picnics or bonfires and so I went and inspected them and that area first. It was very strange from the very beginning.

It was springtime and I took my walk behind lawn mower down to the barns and began clearing the space. It took me about five hours of work, but I got the area to where it was perfect for how I wanted to use it. I then went about looking inside of the two barns. They had stunk to high heaven, and it was a stench that got into my skin almost. I could taste it in my mouth and my hair smelled like it for days. It was something I wasn't familiar with though and no matter how hard I tried I just couldn't place that smell. I had been hunting and camping all my life and there was no animal I had ever smelled, dead or alive, that smelled that rotten. I put a bandana over my mouth and nose and set about cleaning them out too. Eventually I had cleaned and scrubbed enough that the smell was minimal, and I was able to breathe again. I also found some strange droppings that didn't look like they belonged to any known animal either. There were also the carcasses of smaller animals all over the place in the top loft sections of both buildings. I was absolutely disgusted but decided I should just clean it all up and get it nice and sparkly and not ask too many questions. I had locks and new doors for both buildings and because I was in the middle of nowhere and in the middle of the woods in the middle of nowhere, I reasoned that whatever had created those disgusting messes had long ago gone away and it was highly unlikely it/they would be returning any time soon.

I was exhausted by the time I was done with the first building and the outside but there was still a lot left to do on the second building and the surrounding areas. I hadn't had a chance to look around much in those woods and so I made the decision to spend a few nights out there camping and getting to know the land. I went home and grabbed everything that I needed for how long I planned on staying and headed back out there. By the time I got back it was completely dark outside. I had some oil lamps set up in the barns and though I know they're dangerous and people frown upon them nowadays, it didn't even occur to me to be nervous about them at that time. I didn't think electricity would have been an option for the barns at the time and that was the best that I could think of to do. I had bought the land solely for camping and having fun with my family and friends in the woods, with the hopes of eventually having enough money to build my own house on it. I decided to set up a large tent between the two buildings and see how the first night went. I figured I could always move into one of the barns if the weather should get bad or anything else unexpected should happen.

I had nothing but my flashlight outside in the tent with me and once I put the fire out and ate, I was more than ready for bed. I was exhausted from working out in the sun all day and all the work that still needed to be done was somewhat overwhelming for me. I turned in at around eleven and fell right asleep. I woke up an hour later and immediately noticed that the zipper on the outside of my tent, the sky zipper, was unzipped. I know for an absolute fact that I had zipped it up completely and in fact I remembered doing it. I didn't want it to start raining on me in the middle of the night and so I made sure it was zipped and fastened tight. There wasn't any animal that I knew of with both the intelligence and the dexterity to be able to do that and I was immediately all too aware of how alone I was out there and how far away I was from anyone who would hear me scream. I didn't want to get out of my tent, but I knew that I had to, especially when, after sitting there and pondering how the zipper could've become undone so completely, I started hearing strange noises that seemed to be coming from the barn I had worked so hard all day to clean. The noises were loud and sounded like they were coming from several of the same creature. It didn't sound like any animal I was familiar with, and I knew even then that I was familiar with all of them in that area and in that region as well. I grabbed my shotgun and my flashlight and got out of the tent. I immediately saw what must have startled me awake in the first place. Both barn doors were smashed to pieces and the pieces were thrown and scattered all around my tent. The sounds were coming from the clean barn, and I had never been more scared in my life than when I started to approach it. I tiptoed over to it and tried to look inside without being seen from the now gaping hole that was once the door I had only just installed that day.

I couldn't believe what I was seeing but I recognized them for what they were immediately. I was looking at two bigfoot creatures and they seemed pissed off at something. They were frantically running around the barn and looking all over the place for what I assumed were the animal carcasses I had removed and gotten rid of earlier in the day.

They moved extremely fast for how large they were, I mean superhumanly and impossibly fast, and they were hollering and screaming the whole time they were darting all around the place. Though I thought I had gotten rid of it when I was cleaning earlier in the day and I do think that I had done just that, the horrible stench was back with a vengeance, and it was worse than before. I couldn't help it and despite how hard I was trying not to, I accidentally let out a cough. They both turned around so fast it was quicker than it took me to blink. They stared at me and growled. They were both around eleven feet tall with huge feet and large, black eyes. They were covered from head to toe with reddish brown hair, except for their faces. Their hands were gigantic, just like the feet were and they looked from me to one another and then back at me again. I started to back away and realized how hopeless my situation was. The other door on the other barn had been ripped apart and strewn about as well and so there was nowhere for me to run to or hide. Sure, there were acres upon acres of dense and vast wilderness for me to try to escape into, but I knew that they would have known the land and the forest way better than I would have at that time. I didn't know what to do and so, without taking my eyes off them and trying not to blink, I started to silently pray in my head that I would make it out of there alive. Suddenly and without warning the two creatures started phasing in and out. It was like they weren't here, in this three-dimensional world and were only holograms or something. I mean, I know that they were there in front of me, but they were also somewhere else. They were gone before I even finished that thought. I stood there for a few minutes, shock and relief washing over me but then I heard more strange sounds coming from the other barn.

My heart just about sank down to my toes as I tried to fathom having to deal with a bigfoot again, or worse, several. The sounds were a bit different though and it just sounded like something making a lot of noise and wrecking things. I hesitantly walked over to the other barn and really took my time in doing so but once I got there, I realized I had been wrong all along and there wasn't any bigfoot in that barn at all. It was several deer, some of them bucks, and they were agitated by something that I couldn't see. They were kicking the walls and stumbling over one another, almost as if they were very confused as well about how they had gotten there or why they were there to begin with. When they saw me, they looked terrified and started screaming and once again kicking one another to try and get as far away from me as possible. One of them fell over onto its side, almost like it was playing dead. I tried to shoo them out of there, but they were wobbly on their feet, like they had been drugged or extremely shocked or something. I managed to eventually get them all out and running back into the woods beyond the barn, but it took about an hour and a half to do so without putting myself in danger. I finished out what was left of the darkness and at first light I got the hell out of there. I went back there many times, but never alone. Nowadays I will go there alone, but that's only because about ten years after that first night spent there in between those two barns, I had finally saved up enough money to have my own home built on that land. I still own all of it and have bonfires and parties all the time. My friends and family use it for camping, but no one is allowed to hunt on it. One strange thing that happens all the time is that I will go down to that one little clearing between the barns and there will be whole animal carcasses. Most of the time the bones are bleached as though they've been there for a long time when that isn't possible. I am out there once a week keeping the land clear because that's where I bring people most of the time for my parties or when they want to camp on my land.

The only thing I've been able to solidly conclude from all of this is that bigfoot is very real and they're interdimensional. That's the only reasonable explanation for what I saw when I was out there that first night, what appeared to be confusing the deer and why the bones of seemingly fresh animal carcasses were bleached. I share my story often but haven't ever actually seen another one in all these years, despite being there all the time now. I wonder if they're there, but they've been able to make it, so they see me, and I don't see them. I'll probably never have the answer to that though and so I just accept it as what it is until I possibly get more details about them. I am on high alert and hope to see one again someday. This time, I will try to video it or at the very least I will try and take some pictures.

CHAPTER FIFTY-ONE

IN SEPTEMBER OF 1998, I was a drill instructor at Parris Island, Marine Corps Recruiting Depot in South Carolina. I had just finished a rotation, my platoon of recruits had graduated giving me some time. I requested a 72 hour pass and headed to Myrtle Beach for some much needed time off.

The journey started like any other uneventful trip, taking one of the shortcuts I had discovered, specifically Highway 917. It was around 1 am when something caught my attention. I spotted what I initially thought was a dog in a ditch. As I got closer, the creature turned its head and glanced at my car, instantly dispelling any notion that it was a dog.

The animal was hunched over in the ditch, possibly feasting on a deer carcass or some other roadkill. Its facial features stood out to me. The face resembled that of an orangutan, lacking fur and sporting lips that seemed shapeless. The mouth was wider than a human's, and the lips were thin and tightly closed. The creature's head appeared wider than normal, with scruffy fur on top. The fur had an orange-brown hue, which initially led me to consider it as a dog. As it began to stand upright, turning to face me, it became clear that this was no known animal. Unfortunately, I couldn't observe its full height since I had already passed by and couldn't see it in my rearview mirror. I recall it lacked a discernible neck and had a broader shoulder and chest area than I initially perceived. Although I couldn't make out many details about the legs due to their position beneath the animal and hidden by the ditch, I did notice the creature's arms.

The arms were unusually long, and what appeared to be fingers were curled up into its palms, not forming a fist. This observation led me to consider the possibility that it could be some kind of ape, possibly walking on all fours like a chimpanzee. The creature was covered in fur from head to toe, except for the facial region with the orange-brown fur. I could make out two arms clearly, but the legs remained obscured. It was much larger than I had initially estimated. The ditch, which was approximately 3 to 4 feet deep, caused the animal, even while stooped over, to rise about 4 to 5 feet above its level. This disproved the notion that it was a dog. The fact that the creature had to push itself up with its arms (or hands) to turn around indicated it was stooped or bent over when I passed. Initially, it faced the same direction I was driving (SSE) and appeared to be standing, albeit slightly hunched, as I drove by. The encounter took place on a very dark night, with only the car's headlights illuminating the animal. I was traveling at around 65 mph and slowed down, thinking it might run in front of my car, as I had experienced with deer before. I glanced in the rearview mirror after passing, but the darkness made it impossible to discern any distinct shape in the ditch.

After retiring from the Marines in 2007, I have rarely shared this story, fearing that people might think I'm crazy. I now reside in Florida and have never encountered anything similar since.

CHAPTER FIFTY-TWO

IN JULY 2004, a friend and I embarked on a road trip from Portland, OR, to Redding, CA. It was around 10:30 pm, and we were pretty stoked about our journey. Fortunately, the road had just reopened that day after being closed for most of the previous week due to the sour biscuit fire. We were eager to witness the aftermath of the fire, and as luck would have it, there were still some isolated pockets of burning areas along the road. It was a quiet night with very little traffic.

As we drove along, I noticed some movement on the left side of the road. My initial thought was that it might be a hitchhiker. But in a split second, my brain registered something else: a bear? But wait, it was standing upright! And then it happened—the creature stepped onto the road right in front of my high beams, completely visible. I couldn't help but joke, "There he goes right there!" Earlier, I had told my friend about the rumors of Bigfoot sightings in this area. As I looked at the creature, though, I realized it wasn't a bear at all. It was walking on two legs.

That's when it hit me—an intense fear that I had never experienced before. It was as if some primal instinct within me screamed, "Get the hell out of here, now!" I apologize for the language, but that's honestly the closest I can describe the overwhelming feeling I had at the time. As soon as fear took hold, my right foot instinctively slammed down on the accelerator—not to hit the creature, but to put as much distance between us as possible. I must admit, it bothers me now, in hindsight, that I didn't slow down or even stop to investigate further. I've always been intrigued by mysteries and the unexplained, and I'm not someone who can be easily swayed. But at that moment, my instincts completely took over, and any curiosity about the creature vanished from my mind. It was as if my sole focus was to escape. The creature itself was easily seven feet tall, perhaps even eight feet, towering over my Yukon.

I work in construction, so I'm fairly skilled at estimating sizes since I do it all the time. The creature was covered in fur or hair, medium to dark brown. Its arms and legs were long, with no disproportionate lengths between the different parts of each limb. In other words, its calves were not overly long compared to its thighs, and so on. The only time I saw one of its arms descend, it reached past its knee, and I noticed its individual fingers flex. However, I must admit that I didn't catch many details. My attention was drawn to its wide shoulder area, which was remarkably muscular. And here's the detail that makes me believe it wasn't some trick or hoax: the muscles between its shoulders bulged independently. Underneath the fur, I could see these small muscles rippling in different ways as it moved, much like an animal would, as opposed to a bulky costume or a hide worn by a person, which would move more uniformly. The creature had a somewhat cone-shaped head that sat atop a thick, short neck.

Unfortunately, I didn't get a close-up look at its face, so I can't provide clear details about it. But when it first stepped onto the road and spotted us, I did catch a glimpse from a distance. It appeared wide with few discernible features. As soon as the creature noticed us, it seemed to quicken its pace, but it didn't run or even trot—just increased its stride. This creature walked directly in front of my SUV, mere feet away, illuminated by my high beams. If this was some sort of trick, then someone must have devoted an immense amount of time, money, skill, and ingenuity to pull it off on a road that had been closed to all traffic until just a few hours prior. Not impossible, I suppose, but

I highly doubt it. The most unsettling thing for me, apart from the instinctual fear, was the way the creature moved—it felt strangely familiar. I've seen many shows featuring supposed Bigfoot footage, and they often demonstrate how such sightings could be faked. But in those reenactments, the fakes are glaringly obvious. You can tell it's someone in a suit or covered in fur, trying to move like an ape, resulting in mechanical and unnatural movements. However, this creature's motions were incredibly fluid and smooth.

All its limbs moved simultaneously—head turning, legs striding, arms swinging—in perfect harmony. After the creature crossed the road and disappeared into the trees on the right side, my friend and I looked at each other, our eyes wide with disbelief, and simultaneously exclaimed, "No way!" A few minutes later, we reached the first signs of civilization when we passed a truck parked on the side of the road. Three firefighters were inside the vehicle, and both driver's side doors were wide open. I caught a glimpse of the faces of two of the firefighters, and they seemed astonished or shocked. It appeared as though they had encountered something as well, or perhaps they were the masterminds behind an incredibly elaborate and expertly executed hoax. If there were any other reports from the area or if it's possible to speak to the firefighters who were battling the fire in that region, I would love to get in touch with them. Any information they might have could be helpful in piecing together this puzzling encounter.

CHAPTER FIFTY-THREE

I'VE BEEN a reader of all your books and while I don't have a personal story to share, my friend had one. I asked him and he gave me permission to share it with you.

―――――

The incident took place in southeast Oklahoma. According to my friend, he came across a mountain lion while he was in a wooded area where some people were camping. When he arrived at the scene, the campers were hurriedly packing their belongings to leave.

My friend approached them and asked, "What's been going on?" The man replied, "This mountain lion has been walking around our camp, growling at us from time to time. It scared my wife to death, and we're leaving now." After the couple got in their truck and drove away, my friend, holding his rifle, stood next to his truck in the open camping area. He told me that it was unusually quiet, and something felt off, like he was being watched. Naturally, he assumed it was the mountain lion.

As he listened attentively, he mentioned that he could finally hear movement. He said it sounded strange, so I asked him what he meant.

He explained that it sounded like something walking on two feet instead of four paws, and it seemed much heavier than a mountain lion. He made sure the safety was off his rifle, prepared to shoot if necessary. He stayed still, listening, and as the sound kept pacing back and forth, he heard a growl. He described it as a deep, guttural growl, unlike that of a mountain lion. It was much deeper.

My friend grabbed his high-powered flashlight, intending to shine it in the direction of the sound. But just as he was about to do so, he heard a loud roar from about 50 yards behind him. He said the roar was so powerful that it nearly knocked him over. He froze for a moment, and that's when he heard footsteps approaching him. With trembling hands, he switched on his flashlight, and about 20 yards in front of him stood a Sasquatch. He gave me a detailed description, mentioning its towering height of around 8 feet, broad shoulders measuring about 4 feet wide, long black hair, and a squished nose resembling that of an ape. He also emphasized how incredibly muscular the creature appeared, like a massive bodybuilder, with biceps and triceps that seemed as though they were the size of bowling balls.

He said he pointed his rifle at the Sasquatch, but the creature didn't flinch. Just seconds after he aimed the rifle, he heard the roar from behind him once again, but this time it sounded much closer. Fear coursed through him, and he knew his life was in danger. He swiftly jumped into his truck and sped away from there as fast as he possibly could.

My friend has been an experienced hunter all his life, Wes. He knows the sounds and creatures of the woods. He assured me that he had never seen or heard anything like what he witnessed that night. He's so frightened that he won't even go camping alone anymore, something he used to do regularly.

CHAPTER FIFTY-FOUR

BACK IN THE summer of 1972, my cousin and I embarked on a fishing trip along the South Fork of the Nooksack River in Washington State. We were just about to enter the 8th grade, and our parents dropped us off on a Friday with plans to pick us up on Sunday. Looking back, it seems crazy that they left a couple of young boys alone in the wilderness for a whole weekend!

We found a suitable spot to set up camp not too far from the road, approximately 50 feet away from the river. After spending the Friday afternoon fishing, we returned to our campsite and built a cozy fire. Exhausted from the day's activities, we crawled into our sleeping bags and dozed off. To be safe, we stuck our pocket knives in the sand next to us, just in case we needed them during the night.

In the dead of night, I was abruptly awakened by an unfamiliar sound. As I groggily opened my eyes, still half-asleep inside my sleeping bag, I caught sight of a dark figure on the other side of a small fence, slightly elevated above us. It stood about 20 feet away, with the moon casting an eerie glow and outlining its silhouette perfectly.

This creature emitted a series of long, hissing sounds that seemed to go on forever. The best way I can describe it is a prolonged hiss. It would pause for a moment and then start again, repeating this cycle 5 or 6 times.

The silhouette I saw was only from the waist up, revealing broad shoulders and a lack of a noticeable neck. Its forehead sloped backward, and I couldn't make out any distinct ears. The creature seemed to sway slightly from side to side, almost as if it was attempting to catch our scent or get a better view of us lying there. It couldn't have approached us directly without crossing the fence and maneuvering under some low branches. It appeared to be crouching, maybe even on one knee.

Needless to say, I was absolutely petrified. It stayed there for what felt like an eternity, probably lasting about 3 to 5 minutes. When it finally departed, it pivoted its entire body to the right and vanished from sight.

I estimate it was around 3 in the morning when the encounter occurred. I didn't hear any footsteps as it moved away. I remained frozen with fear for the rest of the night, to the point where my body started cramping up from the tension!

Strangely, I didn't hear any sounds as it departed, nor did I notice any peculiar smells. However, not long after the creature left, I heard a series of rapid clicks coming from the direction of the river. It sounded as if rocks were being struck together swiftly, creating a distinctive clicking sound. This clicking happened 3 to 5 times in quick succession. I heard it a few times, initially quite close, and then it gradually faded into the distance, as though moving away from us.

My cousin, on the other hand, didn't stir or hear a thing; he slept soundly throughout the entire ordeal. Despite the harrowing experience, we decided to stay at the same spot the following night. To ease our nerves, we built a massive fire and tied fishing lines to each other's wrists, so we could wake each other up if anything happened.

The next morning, I confided in my cousin about what had transpired. We scoured the area, hoping to find tracks or some evidence of the creature's presence, but came up empty-handed. The field where the encounter occurred had hard, dry soil, making it impossible to spot any footprints or impressions.

I can't emphasize enough that what I saw was neither a man nor a bear, nor was it someone trying to scare us by making growling sounds or anything like that. It was something entirely different, something I can't quite explain. Even after almost 30 years, just recounting this incident gives me goosebumps and sends a shiver down my spine.

CHAPTER FIFTY-FIVE

BACK IN EARLY JUNE 2005, I found myself on an adventurous fishing trip with my brother and a friend. Our goal was to follow a remote tributary that connected to the salmon river, in pursuit of steelhead making their way back to Lake Ontario. We ventured deeper into the woods, approximately a mile down a rugged game trail that ran alongside the tributary.

As we continued along the trail, something peculiar caught my attention. A putrid stench of decaying flesh wafted through the air, assaulting our senses. Soon enough, we stumbled upon scattered deer bones and skulls strewn across the path. I warned my companions to stay alert, suggesting that there might be a den of coyotes nearby.

However, the situation took a more unsettling turn as I rounded a corner on the trail. It was as if an instinctual force froze me in my tracks. My entire body felt charged with electricity, causing every hair on my body to stand on end. Then, an incredibly deep and guttural growl reverberated through the air, making me turn around and ask my brother and Ryan if they heard thunder.

To my dismay, they confirmed that they too had heard the sound, and we all began to feel a growing unease. It was evident that the source of the noise was not thunder. Gathering my courage, I cautiously took a few steps forward, hoping to unravel the mystery. But then, once again, that haunting growl resonated through the forest, shaking me to my core. It was a sound that cut through me like a sharp knife.

As I glanced to my right, desperately trying to make sense of the situation, I caught sight of what can only be described as a large, cow-like eyeball peering at me through a dense, bushy tree. Now I knew without a doubt that we were in the presence of some unknown creature. The distance between us was a mere 50 feet, and my heart raced with a mix of fear and awe. The creature crouched behind the brush, continuously shifting its position to get a better view of us while still concealing itself. The exposed parts of its face lacked hair, and the color of its hair matched the accounts of others who had encountered similar beings, darker than that of an orangutan. The mere thought sent shivers down my spine.

At this point, I urged everyone to make themselves appear as large as possible and slowly start walking backward. However, the creature remained motionless, unresponsive to our vocalizations or our cautious retreat. Finally, when we were out of its line of sight, we all sprinted away, fueled by a surge of adrenaline. Astonishingly, the creature's response was almost immediate. It crashed through the dense woods with such force and intensity that its cacophonous movements drowned out the sounds of two grown men and a 14-year-old boy running for their lives. It seemed as though it was tracking alongside us, keeping pace until we reached a clearing roughly 100 yards away.

We were left shaken and terrified, a jumbled mess of emotions. The encounter had left an indelible mark on our psyches. To this day, I have never returned to that haunting location, haunted by the memory of that chilling encounter with an unknown creature.

CHAPTER FIFTY-SIX

WHEN I WAS fifteen years old, I was a member of a local Boy Scouts club. It was our yearly outing and our adventure took us to Mt. Shasta for a hiking, canoeing, and camping.

Our group consisted of three adults and nine boys, ranging in age from 13 to 16. On the second day of our trip, we set out to canoe the river that led to Lake McCloud. Recently, I looked it up on Google Earth and noticed that the river seemed narrower now, and there were houses along its banks that I didn't recall seeing back then. We started our canoe trip near the waterfalls, where the water was calm and easy to navigate. Each canoe had an adult and three boys.

I was in the middle canoe, and about 30 minutes into our journey, as we approached a bend in the river with thick brush and trees, the guys in the canoe to our right caught a whiff of a foul odor. It's been a while, and I can't speak for everyone in my canoe, but personally, I didn't smell a thing. We teased them, jokingly suggesting that someone had passed gas in the canoe. That's when it happened—a large rock came hurtling out of the bushes, splashing into the water just to the right of our canoe, about 15 feet ahead. The adult leaders urged us to paddle faster.

The guys in the canoe to our right started to holler that they were hearing loud footfalls. All eyes turned to the shore hoping to spy something.

After a few minutes they were giving up, but I wasn't. I kept my eyes glued. And then I saw it, between the trees, I saw this large two legged thing walking.

I called out that I was watching something in the woods. Everyone turned their heads back and as each person caught sight of it, they yelped out with joy and fear.

It appeared huge and was clearly walking on two legs. By my vantage point it was black in color and most definitely wasn't a bear. The adults got spooked and told us to paddle harder. They wanted to get out of there and fast.

I just couldn't keep my eyes off of it. I was mesmerized. I was literally looking at a sasquatch. I mean, what were the odds? I watched until it suddenly disappeared. I don't know if it just stopped behind a tree or went deeper into the woods. It was there and then it wasn't.

As far as details. It was tall and appeared really big and the color was black. Its coat, if that's what you want to call it, looked more like hair than fur. If anyone has seen a bear in real life, they can attest to it having a shine to it, this didn't. The hair looked matted. I couldn't make out fine detail, but enough to know it was walking on two legs and that its arms were really long. Its head sat on its shoulders and it didn't seem to even take notice of us, although I know it had tossed a large rock at us. I think it did this to scare us.

There was much excitement around the campfire that night and by the way the adults acted, they had gotten a bit worried. They kept a vigil all night and I could see their eyes on the shadows throughout the evening.

We never saw or heard anything else that weekend.

CHAPTER FIFTY-SEVEN

THIS INCIDENT TOOK place back in early September 2012 during bear hunting season in Minnesota. As an average person with a passion for hunting, I was excited to run a few bait stations in the hopes of finally harvesting a bear. Out of all the stations I had set up, this particular one seemed the most promising. It had been consistently hit every day since the start of the baiting season.

On that beautiful morning, around 7:20 a.m., I left my house and headed towards my first bait station. The air was cool, and the sun was just beginning to rise over the horizon. This time of day always felt special to me, as if the woods were coming alive. I turned off the dirt road and drove down the logging trail that led to my bait station, located about 150 yards away through the brush.

The area surrounding the bait station was filled with mature poplar trees, along with a few maple and balsam trees scattered about. Before the season began, I had set up a trail camera near the station for a few days to get an idea of when the bears were visiting and the direction they were coming from. As I sat at the fork in the trail, about to exit my truck, I happened to glance down the left trail. Over time, this trail had widened a bit from trying to avoid the muddy areas. And that's when I saw it—something crossing the trail swiftly.

It was only about 50 to 60 yards away from me, and if I hadn't been looking in that exact moment, I might have missed it entirely. Most stories about "Bigfoot" describe the creature as being brown or black, but whatever I saw was massive and had a grayish-white color. I sat there for a moment, trying to shake off the disbelief and convince myself that I was just imagining things. "No," I told myself, "it couldn't be real."

However, my doubts were quickly dispelled when I heard it. The sound of something running through the brush towards my bait station, unmistakably on two legs, reached my ears. Having spent my life bow hunting, I knew the distinct sound that a four-legged animal makes when it runs or trots. It became clear to me that I wasn't imagining things—it had actually happened.

Without wasting any time, I promptly climbed back into my truck and drove away. Despite my long-held goal of harvesting a bear, I was too shaken up to return to that particular bait station. It was a jarring experience that left me feeling unsettled. According to the regulations, all bait stations required the hunter's information to be displayed within a certain distance. So, I knew I had to go back to retrieve my sign.

A few weeks later, I mustered up the courage to revisit the area, but this time I brought along a good friend of mine for support. We quickly retrieved my sign from the bait station, and without lingering any longer, we left. That day marked the last time I set foot in that specific area, the memory of the encounter lingering in the back of my mind.

CHAPTER FIFTY-EIGHT

BACK IN 1990, when I was a 14-year-old kid, I woke up early one Saturday morning with the intention of going squirrel hunting on a small piece of land near my parents' house. This patch of woods was situated in Greenup County, Kentucky, in the northeastern part of the state. The property was bordered by Raccoon Creek, a small creek, and the Little Sandy River. I used to hunt in this area regularly as a youngster and had never encountered anything out of the ordinary. However, on that fateful day in early September, something strange happened.

As I made my way down the ridge overlooking Raccoon Creek, I moved silently, trying not to make any noise. The heavy dew on the trees amplified even the slightest sound, creating a distinct noise as it fell. I had noticed earlier that my neighbor's dog had followed me, but I thought I had chased him away a couple of hours before. The morning was incredibly calm, with barely a hint of wind. Suddenly, I heard the dog start barking and growling in a way I had never heard before. Initially, I tried to ignore the noise, thinking he was just being a nuisance. But after a few minutes, I decided to go and run him off again as he was interfering with my hunt.

Quietly, I crept down the ridge for about 50 yards, and through the trees, I caught sight of what I initially believed to be a young bear. The creature was standing upright on its hind legs, reaching a height of about 6 feet. I noticed that whenever the dog lunged at the animal, it would use its hands to push him back forcefully. The dog would yelp and then go after the creature again. Wanting to protect the dog, I approached slowly, trying to remain as silent as possible. But as I got closer, the animal sensed my presence and turned to face me. It was at this moment that I realized it wasn't a bear.

I couldn't immediately identify the creature as a Sasquatch, but I was incredibly perplexed by what I was seeing. The animal emitted a fierce growl that sent shivers down my spine like never before. When the dog noticed me, he ran toward me, continuously barking at the creature. I briefly considered shooting at the animal with my 20-gauge shotgun, loaded with #6 shot, but I feared it would only make it angrier. Instead, I began slowly walking backward. After taking three or four steps, the creature let out a bone-chilling growl. In sheer terror, I threw my shotgun to the ground and sprinted all the way home. Once I reached home, I wasted no time in telling my father about the terrifying encounter.

My father was initially taken aback by the fact that I had left my gun behind, but eventually, he agreed to grab his rifle and accompany me back to retrieve it. However, he firmly believed that what I had seen was nothing more than a bear. I never spoke about this encounter again because if my own father didn't believe me, who would? While black bears were known to inhabit the area, I had only ever seen one in the wild. I'm not entirely sure about what I witnessed that day. All I know is that it wasn't a bear, and it certainly wasn't a human. The sounds that creature made, at such a volume, were beyond anything a human could produce.

It wasn't until about ten years later, when we stumbled upon a single footprint on the edge of a freshly plowed field, that I mentioned the encounter to the people I was with. Until then, I had kept silent out of fear of being ridiculed. That experience shook me to the core and caused me to stop hunting in the area altogether. I haven't returned to that spot since.

CHAPTER FIFTY-NINE

IT WAS THE EARLY 2000S, and I was a teenager living in Arkansas. In my teens I loved nothing more than high-risk sports. Whether it was racing down the street on my skateboard or tearing up the dirt on my four-wheeler, I was always looking for my next adrenaline fix. My parents weren't thrilled with my love of danger, but they knew they couldn't stop me. So, they did the next best thing: they made sure I had all the safety gear I needed. I had a helmet, knee pads, and elbow pads for every activity. And while I grumbled about having to wear them, I knew deep down that they were important.

My favorite activity was four-wheeling. There was something about the roar of the engine and the wind in my hair that made me feel alive. I loved pushing myself to go faster and take bigger risks. Of course, there were plenty of close calls. I wiped out more times than I could count, and there were a few times when I came dangerously close to serious injury. But that didn't stop me. If anything, it made me more determined to push myself even further.

One summer, I convinced a group of friends to come with me on a four-wheeling trip to the mountains. We spent days exploring the rugged terrain, taking turns leading the pack and trying out new trails. It was on the last day of our trip that things got crazy. We were racing down a steep hill when I hit a rock and lost control of my four-wheeler. I went flying off the machine and tumbled down the hill, hitting rocks and branches along the way.

When I finally came to a stop, I was battered and bruised but miraculously still alive. My friends rushed over to check on me, their faces pale with shock. It was a wake-up call for all of us. We realized that we had been taking too many risks, and that we needed to be more careful in the future.

But even though I knew I had been lucky to survive, I couldn't shake the thrill of the ride. There was something about the danger and excitement that I just couldn't resist.

Do you think for one second, I had learned my lesson? Or that I would start being more careful? Heck no! As far as I was concerned, I was immortal! But I did slow down on the other stuff, but my off-road activities aren't something that I could resist whatsoever. I had always loved four-wheeling. There was something about the rush of the wind in my hair and the roar of the engine that made me feel alive. So, when my friends invited me to go on a weekend trip to the woods, I jumped at the chance.

We arrived at the campsite early on Saturday morning and quickly set up our tents. After a quick breakfast, we headed out on our four-wheelers, eager to explore the rugged terrain. The woods were beautiful. The trees towered over us, casting dappled shadows on the ground. The air was cool and crisp, and I could smell the pine needles and damp earth. We rode for hours, taking turns leading the pack and exploring new trails. But then something strange happened.

I was in the lead, racing down a steep hill, when I saw something move out of the corner of my eye. I remember thinking at that time, did I just see what I think I just saw? I hit the brakes hard, skidding to a stop just inches from a massive creature standing in the middle of the trail.

It was huge, easily seven feet tall, with shaggy brown fur and piercing yellow eyes. It looked like nothing I had ever seen before. It looked irritated with my mere presence, and it was in that moment I realized that fearless or not, one wrong move and I could be eaten alive.

For a moment, we just stared at each other. Me trying not to piss myself over the sheer size of this creature and it is looking at me wondering why I have disturbed its walk through the woods. I could feel my heart pounding in my chest as I tried to make sense of what I was seeing. Was this some kind of bear or a wild animal that had wandered too far from its territory?

But then it moved. It took a step forward, and I could see its massive hands and feet. This wasn't a bear. This was something else entirely. It had a lumbering walk like a bipedal ape. Its arms hung at its sides, and I just continued to gape with my jaw down to the forest floor. I didn't know what to do. My friends had caught up by now, and we all sat frozen on our four-wheelers, staring at this creature in disbelief.

It huffed and let out a bark that rung out in a deep rumbling voice that seemed to shake the ground beneath us. We continued to stare frozen in shock. Then it let out an arching bellow at us. We didn't need to be told twice. We revved our engines and took off down the trail, our hearts racing with fear and excitement. We rode for what felt like hours, trying to put as much distance between us and that creature as possible. When we finally stopped to catch our breath, we all agreed that we had just had the craziest experience of our lives.

CHAPTER SIXTY

I WOKE up early on a Saturday morning, excited to embark on my first Boy Scout camping trip. I had been looking forward to this for weeks, and I couldn't wait to spend the weekend in the great outdoors with my fellow scouts. As I packed my backpack with all the essentials - a sleeping bag, tent, clothes, and food - I felt a sense of anticipation building inside me. This was going to be an adventure.

We met at the local scout hall and loaded up our gear onto a bus. As we drove out of town and into the countryside, I could feel my excitement growing. We were headed to a remote campsite deep in the woods, and I couldn't wait to explore. When we arrived at the campsite, we quickly set up our tents and got to work building a fire pit. We spent the rest of the day learning survival skills - how to start a fire without matches, how to purify water, and how to navigate using a map and compass.

As night fell, we gathered around the fire and cooked our dinner over the flames. The smell of sizzling sausages filled the air, and we laughed and joked as we ate. It was a simple meal, but it tasted amazing after a long day of hiking and learning. After dinner, we sat around the fire and told stories. Some of the older scouts shared tales of their past camping trips, while others told ghost stories that made us all shiver with fear. As we sat there in the darkness, surrounded by nothing but trees and stars, I felt a sense of camaraderie with my fellow scouts. We were all in this together.

As we crawled into our tents for the night, I could hear nature all around me - crickets chirping, owls hooting, and leaves rustling in the wind. It was a peaceful sound, and I felt myself drifting off to sleep. The next morning, we woke up early and set out on a hike through the woods. We followed a trail that wound its way through the forest, past streams and over hills. Along the way, we stopped to identify different plants and animals, and we even saw a deer grazing in a clearing. When we returned to camp, we spent the afternoon practicing our knot-tying skills and learning how to use a hatchet safely. It was hard work, but it felt good to learn new skills and to challenge ourselves.

As the sun began to set on our final night at camp, we gathered around the fire one last time. We shared our favorite memories from the trip and talked about what we had learned. It was bittersweet - we were sad to be leaving, but also excited to go home and share our experiences with our families. It was my first Boy Scout camping trip, and I was excited to spend the weekend in the great outdoors with my friends. We spent the first few day's learning survival skills and exploring the woods. We set up our tents near a small river and spent our days fishing and swimming.

As night fell on the last day of our trip, we gathered around the campfire to share scary stories and roast marshmallows. We were all having a good time, laughing, and joking around. But then we heard a rustling in the bushes. We all froze, listening intently. At first, we thought it might be a deer or a bear. But as the rustling grew louder, we could tell that it was something much bigger. Suddenly, we saw movement in the trees. Something was moving towards us, something big and shaggy. We all stood up, our hearts pounding in our chests.

As the creature emerged from the trees, we could see that it was not a bear or any other animal we had ever seen before. It was tall, at least seven feet tall, with long arms covered in shaggy fur. Its eyes glowed in the firelight, and it stared at us with an intense curiosity. We were all scared out of our minds, but we didn't know what to do. The creature just stood there, watching us. It didn't look aggressive, but it was not something we wanted to mess with.

We slowly backed away from the campfire, hoping that the creature would just leave us alone. But it followed us, step by step, its eyes fixed on us. We could hear its heavy breathing and feel its presence looming over us. Finally, we reached the edge of the clearing. The creature stopped and watched us as we retreated into our tents. We stayed up all night, huddled together in fear, listening to the creature moving around outside.

The next morning, we packed up our gear and left the campsite as quickly as we could. We didn't talk about what had happened until we were safely back home. But even then, we couldn't explain what we had seen that night.

Years later, my friends and I still talk about that camping trip. We still wonder what that creature was and where it came from. And every time we go camping, we keep an eye out for any signs of Bigfoot or any other mysterious creatures that might be lurking in the woods.

Despite the fear we experienced that night, we all became fascinated with the idea of Bigfoot and other cryptids. We started researching sightings and stories, and even went on a few expeditions to try and find evidence of their existence.

One summer, we decided to take a trip to the Pacific Northwest, where there had been many reported Bigfoot sightings. We spent weeks hiking through the dense forests, setting up cameras and recording equipment in hopes of capturing some evidence.

One night, we were sitting around our campfire when we heard a strange noise. It was a low growling sound, coming from the trees nearby. We all froze, listening intently.

Suddenly, we saw movement in the trees again. This time, it was much closer than before. We could see the outline of a large creature moving through the underbrush.

We quickly grabbed our cameras and started filming. The creature was too far away to see any details, but we could tell that it was massive and covered in fur.

As it moved closer, we could hear its heavy footsteps and smell its musky scent. It stopped just at the edge of our campsite, watching us with its glowing eyes.

We were all terrified, but also excited to have finally seen something that could be evidence of Bigfoot. We continued to film as the creature slowly backed away and disappeared into the woods.

When we returned home and reviewed our footage, we couldn't believe what we had captured. The video showed a large, bipedal creature moving through the forest, just as we had seen with our own eyes.

While we can't say for sure that what we saw was Bigfoot or another unknown creature, it was an experience that none of us will ever forget. And it has only fueled our fascination with the mysterious creatures that may be hiding in the wilderness.

CHAPTER SIXTY-ONE

I MOVED to my current location in New Hampshire back in 2001, and over the past few years, I've had several sightings that I can't explain. It might sound strange, but I'm dead serious. You see, my living room has a large picture window that faces a small creek and an empty wooded lot. I've had the pleasure of seeing various wildlife on my property, like deer, bears, turkeys, raccoons, moose, and even foxes. My place is situated in a part of Gilford known as Gunstock Acres. But the sightings I'm talking about happen on dark summer nights, usually in the late evening. There's no specific date or time for these encounters.

Now, let me give you an idea of the layout. The distance from the ground to the top of the window is at least 10 feet. But the creature I've seen is something else entirely. It stands at a towering height of about 9 feet, with long, dark, deep brownish hair. It walks upright, just like a human. Sometimes it passes by in one direction, only to return in the opposite direction several minutes later. Other times, it simply walks away, and I won't see it again until the following year. On occasions when the lights inside my house are on, it appears more like a shadow. I'm always taken aback and startled whenever I catch a glimpse of it. I can hardly believe my eyes, but I can't find any other explanation for what I've witnessed.

Interestingly enough, last summer I happened to mention to my husband and family that I had seen Bigfoot again the previous night. To my surprise, my oldest son chimed in and said he had seen it too, passing by the window, and it had even looked right at him as it went by. He described the same creature, except he saw its face. He swears it's a Bigfoot as well. The encounter gave him the creeps, and I believe he's still spooked by it. Mind you, my son is in his 20s.

Living in an area known as the Great North Woods, surrounded by lakes, mountains, rivers, and caves, there are plenty of hiding places for something like this. I've heard strange grunting noises, the snapping of tree limbs, eerie screams, and unexplained footsteps coming from the wooded lot outside my house. Frankly, after I see the creature, I refuse to venture outside and make sure to turn on all the outside lights until I manage to forget about it again. During winter, we've come across some massive footprints circling the house, but we couldn't identify them. Unfortunately, the tracks often get filled in due to the heavy snowfall we get during storms.

I'll admit, this whole situation spooks me out, but the creature hasn't done anything to harm any of us. It simply peers into the window, observing us. I know what I've seen, but I haven't shared the sightings with many people because I know they'd think we're crazy. So, my family and I are left wondering what this creature could be. Is it possible that it's a Bigfoot? We strongly believe it is, based on what we've witnessed. It definitely can't be a black bear since it's far too tall and walks on two legs like a human. And a moose wouldn't fit the description either. This creature has the build of an incredibly large, broad-shouldered man, with muscles aplenty, all covered in hair. My son mentioned that even its face is hairy, although the skin on the face appears lighter than the rest of its body.

Thank you for letting me share and I love your books.

CHAPTER SIXTY-TWO

BACK IN THE summer of 1988, I went to visit some friends in Huntington, Arkansas. We all had this idea of going to a local lake for some bass fishing. Now, they had warned me beforehand about the abundance of water moccasins lurking around, so I knew I had to be extra careful with every step I took.

As I made my way along the bank, focusing intently on where I placed my feet, something unexpected happened. There was a sudden commotion in the woods about fifteen feet to my right. I turned my head to see what was going on and my eyes widened in surprise. There, standing before me, was an enormous creature, towering at about 7 to 8 feet tall. Its shoulders were incredibly broad, and I could hear this strange, "whoooop whooooop" noise emanating from it. At first, I thought it might be one of my buddies trying to pull a prank on me, so I cautiously approached it. But that's when things took a terrifying turn.

In an instant, the creature grabbed hold of a nearby tree trunk and effortlessly snapped it off. It then slammed the trunk against the ground with a thunderous thud, letting out a deep, guttural growl. Fear coursed through my veins like never before. The sheer intimidation was overwhelming; its muscles were visibly flexed, its head tilted down, and its intense gaze fixed right on me.

Now, my dad had taught me a thing or two about encounters with bears and what to do in those situations. My instinct told me to run, but my dad's advice echoed in my mind — running might only provoke the animal further. So, I quickly dropped my fishing pole, looked down at the ground, and began to back away slowly. The creature followed me for a short distance before simply turning around and disappearing into the woods. When I finally rejoined my friends, I recounted the chilling experience, but all they did was laugh and make fun of me. Needless to say, I haven't returned to that part of the country since then. Now, I find myself living in the desert, far from dense forests and encounters of that kind.

Now, when I reflect on what I saw, I remember certain distinct features of the creature. It resembled a large gorilla, standing with its knees slightly bent and legs bowed outward. Its face was long, and its lower lip jutted out, reminding me of the orangutan Clint Eastwood had as a sidekick. The nose was somewhat like a gorilla's but more pronounced, and the chin stood out with its remarkable length, almost like Jay Leno's. Its eyes were dark brown, resembling those of an ape, and its hair had a reddish-brown hue, much like that of a gorilla, only longer and not as thick. It had a surprisingly beautiful coat of hair, almost like an Irish Setter.

I didn't notice any peculiar smells at the time, but the wind was blowing away from me, towards the creature. I did observe that it touched the ground with the knuckles of its left hand as it approached me after twisting off the tree. Later, I saw similar behavior exhibited by chimpanzees on the Discovery Channel when they felt threatened. Furthermore, I recall that its feet were different from ours—neither like a monkey's nor exactly like a human's. As it growled at me, its mouth formed an "O" shape. That was when I instinctively lowered my head and slowly backed away. One thing I can't forget is that as it walked off, it kept its knees bent and took long strides, with its arms hanging at its sides. If I had to guess, I'd say it appeared to be a female since I noticed what seemed to be large, droopy breasts. Once it turned away, its attention was fixated on a particular bushy spot where it paused, hunched down for a moment, and then swiftly walked away. My best guess was that it either had food or young ones nearby, although I couldn't see either as it disappeared into the trees, roughly 75 feet away from me.

CHAPTER SIXTY-THREE

BACK IN LATE DECEMBER 2014, my wife and I were visiting my parents' house in Southern California. It was a regular evening, and we stepped outside with our new puppy to let him do his business and have a quick smoke. The property sat on top of a hill, encompassing about 5 acres, mostly filled with old oak trees. As we stood there, something strange happened.

First, an eerie silence fell upon us, and the only sound came from some rustling down the hill. Just then, a putrid, foul odor reached our noses, causing both my wife and me to notice it. Now, being a hunter and someone who spends a lot of time outdoors, I immediately assumed it was a cougar. Concerned for our safety, I instructed my wife to take the dog inside. However, as we headed towards the house, I could hear distinct bipedal footsteps parallel to us at the base of the hill.

Mindful of the wildlife in the area, I always carried a gun when I visited my parents' place. And since my dad had been suspecting someone trespassing on the property at night, he had set up an alarm sensor near the driveway. It was meant to alert us whenever something crossed its path, but it had been triggering so frequently that he eventually turned it off. With the scent lingering in the air and the unusual sounds, I decided to investigate further.

Equipped with a flashlight and my gun, I stepped back outside, leaving my wife and daughter inside the house. As I descended the hill, the odor seemed to intensify, and an unnerving feeling of being watched crept over me. Reaching the lower half of the property, I noticed a shadow moving behind a tree. I directed my flashlight towards it and called out, demanding whoever or whatever it was to reveal itself. There was no response. Determined to uncover the source, I cautiously began circling the tree in a clockwise pattern. When I finally reached the point where I should have seen something, there was nothing there. I felt foolish, thinking that perhaps it was all my imagination.

But as I turned around, there it was. About 20 yards in front of me stood a massive figure, partially obscured by another tree. I froze in my tracks, my heart pounding in my chest. The creature, completely black in color, was covered in hair from head to toe, except for its face. Its facial features resembled those of a human, albeit with a flatter nose. The skin on its face had a grayish hue, and its expression remained blank. This unnerving encounter lasted for about 15 seconds, until I heard the front door of the house swing open.

The sound snapped me out of my trance, and I heard my wife calling out to me. The creature glanced up the hill, then back at me, before casually sauntering away towards the neighboring property. Throughout its departure, it kept its gaze fixed on me. As soon as it stepped over the barbed wire fence, fear surged through me, and I sprinted towards the house, fueled by an adrenaline rush like never before. I had never run so fast in my entire life. When I reached the top of the hill, my parents and wife were waiting on the porch. My mom noticed the shock on my face and commented on how pale I looked. I assured them I was fine, though deep inside, I was trembling.

Until now, I haven't shared this story with anyone, and writing it down has brought back the overwhelming emotions. My hands are still shaking as I recount this inexplicable encounter.

CHAPTER SIXTY-FOUR

BACK IN AUGUST, on our sprawling property nestled along the Pacific Ocean, in a town that's gained notoriety for its uncanny Bigfoot encounters – so much so that even the local police accept their existence – I had an experience that defies all explanation and logic.

The evening in question started out like any other. I was going through my usual pre-bed routine – extinguishing the crackling campfire and making my way to the road to catch a glimpse of the deer that often frequented the grassy area between the north and southbound lanes. However, that particular night was different; an almost full moon cast an eerie, silvery glow over the landscape. Strangely absent were the 10 to 20 deer that would typically be there, grazing peacefully.

I stood there for a while, taking in the serene stillness that enveloped the surroundings. Then, movement on the road caught my attention – a massive figure, standing about 200 feet away beneath the illumination of a nearby streetlight. My initial thought was that it was just a very large man, perhaps taking a late-night stroll. This was not entirely unusual, as people often wander around after dark. With an air of nonchalance, he ambled away from me, disappearing from view for a brief moment as he crossed the road and descended into the ditch on the opposite side.

What transpired next is the stuff of nightmares, an image that has been seared into my consciousness. The figure that had entered the ditch on two legs emerged on all fours, crawling its way back across the road. I tried to convince myself that it was a dog – but a dog of truly monstrous proportions. This creature occupied the entire width of a lane of traffic, which, for context, measures a solid 10 feet across. It moved with an eerie, determined purpose, its gaze fixed ahead as if it were following some invisible path. What struck me most was the deliberate avoidance of eye contact; it was as if this being was deliberately ignoring my presence. In that moment, my mind struggled to process the incongruity of it all – an upright figure descending into the ditch only to transform into an immense, crawling entity that seemed utterly out of place.

What further compounded the perplexity of the situation was an incident that occurred during a summit on urban sightings. A speaker delved into an unsettling phenomenon known as the "spider crawl." At the mere mention of this term, memories of that haunting night came rushing back with an intensity that overwhelmed me. Tears welled in my eyes, and I left the room momentarily, grappling with the surge of emotions that had been unexpectedly unleashed.

This encounter has had a profound impact on me, leaving an indelible imprint on my psyche. I find myself continually mulling over the details of that surreal night. The image of the colossal figure, its methodical crawl, and the eerie sense of detachment it projected continue to haunt my thoughts. In the aftermath of this inexplicable encounter, my life has taken a new trajectory, marked by a quest for understanding and a search for answers to the mysteries that linger in the wake of that fateful August night.

CHAPTER SIXTY-FIVE

GREETINGS from the Land of the Long White Cloud! I've got an epic tale straight from the heart of New Zealand, and it involves none other than our very own Bigfoot, or as we like to call it, the Moehau Man. So, brace yourself for a yarn that'll send shivers down your spine!

Picture this: a couple of young blokes fresh out of high school, both 18 and clueless as sheep in a snowstorm about what to do for our end-of-year holidays. My cousin, being the legend he is, comes up with the raddest idea – why not spend a solid week up in the coast with our grandfather? Now, let me set the scene for you. We hail from this tight-knit town called Gisborne, a place with about 40,000 friendly faces. And when we say 'The Coast,' we're talking about this mystical rural wonderland right on the outskirts of town, a haven of untamed bush and forests. Our family's got this cozy homestead nestled in a charming spot called 'Waipiro Bay.' Our granddad was stoked to have us over, and let me tell you, there's something about being out in the wild that just soothes the soul, clears the cobwebs, and sets your spirit free.

Now, after a solid day of tending to sheep and hacking away at wood – I mean, it's a granddad's rite of passage, right? – the old man drops a bombshell on us. He's like, "You lads fancy some eels for dinner? Let's go spotlighting!" Now, imagine the scene: it's around 8 in the evening, the moon's playing peekaboo with the clouds, and we're ready to embark on this adventure of a lifetime. Oh, and here's a little detail that'll make you appreciate the vibe even more – granddad's crib sits perched on this gnarly hill, and right behind it, there's this trail that leads to a creek. About an hour's hike, and the sides of that trail? Well, they're practically painted in lush, dense brush. So there we are, marching along, but guess what? Those eels we were hoping to bag were about as big as a minnow's snack. We march back, spirits still high, and that's when the real magic happens.

From the left side of the bushes, there's this strange symphony of squeals. I'm talking hair-raising, spine-tingling squeals that make you question every decision that led you to this point. We halt, kill our head torches, and turn into stealth mode. It's like we're characters in a survival video game, and we're all ears. In my mind, I'm trying to convince myself it's just a wild boar having a boogie, and turns out, my cousin's got the same thought. Torchlight back on, we trudge on through the creek, but hold up – the plot thickens.

Around five minutes later, those squeals – they're back. But this time, they've cranked up the volume and are practically serenading us. Something's stirring in the bushes, and it's not just your everyday critter. We pull the stealth move again – torches off, senses heightened, and hearts thumping. Lo and behold, we spot it – this towering silhouette, darker than a moonless night, sizing us up like we're the main course at a feast.

But here's where things get freaky. This Moehau Man, as we've come to call it, is no ordinary forest dweller. Its face is swathed in this dense, almost otherworldly black-greyish fur, but its eyes? Oh boy, its eyes are this blazing combo of orange and yellow that send chills down your spine. Its teeth, sharp and canine-like, its hands, massive enough to cradle my noggin – it's like something out of a blockbuster horror flick. We're immobilized, it lets out this deep huff, takes a step back, and just like that, melts into the shadows. My cousin and I? We exchange a look that says it all – relief, disbelief, and a hint of "did that just happen?" We're spooked, but we've got our cool masks on, so we soldier on back to the house, not a word uttered, just the crunch of leaves beneath our boots.

Returning to the old man's house. Granddad had that look on his face like, "No eels, huh?" But my cousin, oh man, he pulls off the poker face of the century and goes, "We might've had a run-in with the Moehau Man." Granddad? He just nods knowingly, like it's all in a day's work. And then, get this, he spills the beans. The Moehau Man, this ancient guardian of the woods, has been making appearances in his life too. He's brushed shoulders with this creature on his hunting escapades, and believe it or not, it's even dropped by the house a few times. Granddad's nonchalant about it – he's like, "I let him be, you know?" But here's the kicker: he lays down the law, tells us not to go Moehau-hunting ourselves (like that was even on the table, right?). He's convinced this Moehau character is this mystical protector of the local woods, a guardian straight out of Māori legend.

Fast forward to today, and here I am, pushing 30, still replaying that night in my mind. The only other soul I've entrusted this tale to is my partner, and luckily, she's got her own stories of the uncanny. So, as the stars twinkle over the New Zealand night, remember – the Moehau Man is out there, watching over the forests, and etching its legend into the very fabric of our land. Epic, right?

CHAPTER SIXTY-SIX

THE JOURNEY through these puzzling occurrences traverses time, beginning in the 1960s, etching memories onto the canvas of my life in the Northern Panhandle of West Virginia. Shadows of unexplained sightings cloaked my childhood home, whispering tales of mysteries intertwined with family routines and the humble homestead. In hushed tones, these "clues" lingered, forming a silent tapestry of enigma that stretched across the years, confined to the inner circle of our small family unit.

A crescendo of whispers transformed into a symphony of undeniable presence, gradually revealing a presence beyond the familiar rhythms of raising a family and tending to a modest homestead. A mysterious thread wove itself through the very fabric of our lives, a thread that weaved through the dirt road, the vast lands, and the very air that we breathed.

It all began on a warm autumn day in 1967, against the backdrop of a serene cow field. This field, nestled behind our family's abode, held within it a small home, a cluster of outbuildings, a sprawling garden, and a little over 6 acres of cherished land. Adjacent to our property, a neighboring farmer's field stood, divided from ours by barbed wire fencing. The landscape unfolded like a portrait, a steep hillside adorned with tall grasses, adorned halfway up by a veil of woods. This is where the first story unfurled, a story woven with innocence and astonishment.

The protagonists of this tale were my sister, a mere 9 years old at the time, and our father. Together, they ventured into the heart of the hillside woods, their eyes drawn skyward by a spectacle that defied explanation. High amidst the treetops, they beheld a sight both baffling and extraordinary: creatures that swung with an uncanny agility, traversing the branches with swift grace. My sister painted a vivid tableau with her words, describing these enigmatic beings as baby orangutans, adorned with stringy orange-ish hair and limbs that moved with almost ethereal fluidity.

Upon their return, our home buzzed with excitement, fueled by the tale of monkeys gracing the West Virginian landscape. Theories tumbled forth like leaves in the wind – perhaps a wandering circus had misplaced its troupe, or maybe our well-heeled neighbor harbored a penchant for pet monkeys. Yet, with the passage of days, each theory waned, revealing a puzzle that resisted easy solution. The tale of the mysterious monkeys slowly faded, leaving us with a sense of wonder that lingered like an echo.

Time flowed onward, carrying with it further enigmatic encounters that added to the tapestry of inexplicability. A mile down the same road, at my grandparent's home, a series of unsettling incidents unfurled. Amidst the shadows of grief following my grandfather's passing, my grandmother and aunt found themselves face to face with an eerie presence. Peering through the kitchen window, they beheld a face that defied reason – a face that gazed back at them from an elevated vantage point, as if borne aloft by an unseen force. The window, elevated from the ground, presented an enigma that lingered in their thoughts, a mystery whose implications echoed like a whisper in the wind.

In the midst of these riddles, a neighbor's voice added a new dimension to the unfolding narrative. His tale unfolded in the shroud of darkness, a nocturnal encounter with a bear that he described with unwavering conviction. Yet, skepticism permeated the air, our parents' raised eyebrows casting doubt upon the veracity of the tale. As the years spun their thread, this particular mystery dissolved, leaving only fragments of a tale that had seemingly lost its way.

Dogs, our loyal companions, became unwitting participants in this unfolding enigma. My father, a seasoned hunter, kept a retinue of hounds that patrolled the night with vigilant barks and fervent energy. Yet, these canine sentinels would often find themselves stirred to uproar by an unseen presence in the neighboring cow field. Nocturnal admonishments were a routine occurrence, a ritual my father undertook to quell the restless baying that echoed through the night.

The tapestry of these unexplained events wove its threads into my adolescent years, remaining a silent enigma that shaped the landscape of my memories. By the time my 15th birthday had come and gone, the landscape had transformed, and my steps were guided by a newfound independence. Alone or with friends, I traversed the fields and woods, tracing shortcuts etched into my memory from years past.

One such shortcut led me to a towering tree adorned with a rope swing, a hidden gem nestled amidst the landscape. The sun-dappled days of summer unfolded beneath the shade of its branches as my friends and I reveled in its simple pleasures. The swing became a cherished escape, a place where laughter intermingled with the rustle of leaves. Yet, an unforeseen encounter shattered this idyllic facade, revealing an undercurrent of disquiet that lurked in the shadows.

As I sat upon a rock, my brother-in-law's ascent to the rope swing was accompanied by an eerie soundtrack – the sound of a woman's scream echoing through the landscape. A chill raced down my spine as the second scream joined the first, reverberating through the hollow like a haunting refrain. An instinctual urge surged within me, propelling me away from that place of innocence and into the realm of uncertainty.

Years rolled by, ushering in new chapters and revelations that added layers to the tapestry of enigma. A son's unsettling discovery of deer carcasses, a family dog's nocturnal symphony of barks, and the chorus of yells and vocalizations that punctuated the night painted a tableau of unease.

Time stretched its fingers further, casting its veil upon my nephew's experiences in the very heart of the land that had birthed these mysteries. A pine tree swaying with unnatural intensity and the specter of a massive entity disturbing the woods evoked a sense of otherworldly presence that defied rational explanation.

Amidst these whispered tales of the uncanny, my family and I would gather, sharing stories that intertwined across decades and generations. Voices would rise and fall, weaving a collective tapestry of experiences that merged the ordinary and the inexplicable.

As I trace back these threads of the unknown, I am reminded of the profound nature of the land that nurtured my childhood and witnessed my journey into adulthood. Each encounter, every enigma, forms a mosaic of the extraordinary lurking beneath the veneer of the familiar. And so, the tapestry of these unexplained mysteries remains a testament to the boundless enigma of the world we inhabit, a world where the ordinary and the extraordinary coexist in a dance of intrigue and wonder.

CHAPTER SIXTY-SEVEN

IN THE SPRING OF 1993, I lived with my parents in a small house in Beaufort, NC. Beaufort is a small town surrounded by water and lots of wild areas. Our house was near the city limits where there were large areas of pastureland that stretched from the highway to the river. The creek that ran nearby was thick with underbrush, making it an ideal area for wildlife to live and kids to play.

One Saturday evening, I was in our front yard with my sister, our friend, a neighbor who was a bit younger than I was, and my mother. We were facing the road when we heard a series of unusual combinations of growling and yelling. They sounded very "guttural". They were sounds that we had not heard before, even though we were used to the usual sounds of wild animals in the area.

We turned towards the sounds and, even though it was already dark, we could make out the figure of a large being. It was under the streetlamp near the bridge of the tributary. It almost looked like an ape, except for the fact that it was extremely tall and stood upright on two legs. It was covered in long, shaggy hair about four or five inches in length. While we were watching it, it raised up its arms and threw them over its head. Then it started to throw its head back each time it made a sound. The screams it made were so deep and I could tell they were coming from deep down in its gut. The figure seemed like it was in some sort of pain or distress. We watched this strange creature for about five minutes before it turned and disappeared into the darkness. It just turned, walked under the bridge, and moved eastward.

We all looked at each other and didn't know what to make of the entire thing. In hindsight, it was very unsettling to watch. While we were all standing out there talking, my mother started making a face. Then we all started to make the same face. There was this horrible, repulsive smell. It was like a mixture of the scent of a goat, a strong wet dog stench, several decaying animals, and a mixture of old skunk. The smells were so bad we all began to gag. My mother went inside but she said we could stay out a little bit longer. The smell was still strong, and we had to cover our noses with our shirts just to continue to stay outside.

We searched that area for the entire weekend for any evidence that might confirm that we really did see that large creature. However, we found nothing concrete. What we had seen was a large, dark, hairy being that moved quickly and with long strides, swinging its arms as it walked. We walked down to the river later that weekend and we found a lot of trees that had been twisted and broken in two. It looked like a tornado or twister had come through and twisted the trees, but we had not had any bad weather for a month or so. We had all been to the river several times since the last storm and no one noticed the trees being twisted or broken like that.

On Monday, we went back to school. My sister and I agreed we weren't going to tell anyone about what had happened that night. During my lunch break Susan, my friend from across the street, came over to my lunch table and started to tell me all the things that had happened at her house over the weekend. Susan has a little dog that stays inside all the time, and she said that the dog went into a frenzy during the night on Saturday. When her dad got up to see what the dog was barking at, he spotted a large, hairy creature walking around in their backyard. When he flipped on the patio light to see what was going on outside, the large figure just turned and disappeared into the darkness near the creek.

At school a few days later I had another friend, who also lives on the same street I did but just a few houses down from us, tell me that during the same Saturday night, her dog also went wild. When her parents got up to see what the matter was, they saw a large, ape-like figure in their backyard. It was also moving towards the creek. She also said that the previous winter, they discovered several large footprints in the snow on their back patio. The prints appeared to be barefoot, showing the outline of toes on several of them.

With all these sightings, our street went on a self-imposed alert. Then the rumors started. Some of our neighbors said that it was a bear or some other known animal wandering around, but we knew it was different. We pieced it all together and we decided that the descriptions of the creature's appearance, behavior, and that horrible smell all added up and that there could be only one answer. We all agreed that we all saw Bigfoot on our block.

CHAPTER SIXTY-EIGHT

IN FEBRUARY OF 2018, my oldest daughter and I were living in Arnold, West Virginia. My youngest daughter was off in school in Roanoke, and she usually came home on the weekends. We were living in an area that was filled with wildlife. My house was on the top of a hill. The house was bordered on three sides by bottomland. I made sure the house was high enough up the hill in case any of the creeks overflowed. The house sits about 125 feet above the creek.

I usually wake up around dawn, let the dogs out and wait for them to finish up. Then I come inside and start the coffee and then get ready for work. However, on that morning, it was cool, and I hadn't had much sleep the night before, so I went back inside to get the coffee started.

The night before, the dogs were barking like crazy and then the coyotes started to howl. It was impossible to get any sleep. After about an hour of listening to that, I stepped out on the porch to see if there was something going on. When I stepped outside, I heard the strangest yell. It almost sounded like an air raid siren. The scream started out on a low note and then warped up to a high pitch yell. Each yell only lasted for about 15 to 20 seconds. After it would yell, then the coyotes and my dogs answered. This went on for a while. When the coyote howls finally stopped, the yell in the woods repeated two more times. I had my dogs inside and had calmed them down. Finally, it was quiet, and I got a few hours of sleep.

I was exhausted that morning and I decided to let the dogs out and start the coffee. I didn't go outside with them like I normally did. The dogs had only been outside for a few seconds before they started going crazy again. The dogs' barks sounded peculiar, almost a whiney quality like they were confused or afraid. I went out to the porch to see what was going on.

I looked over toward the dogs and looked in the direction they were looking. Just beyond the young pine trees, which were about three to four feet tall, I saw something moving not too far away from the house. There was a huge figure standing in my yard. It was about twice as tall as the new trees, so that would make it at least eight feet tall. I called for the dogs and got them back on the porch.

My view was limited to the upper half of the figure since the trees were in the way. I banged on the side of the house, trying to wake up my daughter. She was sleeping in that room. I guess I made too much noise, and the large figure took a few steps backwards and glided back into the woods. By the time my daughter got to the porch, the figure had almost disappeared completely, but she did get there in time to see it before it was completely gone.

A few days later, my youngest daughter came home from college. We told her about what had happened. Of course, she was a skeptic and joked about us seeing a Sasquatch. I thought she was spending the weekend, but she only came out for a visit and a free dinner. She was planning on going back to the dorms that night. It was getting late so she started to gather up her laundry and repack the car so she could leave right after dinner.

After dinner, she grabbed her purse and was headed to her car. We all stepped out on the porch to say goodbye and that is when we were hit with that stench. It's like nothing I have ever smelled before. It was a rancid smell, like rotting garbage, urine, and old skunk spray. She hurried to the car and was going to leave. My youngest daughter went inside, and I stayed on the porch to make sure she got off ok.

Our driveway down the hill is very long and I watched her drive down the driveway. I saw her suddenly slam on the brakes and then turn on her bright lights. She put the car in reverse and drove quickly back up to the house. When she got out, she was shaking and said she saw what she thought was a stump over by the new trees. But then the stump started to sway back and forth. She realized it wasn't a stump, but it was a large, hairy creature standing on two legs and swaying in the darkness. She changed her mind and wanted to spend the night. I went and grabbed my big flashlight and looked all through the trees that surrounded our house. Other than that strange smell, nothing seemed to be out of place.

The next morning, I went out with the dogs. I started to look around the area where the newer trees had been planted. It was the same place we both saw the large, hairy creature. I looked around and I found a very large footprint. It was at least 16 inches long. It looked like something large had stepped on a gopher mound and left a foot-print. The print appeared to have been made within the last 24 hours. That area was still wet from the rain we had the day before.

CHAPTER SIXTY-NINE

DURING THE EARLY spring of 2020, a chapter of my life unfolded as I embarked on a geocaching escapade in the picturesque expanse of Southern New Hampshire, particularly the vicinity near Richmond. My destination was the beguiling Widow Gage Town Forest, a haven adorned with a variety of terrains and an air of mystery. The trail I pursued was circular in nature, an entity in its own right, with a subtle connection to the renowned NET trail, a path that winds along the commanding ridges of Mount Monadnock and delves into the enigmatic heart of the deeper woods. Although the NET's siren call beckoned, my attention was riveted solely on the circular journey I was about to undertake.

As I embarked on this solo expedition, my truck claimed solitary residency in the parking lot, creating an ambiance of solitude. A sense of calm anticipation enveloped me as I embarked on this journey, each step ushering me deeper into the embrace of nature. The voyage began with the discovery of a beaver pond, an idyllic scene that was momentarily disrupted by the startled flight of ducks. Progressing further, faint echoes of distant voices reached my ears, an enigmatic phenomenon reminiscent of waterfowl engaged in their own murmured conversations. Initially, I attributed these voices to the ducks, dismissing them as part of the natural tableau.

Undeterred, I delved deeper into the trail, navigating its twists and turns with steadfast determination. However, the ethereal voices continued to linger, persisting like an enigma that refused to unravel. Convinced that fellow hikers were making their presence known, I quickened my pace, eager to share in the camaraderie of kindred spirits. To my bewilderment, the path remained vacant, the voices mere ephemeral whispers that tantalized without materializing.

The trail led me to the zenith of a modest hill, granting me a moment of reprieve to catch my breath and survey the landscape. Yet, even here, the elusive voices persisted, faint but undeniable. With anticipation coursing through my veins, I positioned myself optimally, preparing to greet the fellow hikers I believed were responsible for these auditory riddles. To my astonishment, no figures materialized, leaving me in a state of confounded bemusement.

In the midst of this enigmatic puzzle, a sudden and distinctly artificial Bard owl call pierced the air, causing me to pivot on my heels in search of the source. Yet, the landscape that met my gaze remained devoid of human presence, as though the very woods themselves were taunting my curiosity.

As I resumed my descent along the trail, a renewed sense of determination filled my every step, a resolve that grew more unyielding as the "owl" call made a dramatic return. This time, the call was accompanied by an almost jubilant "Ya-hooooooo!" In response, my gaze snapped towards the source, and there, about 40 yards away, stood a figure that defied immediate explanation.

Cloaked in the shadowy embrace of twilight, the figure possessed an aura of mystery, its features obscured by either a hood or an afro-like mane. My gaze was transfixed as I witnessed a seemingly fluid transformation, the figure transitioning seamlessly from an upright stance to a swift descent, moving lithely to assume an all-fours posture. With an almost surreal grace, it disappeared from view behind a stone wall, leaving me in a state of awe and disbelief.

The encounter continued to replay in my mind, a mental tapestry woven with threads of incredulity and curiosity. The more I reflected on the experience, the more apparent it became that what I had encountered defied conventional explanation. The notion that I had come face to face with a Bigfoot, a legendary and elusive creature, seemed to linger in the recesses of my thoughts, haunting me with its tantalizing implications.

CHAPTER SEVENTY

BACK WHEN I was 14 years old, I found myself living on a large cattle ranch in the heart of Missouri. The picturesque landscape was adorned with sparsely wooded areas, mysterious caves, and winding, expansive creeks. Hunting had been in my blood from the beginning, starting at the tender age of 4 when I was introduced to firearms. My father, a towering figure standing at 6'5" with a background as a rodeo cowboy, ranch hand, and seasoned professional hunter, was my mentor in the art of outdoor pursuits.

As life would have it, my parents went through a divorce, and it was decided that I would live with my father, starting when I was around nine years old. Being with my dad all the time, except when attending school, allowed me to learn about life as a Midwest cowboy. He had ventured across various states, including Colorado, Montana (where I was born), Wyoming, the Dakotas, and even Canadian territories during his days as an outfitter.

After the parental split, we settled into the old farmhouse situated about half a mile away from a magnificent 6-acre pond and a 60-acre lake to the east. These bodies of water offered endless opportunities for fishing and hunting, and I took advantage of it all. However, there was a smaller 6-acre pond to the north that always gave me an inexplicable sense of unease.

Looking back now, I realize that my experiences on the ranch included something far more mysterious than I ever could have imagined. In recent times, I learned about bigfoot and how they create distinct teepee-like structures using downed logs. It had never occurred to me at the time, but back then, I merely assumed that trees fell in such a pattern during storms due to their proximity to one another.

My black lab became my hunting companion. We were inseparable, and together, we hunted everything that crossed our path. I recall that he would retrieve doves for me, but with a twist – he insisted on devouring the first two before surrendering the others. Our hunting escapades spanned the vast expanse of the ranch, leaving no stone unturned in search of our targets.

One evening, I glanced out of the two-story window and spotted ducks gliding gracefully on the large pond by that eerie place in the woods. Despite its unsettling vibe, I decided to seize the opportunity and thought we could sneak up on the ducks, ensuring a successful hunting session. Being a hick kid in the heart of nowhere, I must admit that migratory bird restrictions were not on my mind that day. I promptly removed the plug from my trusty Remington 1100 shotgun and loaded it with #4 goose and duck loads.

The plan was set in motion as my loyal lab and I embarked on a stealthy approach to the pond. We trekked over half a mile to reach the dam side of the pond, where we hoped to surprise the ducks. Unfortunately, my exuberant dog's enthusiasm got the better of him, and he scared off the ducks before I could take a shot. No duck dinner for us that day.

The small pond's peculiar shape, resembling that of a sperm, was intriguing, and its midsection merged into dense, dark woods that loomed with an aura of mystery. These woods exuded an unmistakable vibe that discouraged anyone from venturing deeper. Consequently, we usually avoided them, but after the failed duck hunt, my curiosity got the better of me, and I decided to follow my dog's lead in the hope of finding other game.

We followed the dam, where the grassland met the edge of the trees. Roughly 60-70 yards past the grassland, the terrain transformed into a dense woodland at the tail end of the pond. My dog was diligently sniffing around, hoping to flush out rabbits, squirrels, or any other potential targets that could serve as supper for my father and me.

It was early October and the sun was starting to dip below the horizon, casting a golden glow across the landscape. However, the area around the bramble bush, I later realized, remained in perpetual shadow, regardless of the time of day. At the time, I merely perceived it as an eerie spot, not something more ominous. My lab was fixated on something ahead, and I kept asking him, "What do you see, boy?" He inched closer to the bramble bush, glancing back at me and our distant house every few steps.

Though I couldn't see what lay within the thorny labyrinth, I felt a mixture of fear and curiosity building up inside me. I persisted, coaxing him to reveal his discovery. After a moment of hesitation, he suddenly lunged into the bramble, only to quickly recoil and stagger backward. The sight of his fear was disconcerting, and before I could react, he turned and sprinted back towards our home, as if he was fleeing from an unseen terror.

Caught off guard and unsure of what just transpired, I stood there for a moment, trying to process my dog's reaction. That's when I heard a sound that sent shivers down my spine. It was a scream or a roar, a guttural noise that I had never heard before and could never recreate accurately. It was a chilling and haunting cry that seemed to echo through the surrounding woods.

My heart pounded in my chest as I saw the bramble bush tremble and shake violently. At that moment, every fiber of my being urged me to retreat, but my instinct to protect myself and my dog kicked in. Without thinking, I raised my shotgun and fired five rounds into the bramble where I thought the source of the disturbance might be.

The shotgun blasts momentarily drowned out the strange noises emanating from the bramble, but when the smoke cleared, I was left with an unsettling silence. Something deep inside me knew that no North American animal could withstand five rounds of that powerful goose load at such close range.

With my shotgun now empty, I couldn't help but feel a sense of vulnerability. My fear was palpable as I peered into the dark heart of the bramble. I caught a glimpse of a dark mass amidst the tangle of thorns, but I couldn't discern what it was. The ominous silence was interrupted by the rapid rustling of vegetation, and I could feel a sense of immense presence lurking just beyond my sight.

My heart pounded loudly in my ears as I weighed my options. Every instinct in me told me to flee, to run back home as fast as I could. But my determination to protect myself and my dog motivated me to hold my ground for a moment longer, preparing for whatever might emerge from the shadows.

And then it happened. Something beyond my comprehension emerged from the darkness of the bramble. It moved swiftly on all fours, its hulking form towering above my 14-year-old frame. It seemed to grunt or growl as it pushed through the dense vegetation, knocking over saplings and small trees in its path. I couldn't see its face or make out any distinct features, but the sight of this mysterious creature sent a shiver down my spine.

My mind was reeling, trying to process the unimaginable encounter. I had encountered numerous wild animals during my life as a hunter, but nothing could have prepared me for this enigmatic and terrifying sight. My adrenaline-fueled instincts took over, and I turned and ran as fast as my legs could carry me, my lab following close behind.

Fear gripped me as I sprinted back to our farmhouse. My heart pounded in my chest, and my breaths came in quick, shallow gasps. I felt an overwhelming sense of vulnerability, as if we had unwittingly intruded upon a realm far beyond our understanding. I couldn't shake the feeling that I had encountered something beyond the ordinary, something that defied rational explanation.

When I finally reached home, I hurriedly reloaded my shotgun with buckshot, knowing that whatever was out there might still pose a threat. I waited anxiously, my faithful lab by my side, for my father to return to the ranch. As an almost 20-year gunsmith, hunter, reloader, and ballistician, my father was a seasoned outdoorsman, experienced in facing the dangers of the wild. I knew that if anyone could help make sense of what had just occurred, it was him.

When my father arrived, I mustered the courage to share the terrifying events that had unfolded in the woods. At first, he seemed hesitant, understandably skeptical of such extraordinary claims. Yet, his own experiences in the wild had taught him not to dismiss the unknown outright.

He decided to investigate, grabbing his .338 Magnum rifle, while I had my shotgun ready, loaded with buckshot. As we made our way back to the area where the encounter had taken place, my heart was still racing with trepidation. I showed him the spot where I had fired my shotgun, and he began tracking the creature's trail. My father was a gifted tracker, with an uncanny ability to follow even the faintest signs left behind by wild animals.

As we delved deeper into the woods, following the blood trail and footprints left behind by the creature, I couldn't help but feel a sense of impending danger. My father was intently focused, his eyes scanning the ground for any signs of the enigmatic being we had encountered. It was a sight to behold, watching him navigate the terrain with skill and precision, the woods seeming to bend to his will.

But as we progressed further, something changed. I could see my father's demeanor shift, and he became visibly more cautious. He slowed his pace, his eyes darting around, as if he sensed that we were not alone. It was as if an invisible force weighed down upon us, suffocating the air with a sense of foreboding.

Suddenly, my father halted in his tracks, his face reflecting a mix of surprise, fear, and something I couldn't quite place. He scanned the area around us, searching for something he couldn't quite see. His grip on his rifle tightened, and he slowly started backing away, motioning for me to follow suit.

I could feel the tension in the air, the hairs on my neck standing on end. Something was amiss, something beyond our comprehension, and my father, who had faced numerous formidable adversaries in the wild, was unnerved.

He reached my side, and without uttering a word, he started walking back towards the safety of the house. We moved in silence, each lost in our own thoughts, haunted by what we had just encountered. As we made our way back to the farmhouse, my mind was a whirlwind of emotions, trying to make sense of the inexplicable events that had transpired.

Back at home, we both agreed never to speak of the encounter again. It became a lingering secret between a father and his son, an experience that defied explanation and lay shrouded in the realm of the unknown.

Over the years, I've become an experienced gunsmith, hunter, and reloader, delving deeper into the world of ballistics and firearms. Yet, no matter how many challenges I face in the field, I can't shake the memory of that haunting day. The strange structures that I once dismissed as mere coincidences now take on a new meaning, leaving me with more questions than answers.

The encounter that took place in the woods on that early October evening will forever remain etched in my memory, an indelible mark of an experience that defied explanation and defied the boundaries of my understanding of the natural world. It is a tale that I have shared with only a few trusted confidants, knowing that the truth of that day lies far beyond what our minds can comprehend. And so, the mystery of that eerie encounter continues to linger, forever haunting my thoughts and shaping my perspective on the enigmatic and unpre-dictable aspects of life in the wild.

CHAPTER SEVENTY-ONE

MY FAMILY and I lived in an area near Deer Mountain, just outside of Estes Park, Colorado. We owned about 60 acres of land at the time. We were in the process of clearing it of brush and timber with bulldozers so we could build on it. We had left about 25 acres as it was, and it was still heavily wooded. In the early fall of 2013, my wife stumbled upon something while out surveying the work that had just been done. While walking along the edge of the wooded area, she discovered unusual footprints on our property. We were excited about the thought of possibly having a Sasquatch on our property, so we took photographs and planned to create a plaster cast of the footprints later in the afternoon. Alongside the footprints, my wife also discovered some feces that she couldn't identify.

During my two visits to this area of the property, I carefully explored the entire land from boundary to boundary to determine if there was an area or a natural habitat that we did not want to disturb. During both visits, I didn't come across any other indications of sasquatch-related activity. Instead, I found tracks of deer, some hogs, and the occasional smaller woodland animal tracks' mixed in. The woods on our property consist of a mix of various trees, and in some areas, the vines were so thick on the trees that it was nearly impossible to navigate on foot. A power line runs through the north end of the acreage, but there is no water source on our land.

Only three tracks were visible in this area. It didn't seem out of the ordinary that we could only find three. The bulldozer had cleared much of the topsoil which resulted in exposing a clay base in some areas. It would be difficult for any animal to leave a clear impression or track. My wife found the tracks in an area that had more sandy loam than clay. I searched for any other potential sasquatch signs such as large broken branches or twisted trees. There were none to be found, at least on this trip.

Based on our initial estimates, we thought the tracks were around 18 inches long. I later came back with tools and when I measured it carefully, I discovered that it was 16 inches in length and 5 inches wide at the ball. There was a well-defined heel. The heel measured four inches in width. The toe was two and a half inches long and one and a half inches wide. The length to width ratio was well beyond what is normally expected for a human foot. Again, I thought that it was almost certainly sasquatch tracks. The tracks itself did not clearly register the third and fourth toes in the loam. This is most likely due to the end of a root lying on the ground and under the toes when the impression was made.

Since our property did not contain a water source, it would make sense that a sasquatch could have been traveling through our property. That would also explain the lack of physical evidence in the general area.

Regarding vocalizations or yells, several members of my family reported that they had occasionally heard a low moaning sound coming from our property or the adjacent land, usually occurring late in the evening or early at night. I do not recall hearing any type of screams or yells coming from our general area but until this find, we were not concentrating on listening for these sounds. I do remember encountering a very foul stench that came from the woods when we first began to clear the area. I naturally assumed we had disturbed a group of skunks when we began to clear the area with the bull dozers.

After seeing these tracks, I decided to reexamine the barbed wire fence that borders our property. I walked near the woods towards the barbed wire fence, staying in the shade and looking for more tracks. When I reached the fence, I carefully bent down and examined the area. Tangled on the strands of wire, I spotted a tuft of hair. The hair was long, coarse, and appeared to be a deep shade of brown, with hints of reddish gold. I reached out and gently touched the hair and as I looked at it closely, I noticed that some strands were interwoven with tiny twigs and leaves.

I reached inside my pocket, wishing I had a plastic bag. I did have an old receipt in my pocket, so I gathered the hair, being sure not to disturb it any further. I wrapped it in the paper, and I put it in the pocket of my shirt. I added that to the evidence that I was collecting. I found no other evidence of a sasquatch in the area.

CHAPTER SEVENTY-TWO

IT WAS early August of 2011, and I had planned a family vacation. We were heading to a rather isolated cabin near Horse Creek in northwest California. I had heard about the cabin from a friend and quickly booked it online. My wife and children were all excited to head off into the wilderness. On the way to the cabin, I told my family about the Sasquatch stories from this area, and they were all excited and wanted to find one.

Once we settled into the cabin, my children and I decided to head to the office to get a canoe. We wanted to go rowing in the river near our cabin. As we walked down a narrow road, we noticed something on the side of the road. There were enormous human-like footprints pressed about an inch into the soft soil along the side of the road. Both my kids and I couldn't help but notice that the footprints were too big for a man, yet it looked almost human-like, The prints had five distinct toe prints, an obvious heel, and a break at the mid-tarsal area with a ridge that reminded me of the lines on the palm of a hand. It was unmistakably a unique print unlike any other.

I wasn't expecting to see anything this quickly into our trip and I hadn't brought a camera with me. I used my cell phone to take pictures. I put a dollar bill next to the footprint for scale. From my estimate using the dollar bill, it seemed that the possible track was at least sixteen inches long or maybe even more.

We began to thoroughly look around for other prints or any evidence of where the creature might have come from. There were no signs of disturbance or any depressions, telling us if it had walked into the grass or wooded area. On the other side of the road, there was a large open field that was enclosed with a six-strand barbed wire fence. The fence was too tall for even a 7- or 8-foot-tall creature to step over. Other than the one distinct footprint, there was nothing else to be found.

Later that day, around dusk, I was outside alone. I heard two howls coming from a distance downriver. It was probably around 9 PM. It was at least six hours since we discovered the footprint along the side of the road.

I stood in front of the cabin, and I could hear everything that surrounded us. Later that evening after we all came inside, my wife mentioned that she heard strange animal sounds when she was sitting on the porch. The porch overlooked the river in the back of the cabin. It was about 30 minutes after I first heard the howls. She said it wasn't like any sound she was familiar with. I asked her where she thought it came from and she pointed in the same direction as I had heard the howls earlier, but she heard them a bit further down the river. It was odd that we each heard something distinct and different, and our children didn't hear anything unusual at all.

The howls I heard sounded somewhat like the recorded sounds on the internet that others claimed to have been made by a Sasquatch. The howls were clear and distinct and lasted roughly around 5 to10 seconds each. I started to pay attention to them, and I noticed there was a gap of about 3 minutes between them. The sound seemed to be far off in the distance, maybe about 100 yards from where I stood outside the cabin. They sounded somewhat human-like but with a distinct difference that I couldn't quite put into words.

Throughout the rest of our stay at the cabin, neither my family nor I heard anything else like those howls from the first night. As my children and I walked around, we would pay attention to the ground. We didn't find any additional footprints for the rest of our stay.

However, the second day that we were here, I was standing outside in front of the cabin again and waiting for everyone to get ready for a hike. I heard a crashing sound coming from the forest. It sounded like something very large was walking through. I walked over to the fence in front of our cabin and looked across the field.

I spotted a small muddy cattle tank at the edge of the woods, about 25 yards across. The tank was about 150 yards or so from where I stood. I looked around the area where I thought I heard the crashing sounds and a large group of crows suddenly burst out of the trees. They were flying in all directions and looked very agitated. This happened just on the other side of the tank. I couldn't see or hear anything else or anything that might have made the crows take flight suddenly. It was a brief, isolated event and never happened again. All the cattle were together in the smaller east field and not in the field where I heard the disturbance. After hearing that noise in the woods, I quickly changed our plans from hiking and exploring to a day on the water.

CHAPTER SEVENTY-THREE

IT WAS the summer of 1979 and my family, and I were living north of Bradley, Maine. One day, my high school boyfriend and I went on a picnic. We drove to a pasture area on my boyfriend's farm, not too far from where I lived with my parents. There was a lot of shade from the trees and a small pond surrounded by tall reeds. Lots of times we'd see wildlife come walking out of the trees and they would walk out into the open field.

The area around Bradley was mainly surrounded by a few small creeks and a lot of dense woods. Every now and then there would be an open area of flat farmland and pastures, but for the most part, it remained wild. At that time, the area was sparsely populated and provided a somewhat isolated environment which was home to many kinds of wild animals. Since it was an isolated part of the community, my boyfriend had brought his rifle along, and his German Shepherd, Ralphie, came along with us. The area I went to was on my boyfriend's parents' property. It was located on a pasture that sloped down to a pond at the bottom. We had a handful of other friends join us and we were enjoying ourselves with the boombox turned up and the music was drowning out the sounds of our surroundings.

I was the first one to notice that Ralphie was acting out of the ordinary. At first, we thought he was just playing, but when we turned the music down, we started to hear a low growling and grunting coming from the wooded area. Ralphie started pacing, growling, and making unusual noises and never took his eyes from the treeline. His back and neck were arched, and his hair stood straight up. I had never really seen Ralphie act like that before. We turned the boombox down a bit more and we all started to look over to the tree area just like the dog. I scanned the area, and, in the trees, I spotted an ape-like creature. It was standing over by the trail that led to the pond, and it looked like it was just watching us. At first, I struggled to make sure I was really seeing what I thought I was seeing. If it hadn't been for Ralphie's weird behavior, I might have brushed it off as a prank.

The creature was ape-like, but not really an ape. It looked like what I imagined a Neanderthal man would look like, morphing into a human but keeping some ape-like qualities. The sun was starting to dip behind the trees and the entire area was getting more shaded. Some of the details were harder to see than others. The creature's appearance remained mostly silhouetted at the edge of the trees.

Its right arm was sticking out to its side. It looked like it was holding tree branches to one side as it peeked around them and was just watching us. The creature was huge and at least seven feet tall. It had an imposing build, especially in the shoulder and chest areas. The creature had thicker fur on its head and shoulders, and not so much across the chest. That's how I could see all the muscles in the chest area. The creature was covered in long, shaggy hair, almost like a sheepdog. It appeared to look like it didn't have a neck, but I knew that was probably impossible. Its left arm hung down to its knees and it had huge hands. It was standing upright on two legs like a human. Everything happened so quickly, and I couldn't get a very good look at its face, but what I did quickly see was that for the most part, the face was very flat. Not rounded like an ape or human face. It had a wide nose too and was also very flat.

I was certain the creature was not human because it was much larger and hairier than any human could be. Its head seemed slightly pointed, with hair brushed back from its forehead. It looked like one of those "Trolls" dolls with its hair sticking up the way it was. The entire time it was watching the group, it seemed fixated on just us and Ralphie.

I was terrorized at just the sight of the creature, and I was utterly frightened. My boyfriend shouted out for everyone to get into their cars and go. My boyfriend was so panicked he jumped up, grabbed the boombox which was still playing, and then wrapped up everything into the blanket we had been sitting on. We ran to the car, I opened the door and let Ralphie jump in and then we drove away. I was afraid that the creature was going to attack us. I forgot we had to stop and open a gate. I knew that would give the creature time to catch up with us. I didn't dare look back. I asked my boyfriend what he thought he had seen. He refused to discuss it and said that he didn't want to talk about the incident again.

CHAPTER SEVENTY-FOUR

BACK IN THE LATE 1970S, around 1979, during my youthful days of about 17 years old, I embarked on a thrilling adventure as part of an Outward Bound two-week course. Our expedition was set in the rugged wilderness near Tharwa, just south of the vibrant city of Canberra. This exhilarating journey led a group of approximately ten spirited individuals, including myself, on a challenging navigation through the enchanting landscapes of the Tidbinbilla ranges. Our intrepid quest culminated in a river trek along the meandering Murrumbidgee River, eventually guiding us back to the base camp.

The rhythm of our days was dictated by the sun's ascent, compelling us to rise with the first light of dawn. With spirits high, we'd embark on daily bush treks that spanned an impressive 7 to 8 hours, forging our path through the untamed beauty of the wilderness.

As the trek neared its conclusion, we established our campsite atop a ridge, the golden hues of dusk casting an ethereal glow over the surroundings. Our humble shelters were crafted from plastic ground sheets stretched between sturdy trees or shrubs, providing us with a modicum of protection. It was a rudimentary arrangement, the kind that fostered a strong connection to the raw elements of nature. And yet, despite the simplicity, there was an air of camaraderie and shared adventure that enveloped our group.

Our evenings were illuminated by a central light, for a fire was out of the question due to fire bans in effect at the time. Seated around this modest beacon, we'd converse and share stories, cementing the bonds forged during our arduous journey. It was during one such evening that an incident occurred, an incident that would etch an indelible memory into my consciousness.

In need of a brief respite before retiring to my sleeping bag for the night, I decided to venture into the darkness to relieve myself. Armed with nothing more than a roll of toilet paper and a shovel, I stepped out from the circle of light, my senses attuned to the world beyond. The moon cast eerie shadows, creating an ambiance that oscillated between enchantment and apprehension. As I positioned myself at a discreet distance from camp, the thought of fetching a torch crossed my mind, only to be swiftly dismissed. After all, I reasoned, there was no need to stray far from the group.

As I squatted, engrossed in a moment of privacy, the stillness of the night was shattered by an abrupt cacophony. The unmistakable sound of breaking branches reverberated through the air, a tumultuous symphony of movement that seemed to originate just 20 meters away from my position. In the wilderness, such noises could easily be attributed to various creatures traversing the underbrush, and I initially dismissed it as such. However, what ensued defied rational explanation and plunged me into a realm of unnerving uncertainty.

Instead of the sound gradually fading away as one would expect, it drew nearer with a disconcerting urgency. Within moments, a powerful presence tore through the foliage, covering the short distance with astonishing speed. It was almost as if the creature was propelled by an innate purpose, a purpose that led it directly behind me. Inexplicably frozen in place, I strained to detect any hint of movement or sound, my heart pounding within my chest. And then, amidst the symphony of my own racing pulse, I became acutely aware of the creature's breath – an audible, rhythmic cadence that resonated just inches from my being.

In that suspended moment, my mind was a whirlwind of

conflicting emotions. I marveled at the proximity of this enigmatic being, a profound curiosity mingling with an undercurrent of primal fear. Questions raced through my thoughts – how close would it venture? Was danger imminent? And yet, an instinctual intuition reassured me that if malevolence were its intent, it would have struck already.

As the enigmatic entity remained cloaked in darkness, I grappled with a decision. Should I confront the unknown, stand and face it head-on? Or should I retreat to the safety of the camp? Unwilling to gaze upon the entity, I chose the latter, rising slowly to my feet and swiftly departing from the scene. Fear, curiosity, and a myriad of emotions swirled within me, culminating in a realization that this encounter had forever altered my perception of the natural world.

Upon rejoining the group, I was compelled to share my experience, seeking validation or a shred of acknowledgment from my companions. However, my revelations were met with indifference, my account falling upon deaf ears. In the subsequent decades, I've revisited this extraordinary incident, grappling with its implications and piecing together the puzzle that it presents.

Looking back, I've reached certain conclusions. This was no kangaroo or wild boar – of that, I'm unequivocally certain. The entity that crossed my path that fateful night was an observer, an enigmatic presence that had likely been shadowing our group for days. While its intent remains a mystery, I'm inclined to believe that its curiosity surpassed any malevolent intentions.

CHAPTER SEVENTY-FIVE

IN MARCH OF 1997, my husband and I went on our annual hiking adventure. Being seasoned long-distance hikers, we had previously hiked across various challenging trails, including a journey from Mexico to Canada. This year we chose an area in Oregon. This area was about 175 miles and had dense forests, steep terrains, meadows, and streams. The elevations range from 500 feet to well over 6,000 feet.

On this day, my husband and I were hiking through the heart of the Oregon wilderness. We stopped for a break and to have a bit of lunch and that is when we heard an unfamiliar sound that was echoing through the forest. Even though my husband also heard it, I was the only one who got up and went to investigate the noise. I walked around for a little bit and started to move closer to the creek. Before I could get to the water's edge, I glanced across the creek. That is when I saw a very curious creature. The creature was about 20 feet below me and approximately 30 feet away. By the overall shape of the creature, I guessed it was a young female, busy drinking water by using her hands to cup the water.

The creature almost looked like a primate, and by that, I mean it was covered in thick hair all over its body. It was rather shaggy and unkempt and ranged in length, probably between four to five inches.

The creature was covered in a "bark-like" color - the hair was mottled and varied in color in a mixture of browns and grays. From my vantage point, I could not see any ears, but they may have been obscured with hair.

The moment the animal noticed my presence, it reacted with fear and began to "call out" again. This time, the calls shifted from its previous relaxed demeanor to ones that were filled with panic or distress. I could sense it was a young being, perhaps given the chance to explore independently. However, I do feel my unexpected appearance startled it which resulted in the creature to run back towards its parents. The cries of the animal seemed like that of a frightened child. The creature quickly left the edge of the water and began scrambling on all fours. It was running with its knees bent and tried to remain low and hidden. I noticed that the creature was running in a serpentine pattern.

I walked back in the direction of my husband and began to tell him what I had just seen. We continued with our hike. We were now determined to catch another glimpse of the creature. My husband noticed movement across the creek. There, we both saw the creature as it darted along the opposite bank and the mountainside. Unfortunately, our view was partially obscured by trees and debris. We watched for as long as we could and in an unexpected turn, the creature changed its trajectory and its "scrambling" run. It began scaling a steep hill and to our amazement, the creature stood upright on two legs and began to move quickly up the mountainside.

By this time, the creature had moved far enough away from the underbrush, and I could now see with an unobstructed view. I was able to see that the creature had very distinctive features. It had a very a tall and skinny frame with legs about four feet long. The legs were very thin and covered with hair like the rest of the body. Its head was large and oval shaped. Most of the head was covered with the same type of hair that was on the body, except for parts of the face. The eye, nose and mouth areas seemed to be relatively hair free, much like a primate. As the creature ran up the steep hill, I could see that its movements resembled those of a human, fast-paced and with arms swinging. The entire time the creature ran up the hill it was anxiously calling out to someone or something. We were only able to see the animal for another minute or two and then it disappeared into a denser part of the woods.

Satisfied that he had seen enough, my husband urged that we continue our hike. We were camping at a campsite within the forest and still had about an hour before we reached the spot. We wanted to reach the area before it got dark.

We made it to our destination and set up our camp. The following two nights we were disturbed by an extremely unpleasant odor that drifted in the air while we were sleeping. This smell was extremely toxic and overpowering, enough to wake us from a deep sleep. The only way it could be described was a mixture of something very organic and decomposing, almost a skunk-like musk smell with a rancid sewer mixed in. The smell drifted into our tent and within 30 minutes the smell had dissipated. This smell was the sole indication that we possible had any visits at night by what I am assuming was Bigfoot during that period. Each morning I check around our campsite for any evidence or footprints. Other than a few broken branches and that nightly overpowering stench, there were no other unusual sights or sounds.

CHAPTER SEVENTY-SIX

IN EARLY SPRING OF 1998, my friend and I went on a fishing trip. We were fishing from one of the tributaries of the Snake River in Arkansas. That day we were fishing for smallmouth bass and crappie fish. The water level was a bit too low for a boat, so we were sitting on the wooded side of the bank and casting from there. It was a nice partly sunny day with just a little breeze.

We were on the bank, not really speaking to each other while we were busy fishing. We were just enjoying the quiet. While I was sitting on the bank, I started to get a whiff of something foul smelling. I looked over at my friend, who was about 80 feet away and down the bank from me. He wasn't reacting to it, so I thought it was closer to me. I am not sure how to even describe it really. The closest thing I can think of is a pungent body odor mixed with a rotting sewer with something dead dumped into it. It was starting to make me gag a bit, so I reached for my drink out of the cooler. I splashed some of the ice water on my face and that helped for a bit, but then the stench overtook that. I looked over to my friend. His cap was initially pulled way down, almost to his nose. Now I saw it was pushed back. He was looking around for the source of the smell. He looked at me and I shook my head "no" and shrugged.

We both sat up in our chairs and began to look around. I looked over to my left and I saw through the thick brush, a figure walking out of the woods. It was covered completely in shaggy brown hair. I watched as it walked out of the woods and down to the edge of the river. It bent down and stuck its arm in the river. It looked like it was reaching for a fish. It went from bending over the edge of the water to standing upright on the bank. I let out a startled shout, which immediately got my friend's attention. He looked over and saw the hairy figure too.

The creature made a combination sound that was a mix of a grunt and a snort. I was able to get a good look at the creature while it was grunting. I was too afraid to move, so I just stared at it.

The creature that stood there was huge. It was at least eight feet tall. Its body was completely covered in a thick coat of brown hair. As it stood there looking at me, it put a fish in its mouth. It just looked at me and started to eat a live fish. It then made a sudden and very loud noise. It was a combination of a grunt and a yell. It looked at me for about 30 seconds. It seemed more concerned with what it was eating than it was with me looking at it. It turned and walked up the bank. It had very long legs, so it didn't take any time at all for the creature to make it up the bank. In just a few steps it had disappeared into the woods.

It was almost ape-like in overall characteristic, but it was a bit different. The face wasn't covered with fur like an ape face would be. The hair on this creature did come down low and stopped just above the eyes. I couldn't tell if it had eyebrows or a brow ridge, but that's where the hair stopped. Its head was slightly conical, and the hair went straight up to the top of its head, and it had a bit of a "tuft" of hair that sat on the top. The eyes were deep set, in fact, the entire face was rather flat. It had a wide nose, also flat, and a very wide mouth. The lower lip seemed to stick out a bit more, but that might have been because it was chewing with its mouth open. As it ripped apart the fish, I could see the creature had a lot of teeth. The ones in the front were jagged, ripping at the fish like a set of knives. It really didn't look like it had a very long neck. It was short and stumpy as far as necks go.

The creature had huge, muscular shoulders and very long arms. Of course, huge hands too, which really aided in his fishing technique.

I looked at my friend. He had already read my mind and was packing up. We left rather swiftly from that particular spot along the lake. We chose to relocate to another area for fishing, someplace not so wooded. However, before calling it a day and departing entirely, we felt the need to return to the spot where we had encountered the large creature.

We looked around and didn't see the creature, so we walked to the area where I had seen it. I discovered large tracks that led from the edge of the water, up the bank, and into the woods. The tracks were around 18 to 19 inches in length. Along the bank, we noticed the remains of several dead fish.

CHAPTER SEVENTY-SEVEN

WHEN I WAS twelve years old, I had my first encounter with bigfoot, but it wouldn't be the last. I hadn't ever heard of bigfoot before but once I found out what it was a lot of the strange things I had been seeing and the odd sounds I had been hearing, all of which had been coming from the woods that surrounded my house, started to make a lot more sense. I grew up in the Pacific Northwest and nowadays it could realistically be called bigfoot central instead. I lived in a huge old estate house that had been built in the seventeen hundreds and it was old and drafty but the best part about it for me, growing up, was the woods. As soon as you walked outside or looked out of any window in the house, all you saw were trees, bushes and woods and it went on as far as the eyes could see, too. Since my parent's house had been passed down through the generations and it was so large, throughout the years it had been used for many things, and though I don't know really anything about the history of the property, the home, or the land, I can tell you I've had some very strange and oftentimes frightening experiences and encounters there. There were several other, smaller cabins scattered all over the property and I think there were five in total, aside from the main house. I guess they were for people who worked on the land back when it was a farm or something but like I said, I have no idea. I have four older siblings but all of them are so much older than me that I never really hung out with or did anything with any of them. One of the extra houses my parents let my eldest sister move into with her husband and their one child but other than that and for as far as I can remember, the others were all empty. Until, one day when I was twelve years old back in 1976, My father introduced me to his cousin and his cousin's sons. The one boy, who we all called Hank, was my age and he had an older brother the same age as one of my older brothers. Dad said that they would be staying in the largest of the extra homes on the property and that they were family and should be treated as such.

This was such an amazing surprise for me because aside from when I was at school, I never had anyone to play or do anything with and spent almost all my free time alone and wandering the woods. I remember thinking that I really hoped he would love camping and being in the woods just like I did and that we had some things in common. Hank and I immediately took to one another and were instant best friends. It turned out he did enjoy all the same things that I did, and he would also be starting at the same school that I went to, once the summer was over. His mother was very sick and, in the hospital, and would be there for a while and his dad couldn't afford to pay for somewhere for them to live, everything taking care of two growing boys entails and everything in between plus the medical bills so my father had offered them one of the cabins. They were small but the one they were staying in had two bedrooms at least. Okay, now let me get to the encounter. Hank and his family had been there about two weeks and he and I had basically spent every waking hour together in that time. His older brother was mean and picked on us all the time so when we had sleepovers Hank would always come to my house. One night when he was staying over, he told me that when he was asleep at his house, usually on the couch because his brother wanted the bedroom to himself, he heard strange noises like someone scratching along the side of the house and sometimes he would even see and hear the doorknob jiggling and turning. It always happened in the middle of the night. I was fascinated but also a little scared. I told him about all the times I had heard strange wailing, hollering, and howling noises

THE BIG BIGFOOT BOOK

coming from the woods and there had been times when I also heard strange noises outside of my bedroom window. He seemed like he wanted to tell me something and I asked him if there was anything else, but he said no.

One night around this same time I asked Hank if he had ever been camping and he said that he had and that he had been asking his father if they could go ever since his mom got sick, but his dad had too much on his mind. I told him that I had a spot right in the woods that surrounded our houses and property and that I was allowed to go out there alone and often I did. He seemed so excited, if not a little apprehensive because all the activity that had been happening at both our houses in the middle of the night. We decided to ask our dads if Hank could come with me camping for a night at my spot in the woods. They both said yes and one night, about a month from when Hank first moved in, we went down by this creek in the woods and set up our tents. I built a fire, and we had some snacks. We talked and read comic books until one in the morning when finally, we were both ready for bed. It was the middle of the night when we were both woken up from sleeping deeply from a very loud and scary sounding growl. It was close to our tents and camp, whatever it was, and Hank and I were both peeking out of our tents almost instantly upon hearing it. We whispered to one another about what it could be. It was one growl and then a noise that sounded like someone was dragging a heavy metal chair across a floor. We were terrified at first and I crawled from my tent into his. We whispered some more and discussed what to do next when suddenly Hank smiled. He insisted that it must have been his brother out there, probably with my brother in tow, trying to scare us. They were sixteen and didn't have curfews so no one would notice if they weren't' home or anything like that. They liked to hang out in the woods too at night, but they drank and blasted music all the time. We didn't hear any loud talking, or any talking at all, but the growling sound was so foreign to the both of us that we thought for sure that it was them, and we were done being their victims. We got out of the tent confident that we were going to trick them and scare them first.

We each got out of the tent and grabbed some small rocks when suddenly, before we could even take two steps, a large rock whizzed by my head and hit Hank right in the middle of the forehead. He yelled and his eyes welled up with tears. We knew which direction the rocks had come from, but we couldn't see much because it was so dark out there in the middle of the forest. So, I turned on my flashlight and the both of us saw something coming towards us through the trees and I turned my light in that direction. The problem was, whoever it was stopped right before it reached the light, and it looked like nothing but a gigantic shadow. As soon as we heard the breathing, we thought for sure it was our brothers and we both ran towards it with our flash-lights, yelling as loud as we could. We were hoping they were distracted enough to not be expecting that and that we would get them instead of them getting us. We realized almost instantly that we had made a terrible mistake. Our lights both hit the massive creature in front of us at the exact same time and we stopped screaming and just stood there, the second we realized it wasn't our brothers. The creature roared at us, deep from in its belly and as I moved my flashlight, I real-ized it had a giant rock in its hand. It pounded its chest and bellowed and then it started smacking the side of one of the trees hard. It looked like it could legitimately break the tree in half if it wanted to. The thing looked like giant, hairy ape man with brown hair all over it and giant feet. However, its face looked so human, especially in the big brown eyes, that we didn't know what to do. We begged it to let us go and not to hurt us. Hank and I were both crying, and he was bleeding all down the middle of his face from where he had been hit with the rock. The creature was around thirteen feet tall and six or seven feet wide, give or take a few inches. It cocked its head to the side like a dog does when it's confused, and its eyebrows crinkled as though it were very concerned about something. Then, it let out a sound that sounded to us like some sort of cry. Then around us other creatures were banging on trees.

Then, it turned and ran away, moving faster than anything we had ever seen in our entire lives. We were so terrified and confused it took us a few minutes to calm down, stop shaking and to be able to talk again. We knew we couldn't risk walking through the woods half a mile to get back to our houses and so we huddled in his tent for the rest of the night, waiting for the sun to rise. We weren't really scared, because if it had wanted to hurt us, it could have but instead it looked confused and concerned and then it chose to run away from us. We both fell asleep in Hank's tent and he and I left all our stuff there and went home first thing in the morning. We immediately went to get our dad who were doing work on the fences surrounding the property.

We were wild with excitement and our adrenaline was pumping as we yelled and talked over each other to tell them what happened to us the night before. I don't know what we expected but it wasn't the reaction we got, that's for sure. Our dads just looked at one another and they both said, "bigfoot again" at the same time. Hank and I asked them what they meant, and they told us they had been seeing and hearing bigfoot all summer and that they were certain it was what damaged the fence they were there mending at the time and that it had also broken into the shed and had been trying to get into the houses. My dad said one of the vacant houses on the property had a bunch of leaves and branches, twigs and even whole tree pieces that looked like they had been ripped right from the ground, on the inside and all over the place. He cleaned it all out and that's when the activity started. We were forbidden to go into the woods anymore for the rest of the summer but though our dads and brothers searched diligently, they never found the creatures or any other signs they had ever been there at all. The visits to the houses, the nesting and even the damage to the property all ceased and by the time the fall came they were convinced the creatures had moved on. After all, our property was completely forested, and the woods went to who knows where and stretched for who knows how far. It wasn't until a year later that any sign of them was evident in the woods but there was no more damage to anything. I had several more encounters with them but every time they seemed angry but then ran off into the woods. I am convinced bigfoot lives underground but I will tell you why in the next encounter story.

CHAPTER SEVENTY-EIGHT

WHEN I WAS APPROXIMATELY 12 years old, an unforgettable deer hunting experience with my father took place in the enchanting Salt Fork State Park. Before I delve into the extraordinary encounter, let me emphasize that my father had always instilled in me a deep respect for nature, cautioning me to approach everything in the woods with reverence.

Our adventure began when we arrived at the primitive campground within the park, now apparently known as Sasquatch Ridge or something of the sort. After dark, we parked and decided to spend the night in the back of our pickup truck, which had a cap. As we settled in and the night enveloped us, my father's rhythmic snoring eventually lulled me to sleep.

However, in the midst of the tranquil night, something inexplicable shattered the serenity. Awakened by strange noises, I found myself lying in the darkness, the atmosphere thick with suspense. I could distinctly hear footsteps approaching, and then the unnerving sound of something running its hand along the side of the truck's cap. Peering up, I caught sight of an immense, dark shape looming beside the truck. The intensity of the moment overwhelmed me, and I instinctively pulled the blanket over my head, trying to shield myself from whatever mysterious presence lurked outside. Amid the tense silence, a low grunt echoed through the night, followed by receding footsteps. I managed to drift back to sleep, only to be jolted awake by the alarm on my father's watch signaling the start of a new day.

As the sun rose, we embarked on our hunting expedition, positioning ourselves on the side of a hill where three hollers converged. It was around 8:30 a.m. when a sizeable buck leisurely strolled down the path in the bottom of the holler. Seizing the opportunity, I aimed my weapon and took the shot, hitting the buck. It darted up the opposite side of the holler, disappearing from sight after falling down. My father suggested we give it some time and allow the area to settle, in hopes that other potential prey might come our way before we retrieved the deer.

After some time, we decided it was time to collect our hard-earned prize. As we ascended the opposite side of the holler, I spotted the deer first and then noticed something perplexing emerging from behind a tree near the fallen buck. My senses were on high alert as I attempted to make sense of what was before me. Just as I was processing the bizarre sight, my father reached the hill's crest behind me, revealing the full picture of the astonishing encounter.

There, standing over the deer, was a creature of immense proportions, unlike anything we had ever seen before. It seemed uncertain, swaying back and forth, as if contemplating its next move. Emitting a low, guttural growl, it conveyed a mixture of curiosity and intimidation. My father quickly stepped forward, forming a protective barrier between me and the enigmatic entity, instructing me not to interfere, as he whispered firmly, "No, no, no... it's his deer now."

Backing away cautiously, we maintained a watchful eye on the creature, which continued to regard us with an eerie intensity. In that moment, it felt as if we were spectators in a surreal performance orchestrated by nature itself. The aura of mystery and fear enveloped us, silencing our words and heightening our instincts to retreat.

Making our way out of the woods, our minds were abuzz with countless questions, yet neither of us uttered a word. Despite the allure of hunting for the rest of the day and the next, my father abruptly decided to abandon our original plans. Without any explanation, he drove us home in silence. It was as though an unspoken agreement had formed between us never to discuss the peculiar encounter.

Over the years, I have recounted this extraordinary tale to a few researchers, hoping to find answers and perhaps even validation for what I witnessed. However, despite my efforts, the enigma remains unresolved. To this day, I am left pondering the identity of the enigmatic creature and the purpose of its encounter with us that fateful day in Salt Fork State Park. My father, too, has remained tight-lipped about the incident, redirecting any mention of it, perhaps believing that some mysteries are best left untouched in the realm of the unexplained.

CHAPTER SEVENTY-NINE

DURING MY TEENAGE YEARS, my family relocated to the picturesque landscape of South Carolina, settling in a rural area near the northern central Savannah river region. Our new home was an ancient farmhouse encompassed by approximately 80 acres of land. Although the fields hadn't been cultivated in years, their outlines were still visible, serving as a testament to the area's rich history. The property, surrounded by vast hunting club territories and dense tree-covered areas belonging to the paper company, was undeniably beautiful, but there was something about the woods that never sat well with me. The feeling of being watched, especially at night, gnawed at my senses, unsettling me even when I carried a shotgun or rifle for protection. I tried to dismiss these unsettling sensations as mere figments of my imagination, convincing myself that there was no real danger lurking in the woods.

One fateful day, around the age of 16, my father and I ventured out to inspect some food plots he had meticulously planted on the property. Engaged in casual conversation while walking back from the back 40, we were suddenly interrupted by a spine-chilling guttural roaring sound that echoed through the air, seemingly lasting an eternity. Instantly, we both froze in our tracks, our instincts kicking into high gear as we scanned our surroundings for any sign of danger. The sound emanated from behind and above us, as if some unseen entity lurked in the hills surrounding the bottom where we stood. A surge of fear washed over me, and even though we were armed with 12-gauge shotguns loaded with buckshot, I couldn't shake the feeling of vulnerability. Turning to each other, our eyes wide with trepidation, we acknowledged having heard the strange sound. Hastening our pace, we made our way back to the house, each step punctuated by the eerie silence that followed the unsettling roar. Upon our return, we questioned my mother if she had heard anything unusual, but she had not. However, she mentioned that the dogs had been barking for about 20-30 minutes before our arrival, a fact that intensified our sense of unease. That mysterious roaring sound, unlike anything I had encountered before, haunted my memory for days on end until months later when my brother and I watched a television show about the legendary Skunk Ape. To my astonishment, the show played a scream that resonated eerily with the noise I had heard that day. The unsettling feeling never left me, even after that enigmatic encounter.

Months passed, and my father experienced a chilling incident while reading out in the garage one evening. Overwhelmed by the sensation of being watched, he looked up and spotted a strange silhouette about 15 feet away, lurking in the shadow of a tree along the old fence line. The figure was approximately 4-5 feet tall, covered in hair, and appeared to be observing him intently. My father's heart raced as he stared back at the mysterious entity, which made no sound but continued to lean out from behind the tree, peering at him in an eerie manner. This bizarre observation lasted for about 30 minutes before ceasing abruptly, leaving my father bewildered and disturbed. He later confided in me about the encounter, and together, we speculated about the nature of the mysterious creature that seemed to inhabit our property.

A few months after my father's unnerving experience, my aunt was visiting us late one night, around 12-1 a.m. Seeking a moment of solace, she stepped out to the back of the house to have a smoke. However, her moment of tranquility was shattered when a small, bipedal, furry creature, measuring around 2-3 feet in height, emerged from behind the pump house and fixed its gaze upon her. The little being had dark hair and skin, an almost monkey-like appearance that was both intriguing and unsettling. It stared at her silently for a couple of minutes, seemingly assessing her presence before nonchalantly retreating back into the woods. My aunt, visibly shaken, returned to the house, recounting her surreal encounter to the curious and bewildered family members.

Over the years, I had a couple of frightening experiences while home alone. Seated in front of the television or engrossed in some task, I would suddenly hear loud bangs on the exterior walls, startling me into immediate alertness. Rushing to investigate, I would find our dogs barking frantically, but there would be no signs of anything amiss, leaving me perplexed and on edge. These unexplained incidents persisted for a span of 2-3 years, adding to the air of mystery that surrounded our property.

Remarkably, as if the presence of these enigmatic creatures was somehow connected to the nearby tree-covered lands owned by the paper company, the uncanny happenings ceased when they cleared out their territory. The eerie sense of being watched, the terrifying roars in the woods, and the mysterious glimpses of small, furry bipeds all faded into memory, leaving us with a collection of unforgettable experiences that defied rational explanation.

Throughout this time, I had always been skeptical about the existence of creatures like Sasquatch, considering them to be the stuff of myths and legends. However, the connection between the howl I heard during that television show and the terrifying roars in the woods during my own encounter led me to reconsider. It became apparent that there might be more to these ancient woods and the legends that had been passed down through generations. While I couldn't definitively explain the inexplicable occurrences that unfolded on our property, I couldn't deny the profound impact they had on my perception of the natural world.

As time moved on, my fascination with the enigmatic creatures only grew. I delved deeper into the realm of cryptozoology and the many stories of Sasquatch and similar beings that have captivated the minds of adventurers, scientists, and enthusiasts alike. The possibility that these creatures, once dismissed as mere folklore, might be real beings dwelling in the remote corners of the world became a source of endless wonder and intrigue for me.

Today, I remain awestruck by the memories of my time in South Carolina and the encounters that forever solidified my belief in the existence of beings beyond our conventional understanding. The dense woods, with their secrets and mysteries, continue to beckon to those willing to explore the unknown and challenge the boundaries of our knowledge. The enigmatic encounters during my time in South Carolina have forever instilled in me the understanding that the natural world is vast and teeming with marvels, forever shrouded in the mysteries of the dense woods.

CHAPTER EIGHTY

IN THE EARLY fall of 2017, a picturesque hunting trip led me to the southern portion of the Siuslaw National Forest near Newport, Oregon. With my engine captain as my companion, we embarked on an adventure through the wilderness, driven by the excitement of exploring the vast expanse of nature. As my buddy dropped me off he pointed out on the map where we would rendezvous later. The air was crisp, carrying the scent of the forest, and I felt an exhilarating anticipation for the day's hunt.

As I commenced my descent down the road, I felt a sense of connection to the natural world around me. The bank on my right guided my path, and all was quiet as I made my way through the tranquil woods. The journey seemed promising, and I looked forward to the prospect of encountering majestic wildlife along the way.

Eventually, I reached a recognizable point on the road that I had seen on the map. With excitement brewing, I decided to cut up the bank and explore a clearing nestled beside a National Forest boundary sign. The terrain unfolded before me, revealing a beautiful low area adorned with bark and fern-covered ground, while a hill beckoned for me to explore further. I made my way over the hill and discovered the other portion of the road that would lead me to the designated drop point where I was to meet my buddy later in the day.

Time passed, and I waited patiently for my engine captain to arrive, but as the day wore on, my patience began to wane. Impatience got the better of me, and I decided to head back up towards the ridge of the draw I was in, charting a path that seemed more efficient than retracing my steps along the old road. My boldness led me to climb up the bank on the side of the road, where I found myself immersed in a dense thicket of Pacific bamboo, with the towering plants standing a foot or two over my head.

As I forged through the bamboo, the atmosphere seemed to change, and a hush fell over the woods. The silence was deafening, devoid of the usual symphony of chirping birds and rustling leaves. An inexplicable chill ran down my spine, and my senses heightened, as if an unseen presence lurked nearby. My instincts screamed at me to be cautious, and before I knew it, I heard a loud thud followed by the snapping of bamboo to the southwest. The sudden intrusion of this unfamiliar sound filled me with unease, and I couldn't shake the feeling that I was not alone in the thicket.

A heightened state of alertness took over as I navigated the bamboo, and what happened next left me in a state of both dread and fascination. As I moved, whatever was out there seemed to mimic my steps with uncanny precision. Every move I made, it copied almost perfectly, matching my speed and direction. It was as if I had an unseen shadow, mirroring my every movement. Fear tightened its grip on me, and I could feel an unnerving sense of being followed and chased. With each step, the eerie feeling intensified, and the dense bamboo seemed to close in on me.

Despite my growing apprehension, I mustered the courage to take quiet, careful steps forward, hoping to catch a glimpse of what was lurking behind the bamboo. Every fiber of my being told me that I wasn't alone, and I couldn't shake the unsettling feeling that something was watching my every move. However, the entity cleverly remained just out of sight, shrouded in the dense foliage.

Growing increasingly tired of this mysterious pursuit, I decided to push my way out of the thicket with determination. To my surprise, the unseen presence seemed to speed up, as if matching my urgency to escape. It felt as though I was being chased by an enigmatic force, invisible yet undeniably real. My heart raced, and adrenaline surged through my veins as I cleared the bamboo and finally found myself free from the claustrophobic embrace of the thicket.

Still gripped by an unshakable sense of urgency, I pushed my way further north and then veered west, intent on finding the road that would lead me back to safety. As I continued on my quest, I arrived at an embankment, affording me a vantage point to look south. From there, I could see the clearing where the National Forest sign stood, a bit off in the distance. However, what caught my eye was an anomaly that sent shivers down my spine. Right where I had walked hours earlier, there appeared to be a large stump. But something didn't feel right. My instincts screamed that what I was seeing wasn't a stump at all. Despite the distance obscuring my vision, I couldn't shake the feeling that the stump had transformed into something else, something large and hairy, crouched down with its back turned to me.

Fear surged within me as I realized that the creature, whatever it was, had been watching me the entire time. Its presence in the thicket, its mimicry of my movements, and now its crouched position nearby sent a wave of dread coursing through my veins. The creature's reddish-brown hair concealed its features, leaving me unable to discern its true identity. A primal instinct warned me to leave this enigmatic being undisturbed, and my gut told me to get out of there as quickly and silently as possible.

With adrenaline driving me forward, I slung my shotgun over my shoulder and proceeded to slide down the embankment, quietly and swiftly making my way to the old road. The woods seemed to close in around me, and I couldn't shake the feeling of being pursued, as if the creature was silently trailing my every move. My steps became more determined and less concerned with making noise, for all I wanted was to put distance between me and whatever inexplicable force seemed to stalk me.

Suddenly, the sounds of movement behind me stirred an even deeper fear. A low growl resonated through the forest, vibrating within my chest. I recognized it instantly – the same type of growl I had heard during a previous unsettling encounter on a farm. Fear, now mixed with a growing sense of urgency, drove me to turn around and face whatever was approaching. My hand gripped my shotgun firmly as I pumped it once to chamber a slug, ready to defend myself if need be. But the unseen creature remained hidden, its presence felt but not seen.

With the eerie growl echoing in my ears, I decided it was time to exit this forest realm as quickly as possible. My heart pounded, and my senses were on high alert as I retreated, keeping my shotgun at the ready. Navigating the challenging terrain, I covered nearly three-quarters of a mile before finally reaching the berm where my anxiety began to subside. At that moment, a familiar voice broke the tension – it was my buddy John, my engine captain. His unexpected appearance brought a sense of relief like no other, and I felt a flood of gratitude and safety wash over me.

Exhausted, emotionally and physically, I recounted my harrowing experience to John. His presence brought comfort and reassurance, but the memory of the enigmatic encounter stayed with me long after the day's events had passed. The eerie happenings of that day in 2017 left an indelible mark on my psyche, forever altering my perception of the wilderness and the potential mysteries it holds.

Since that unnerving experience, I have never ventured down that particular road again. The enigmatic encounter served as a poignant reminder that the natural world holds secrets that may defy our understanding. It also instilled in me a sense of reverence for the wilderness, acknowledging that there may be more to it than meets the eye.

CHAPTER EIGHTY-ONE

MY WIFE and I had always gone camping and on other outdoor adventures together, even when we were dating. We met in college and both of us had an innate and deep love for all things outdoors. Once we started our own family it was only natural that we brought our kids along on all our excursions and they also seemed to have a deeply ingrained love of nature. I've had many strange encounters in my life, but this was the first one, which is weird because it happened when my first son was five and I had been in and out of all different types of woodlands and forested areas since I was at least that age myself. I think that it's more than likely that I had experienced things before this but that I merely didn't notice or investigate enough to be able to pinpoint anything too far out of the ordinary. I was taught if I heard something strange or felt uncomfortable and scared in any way, to leave where I was if possible or try to blend in. This was the first time I ever actually went and investigated something odd, and I admit I got the shock of my life. It started out as a joke, to be honest, when my oldest son was just five years old and our only child. My wife and I were amused one day when he came home from summer camp talking about bigfoot. She and I knew the legends, of course, with the both of us being from the Pacific Northwest, but we never put too much stock in any of it and that was mainly because, as I already stated, we figured we would have certainly come across something as obvious as bigfoot is said to be once you spot it, in all the years we had been exploring the wilderness every chance we got.

We had a camping trip planned for the following weekend and we told our son that we were going to a place where bigfoot was known to live. We saw his eyes light up and how fascinated he was by it and even though this happened in the eighties, our oldest son today is a paranormalist and bigfoot hunter. This must've been the start of it all. We went to a different campsite than the ones we normally would go to, and it was a lot more isolated than we initially thought it was going to be. My son was excited and jumping at every little noise but he wasn't scared or anything so I thought it would be a good idea to tell him that the next day he and I would go and see if we could bang on some trees and find bigfoot. He was all about us doing that and once we set up the camp and got everything done, it was all he could talk about. My son, my wife and I all slept in an extra-large tent but spent most of the time when we were lying down to sleep outside of it in our sleeping bags. Things started to get very weird from that first night we were out there. We heard strange banging sounds all around the forest, but we couldn't tell exactly where it was coming from because of how the sounds reverberated through the trees and they seemed like they were coming from many different places at once. My son and I were awake listening and my wife, though she heard it, was very tired and a few months pregnant, so she wasn't as interested as we both were of the noises and went to bed earlier than us. While my son was hoping to see a bigfoot, it was only right then at that moment that I had ever even contemplated that being a possibility. We were hearing what sounded like definite knocking and I didn't know of a single other animal that was a likely culprit. It was strange to say the least but as soon as the thought of seeing bigfoot was in my head, the forest took on a whole new form of eeriness that I had never experienced before.

It was too quiet, aside from the knocking and only then did I realize there were no other animals out or around anywhere and there was nothing else out there making any noise. It was unnatural, at least for my experience and what I was used to, and eventually after about fifteen minutes I told him it was time for us to go to bed. No sooner did we join my wife in our tent than did the hollering and whooping noises start. My son fell asleep rather quickly, even with all the excitement, leaving me alone and awake to notice whatever was out there was moving closer to our camp. I checked my watch and at around three in the morning I heard chattering sounds that sounded like a mix between the sounds an ape makes and a human being mumbling, somewhere very close to our campsite. I closed my eyes and prayed that whatever it was wouldn't attack us. Between the knocking and then the eventual chattering and everything in between, all told it had been going on for more than an hour before suddenly and all at once, the forest seemed to burst to life again in its usual cacophony of sounds and noises. I finally fell asleep, but it was a restless one. The next morning, we were all up bright and early and had breakfast. Everything seemed very normal, and I easily put aside what happened the night before as a fluke and figured it was a one off and wouldn't happen again. I didn't tell my wife or son about what I had heard once they were both asleep. I was pretty sure we were during bigfoot but didn't really know what to do with that information. My wife wasn't feeling too well, she was almost out of the morning sickness part of pregnancy, but she wanted to just rest in the tent at the camp. My son and I were going fishing on a nearby lake, and we were supposed to "look for bigfoot" still because he didn't know my wife and I had only been kidding. I was worried about that little fact but figured I would just follow his lead and because it was broad daylight, I thought we would be okay. I was under the impression bigfoot only comes out at night. Boy, was I wrong about a lot of things back then. My son and I packed up and went to rent a small boat for fishing. There were a couple other dads there with their kids and as we got everything together my son and one of the other boys made fast friends with one another and the dad seemed cool, so I was talking to him. The kids were in the middle of talking about something or other and the dad asked me if I had heard the strange sounds in the woods the night before I said that I had, and he told me he knew it was bigfoot. We got to talking about that for a good twenty minutes before the kids pulled us away from the conversation, both anxious to go fishing. We shook hands and told one another where we were camped in case, we wanted to introduce the wives. Then, we went our separate ways.

My son and I caught a few fish and by the time we were ready to bring the boat back it was just us and the other father and son we had become friendly with. My son and the other kid were talking, and the dad was talking about getting his wife and grilling for lunch. Remember it was the eighties and a different time. I went and got my wife and left my son to play with his kid. The boat rental employee was there too, so I figured it was safe. To make a long story short, as my wife and I were slowly making our way back to the lake, we heard our son and another kid, who I assumed was the other little boy, screaming. We started running and when we got there, he and the other kid were running out of the water. I looked for the other dad and he was standing there with his wife. They were next to the boat rental guy and as the kids ran for their lives, screaming from the water, it was an odd scene because all the adults were just standing there next to each other, with their mouths open and seemingly unmoving. I followed their gaze and stopped dead in my tracks. My son ran up to us and was yelling something, but I was so shocked by what I was seeing that I really couldn't hear what he was saying. He was tugging at my legs and jumping up and down but all I could do was stare at what I saw in the middle of the lake. It looked like it was floating, and I could only see from the waist up. It was massive even when I could only see that much of it, and it had grayish brown hair all over it. The smell of wet dog wasn't overwhelming, but it was there in the air. The creature was staring back at us as we all stood there staring at it. No one was moving except the kids and after a minute or so I snapped out of it and told my son to go back to the camp with my wife. I said it in such a way they both knew I meant business and I think the magic of bigfoot had worn off for my son with his seeing one. He took off running towards the camp without even saying goodbye to his news friend. The other kid and both parents took off and the boat guy was on his walkie talkie with someone, telling them what was happening.

I didn't plan on doing anything but wanted to see what would happen next. The bigfoot suddenly turned around and started swimming, like a dog swims, to the shore over to the right side of the lake. It got there extremely quickly, and I watched in awe and horror as it exited the water, in broad daylight and shook itself off just like a dog would do as well. I could see it had something in its hands that I recognized after a few seconds as fish, and it looked like there were several grasped in each of its massive hands. It was ten feet tall or more and after shaking itself off it turned back around to look at me and the boat guy. It roared so loudly that the ground shook and you could see the vibrations of it ripple across the water. Then it took off as fast as lightning back into the woods and we didn't see it anymore. I looked at the only guy left with me, shocked and at a loss for words, and he just shrugged back and walked off, back to his little hut where he had been renting the boats out of.

My family and I packed up and got out of there and it was a few years before we ventured back out into the woods again, but the experience had a lasting impression on my son. It started off as a hobby but his passion to find the truth turned into a career. He's gotten some clear and convincing evidence over the years and is writing a book about all his experiences where I'm sure he will write about the first time he ever saw the creature in the first place. I can write about some other experiences I've had since then and I think that I will, and I also want to tell some of the stories of the times my son and I saw bigfoot after this one, years later, but I need to ask his permission first. Thanks for letting me share.

CHAPTER EIGHTY-TWO

DURING THE SPRING and summer of 2019, heavy rainfall led to significant flooding in our area of Big Falls, Minnesota. The storms and constant rains brought about an unusually wet period that caused major flooding for the county and the entire region of Minnesota.

It was during the flooding that my family and I noticed something unusual on our property. Our farm was about three miles from a family park which, for the most part, was flooded for a few weeks. We lived several feet above the floodplain and had several days where I thought we were going to have our home flooded. Our home was near a heavily wooded area. When the river would crest, we noticed a lot of animals from the park fleeing the flood and getting closer to our house. One afternoon, my family and I had a run in with what appeared to be an ape-like creature. It was hiding in the wooded areas of our property. It was my wife who noticed it first.

The first instance happened early in the spring. We have a small herd of cows who are typically calm and composed. One afternoon, the cows were showing signs of distress. One cow broke away from the herd and ran to the other side of the field, away from the grove of trees. The cow was unwilling to cross the field and rejoin the herd. While it remains uncertain whether this cow's behavior was directly connected to the subsequent events, I thought it was worth noting that this incident coincided with the onset of our encounters, the abnormally heavy rainfall, along with the river coming out of its banks.

Shortly thereafter, my daughters reported seeing a huge gray creature beneath an old tree in our front yard. They described the creature as massive and said that it had a very threatening growl. It growled when they accidentally got too close. Of course, it scared them, and they quickly ran away. On one occasion when they saw it while they were in the yard, the creature ran away and headed towards an abandoned trailer house located on our property. This was around the time when the Big Fork River crested and flooded the valley, making a lot of the animals that lived in the family park near us evacuate their woodland homes and head up toward our house.

Our house is approximately a quarter mile from the river. With all the animals running and seeking shelter from the flood waters, my wife would often sit out on our front porch and watch the animals. My wife is the one who experienced the closest encounter with Bigfoot. One night, as she walked out to the front porch, she came face to face with the creature. It was only a few feet away from her and was standing in our flower bed. She stepped back and was flat against the house, afraid it was going to run at her. She said the creature was close to seven feet tall and had gray hair covering its body. It had very distinct ape-like features and it just stared at her. She said it seemed as shocked to see her as she was to see it. Startled by her presence, the creature turned and ran through the overgrown weeds and back into the woods. My wife said that the creature ran like a human, on two legs and swung its very long arms as it ran. When it went to the electric horse fence it jumped and cleared it without an issue. The fence is about six feet high. After it cleared the fence, it kept running.

After my wife told me of this event, I was eager to investigate further. The next morning, I walked into the pasture. My eldest daughter was interested in what her mom saw the night before, so she came along. Though I didn't feel threatened, I had a feeling of being watched while I was out there. My daughter shared this feeling too, although she initially brushed it off as paranoia. As we walked around the area, I found only one piece of "evidence". I found a very large handprint that was imprinted in the grass and mud. It resembled the impression one might make if bending down with your knuckles flexed and your thumb extended for support, almost like a football player would do in a game.

A few days later I had my own encounter. While walking over to the barn, I saw a gray creature in the yard. It was easily seven feet tall. It matched the description my wife told me. When the hairy creature saw me, it turned and headed back towards the woods. It effortlessly leapt over a bush that was between five and six feet tall. This was my family's final sighting of the Bigfoot creature.

The massive amounts of rain had been making the night's much cooler. We would often leave the front door open, letting the air flow in through the screen door. While we were watching TV one night after dinner, there was an unpleasant and overpowering odor that came in through the screen. Initially, I thought that an animal might have died at the edge of the woods and that was what we were experiencing. The next morning, I walked the property line closest to the woods. There was no evidence of a carcass. This unpleasant smell lasted on and off for approximately six weeks. It was also during the period of elevated river levels and flooding. As the river receded and the flooding stopped, both the foul odor and the sightings of the Bigfoot creature stopped.

CHAPTER EIGHTY-THREE

WHEN I WAS ABOUT 12 years old, my uncle and I embarked on a memorable trip to visit some family and enjoy a fishing adventure on our family's charter boat in northern California. Our cousin owned and operated the charter fishing boat, and so we would often drive up to stay with our cousins, relishing the opportunity to fish, pull up crab pots, and have a great time together. Their home was nestled in the heart of the forest, just outside of town, surrounded by a few acres of wilderness.

One day during our trip, I found myself outside with two of my younger cousins. We ventured into the woods near the house to play a game of baseball. Being the eldest, I took on the role of soft tossing the ball to my younger cousins so they could take some swings. We found ourselves in an area where the forest had been cleared and cut, creating a makeshift baseball field.

As we played, one of my cousins hit the ball with surprising force, sending it flying into the forest, not too far from the cleared section. I quickly dashed to retrieve the ball, excited to keep the game going. However, as I approached the edge of the forest, I suddenly froze in my tracks. Standing there, just behind a tree stump from a fallen tree, was a massive and dark creature. My heart pounded in my chest as my mind immediately jumped to the thought of encountering a bear. My instincts kicked in, and I remembered not to run, as running could trigger a predator/prey response.

With caution, I maintained my gaze on the creature, which was standing upright and had an almost human-like appearance. Its behavior was distinct from that of a bear, further solidifying my belief that this was something entirely different. The creature leaned over at its hips to peer around the tree stump, seemingly observing me curiously. I couldn't believe my eyes; it was like witnessing a creature from a storybook.

After what seemed like an eternity, the creature straightened up and calmly walked across the edge of the clearing and disappeared into the thicker parts of the forest. Its appearance was striking, as it was very dark brown to black in color. Despite the initial fear, I couldn't help but feel a sense of wonder and intrigue at this unexpected encounter. The creature's demeanor conveyed a certain level of awareness, as if it knew we were there but didn't anticipate one of us intercepting its path.

Upon realizing that it wasn't a bear and that I had encountered something truly extraordinary, I wasted no time in making my way back to my cousins as swiftly as I could. I conveyed my urgency, telling them that we needed to leave immediately and return to the safety of the house. This encounter took place on a bright morning in early summer, adding an element of surrealism to the entire experience.

The creature's appearance wasn't menacing or frightening; in fact, I got the sense that it wasn't fully grown. It stood still at first, as if caught off guard by my presence. From my estimation, based on the size of the broken tree it stood behind, I would say it was at least six feet tall. Despite the initial surprise, it didn't display any aggression or intense fear. It almost felt as though I was observing another kid who didn't want any trouble and simply wished to continue on its way.

Since that extraordinary encounter, I've remained fascinated by the mysterious creature I encountered that day. While I cannot say for certain what it was, the experience left an indelible mark on my memory, sparking a curiosity about the vast mysteries that may lie hidden within the wilderness. The encounter also served as a reminder of the wonders and enigmas that nature has to offer, leaving me with a sense of awe and reverence for the untamed beauty of the great outdoors.

CHAPTER EIGHTY-FOUR

LET me tell you about this unbelievable encounter I had in Spotsylvania, Virginia, just this past Friday. You see, I'm a 53-year-old construction guy, a former Marine, and to top it off, a seminary grad. Quite the combination, right? Anyway, I was driving home from work and decided to take the back roads because I had to drop off my laborer at his house. After bidding him farewell, I continued on the last stretch of road, about 3 miles away from my own home.

The road, known as Post Oak Road, offered a picturesque landscape with a mix of woods, farms, and a few houses scattered here and there. It's a peaceful route, perfect for winding down after a hard day's work. Little did I know that this routine drive would turn into an extraordinary and baffling experience.

As I approached a wooded section of the road, I couldn't quite believe my eyes. I saw something that defied easy description. It was as if a sasquatch or a woodbooger—or maybe something entirely different—suddenly emerged from the dense woods, catching me completely off guard. This mysterious creature was unlike anything I had ever encountered before.

In the blink of an eye, this enigmatic being crossed the street with astounding speed. One step, two steps, and it was gone, disappearing into the wilderness before I could even process what I had just witnessed. Its movements were unlike anything I had ever seen, leaving me awestruck and perplexed.

Trying to convey its appearance is no easy task. The creature had a dark mocha color, tinged with hints of red and orange, making it stand out from any ordinary wildlife in the area. This was no ordinary bear; of that, I'm certain. Its immense size, probably around 8 or 9 feet tall, was evident as it effortlessly brushed against the overhanging branches while crossing the road.

One distinctive physical trait that stuck in my mind was the extremely long and thick hair on the underside of its arms. It was a feature that set this creature apart from anything I had ever seen before. I found myself mesmerized by the majesty and mystery of this enigmatic being.

The area from which it emerged only added to the intrigue. It was a wooded patch with a 3-foot bank that dropped down to the road and then rose back up another 3 feet before a 4-foot farm fence. This creature navigated through this challenging terrain with an ease that seemed otherworldly.

As someone with a practical background, I usually seek rational explanations for the events I encounter. However, this sighting defied easy categorization, leaving me with a sense of wonder and curiosity that has stayed with me ever since.

Sharing this experience with others has been a mix of excitement and apprehension. Some may doubt the veracity of what I saw, but I know in my heart that I witnessed something extraordinary. The woods of Spotsylvania, Virginia, hold secrets that extend far beyond our comprehension, and I feel grateful to have had this unforgettable encounter.

CHAPTER EIGHTY-FIVE

WHEN I WAS twenty years old, I was camping alone in the Blue Mountains in Oregon. The Blue Mountains are a place I am and always have been very familiar with. My family and I lived in the middle of nowhere very close to the mountains and we spent most of our time in them doing one thing or another. We would go on vacations there camping, and, in the summer, we would visit one of many popular swimming holes not to mention all the time my siblings and I would wander off into the woods in our backyard and that surrounded our house that were somewhat considered to be a part of the Blue Mountains. I preface my encounter story with that because I want anyone reading this to understand that, while the mountains are so vast, I don't think anyone could be familiar with every single inch of them, I feel as though I were familiar enough with them in general to understand what sort of wildlife lurked out there and what the most prominent dangers were. I was simply going camping for a week in the Blue Mountains and there wasn't any reason, and it wasn't anything unusual. Until, that is, it became unusual because of what I encountered when I was out there.

Some people say some of the things I did while camping there were highly unusual but if you understand how incredible a night swim in one of the mountain's swimming holes under the light of the moon and a sky full of stars can be then maybe you wouldn't think it was so strange. I would eat supper early and then go to bed early as well. At around two in the morning, I would get up and hike in the dark to one of the swimming holes. I had two industrial sized flashlights and a shotgun. The lights combined with the stars and the moon provided more than enough to illuminate my path very well and I hadn't ever had to use the gun except to scare off a predatory animal or two. I was more than comfortable out there at night and in fact I preferred it to being out there during the daytime. It can get hot out there and while day hiking is something I often do and enjoy very much; in my opinion nothing compares to the fresh night air and the feel of the water at night. That's just me though and the reason I had to explain all of that is because it was one of the times when I was making my way to the swimming hole that I started to feel very strange. Out of nowhere the forest went silent and I almost felt as though I had walked into some sort of interdimensional portal or something. The forest already seemed like a whole other world when looking at it through the nighttime lens, but this was something altogether different. It was eerie and I stopped for a minute to wait for the sounds to start up again, but they didn't and as I stood there listening the hairs on the back of my neck started to stand up on end and my skin started to prickle in goosebumps that I knew had nothing to do with the chill in the air.

I didn't hear anything at first and so I rationalized it in my head and told myself it had nothing to do with me and was none of my business. I kept on walking but after taking only a few steps I felt like I was being not only intensely watched but followed as well. Before long I was close to the one swimming hole, I would take my nighttime swims in, but I stopped and peeked through some trees first because I heard strange noises coming from that area and I didn't want whatever was out there to see me. I hadn't seen another human being the entire time I had been there up to that point and anyway the sounds were more animalistic than anything else. I heard loud splashing coming from the water and strange whooping and hollering sounds. At one point I heard what sounded to me like something like a chuckle but when I looked, I didn't see anything at all. I was scared but knew I couldn't turn back, mainly because I knew with absolute certainty that something had been following me and that whatever it was it was still behind me somewhere. I reluctantly but with as much confidence and nonchalance as I could possibly muster stepped out from behind the trees and laid my bag down. I didn't hear any of the strange noises anymore and honestly at that point I thought I had been going crazy or was overtired or something because it seemed then like the noises had been coming from literally nowhere. I felt like there weren't just one set of eyes on me at that point and like I had stepped into a group of people who knew I didn't fit in. I don't know how else to explain it except I felt like how someone does when they walk into a room full of people and everyone stops, stares at them and then the whole room goes silent. It felt like that, only I was out in a very open area of the forest and could clearly see there wasn't anyone or anything out there with me. I was very confused, but I decided I had hiked for over an hour in the middle of the night to swim and that's exactly what I was going to do. I ran and jumped into the water.

It was even stranger when I did jump in because I felt like when I landed, I had touched something that didn't feel like it belonged in a swimming hole. It felt like fur or hair but again there was nothing there. I looked around with my flashlight, one of which was now around my neck, and searched for what I could have possibly acciden-tally touched but again, I saw nothing. I stood very still for a moment and the water came almost up to my neck. I still didn't see or hear anything but noticed the water parted right next to me and knew it wasn't from me because I hadn't moved at all and was even trying not to breathe too heavily. I was immediately terrified but didn't know what to do so I just stood there, perfectly still, watching and waiting to see what happened next. Suddenly it looked like some of the trees in the forest surrounding me were parting but there was nothing there. They were parting up top and, in the middle, so I knew it wasn't just some small and incredibly silent animal or creature that was cutting or passing through them. I was stunned and thought that maybe I was dreaming, or I had suffered a head injury or something and was in some sort of daze, trance, or coma. I was beyond scared and slowly made my way back out of the water. I started to walk towards where I had left my backpack, my gun and my other flashlight and I saw footprints. There was a bit of sandy mud there on the ground surrounding the water, I don't know what it's called, but there were several sets of giant footprints all seemingly going in different directions. They were gone just as quickly as I was able to look at them and then blink. What the hell was happening? I had no idea.

I noticed almost immediately too that a lot of the footprints were headed in one direction and that was towards where I had just seen the trees parting a minute or two before. Before that even had time to register, I saw something move out of the corner of my eye. I looked quickly and saw a set of eyes watching me from behind some trees clumped together right there at the tree line that separated the sandy dirt that surrounded the swimming hole and the woods. I froze and all I could hear at that point was my heart beating loudly in my chest. I just stood there, staring at the eyes as they stared back at me. The creature had to have been ten feet tall or more just based on where the eyes were peering at me from. Then, it stepped out of the shadows and out from behind the trees. I knew what the creature was the second I saw it, but I still had no idea what the hell was going on with the rest of it; the rest of everything else I had just experienced. The figure was covered in brown fur or hair all over its body. It had extremely long arms and bright yellow eyes. The eyes almost looked like they were glowing and like they were peering into my soul. Its face had a human quality to it that I still can't quite put my finger on, and it looked more curious about me than anything. Nothing about it seemed aggressive or threatening. That didn't do anything for the panic and terror settling into my body and stomach at the time though. It muttered or mumbled something but to me it only sounded like gurgling noises, although I somehow knew or at least I suspected that it was trying to communicate something either to me or others like it that I couldn't see at that moment.

Suddenly the bigfoot started shaking the tree next to it and it was doing so violently. As it did that it was loudly making the same gurgling sounds, I was so sure was a form of communication for it. Before I knew it the whole forest seemed to be going nuts with the same types of noises. More gurgling, echoing throughout the woods and trees shaking everywhere. I couldn't see anything else and was afraid if I lifted my flashlight and turned it on that I would somehow upset the one right there in front of me. It was no more than ten feet away from me and if it had wanted to hurt me it easily could have. That didn't seem to be the motive behind whatever it was doing though because it never came any closer and like I said, there seemed to be nothing aggressive about it. Finally, after a full two minutes of listening to the cacophony of trees shaking all around me and echoing gurgling sounds all throughout the forest, the one in front of me stopped, turned to survey the forest and then it ran off into the woods. Everything stopped. It was dead silent again and the bigfoot had taken off so fast that had I been in the middle of blinking when it left, I wouldn't have seen it go at all or in which direction it went. One thing I did see was several sets of tall bushes and some shrubbery move aside as though something large had walked through it. While I was still standing there trying to understand what I had just witnessed, the regular sounds of the forest at night started up again and owls were hitting in the trees right above me. The insects came to life again and several small rodents ran past me.

For whatever reason I wasn't panicking anymore and believe it or not I went right back into the water and swam for another hour. I didn't have any other incidents the whole time I was out there and no other encounters with anything out of the ordinary. I think bigfoot can phase in and out of this dimension and comes from another realm. I think there were a lot of them at the swimming hole and that I surprised them, and they were forced to make themselves invisible. Maybe the one who somewhat confronted me was some sort of leader or something and that's why it allowed me to see it, but I didn't see any of the others. I knew there were a lot of them because of the noises, the footprints, and the parting of the trees but I only ever saw that one. Also, I think I accidentally touched one who had been in the water when I carelessly jumped in without looking. Not that I would have been able to see it anyway. There's nothing more to it and I'll write some more about other encounters I had with a group of bigfoots in that exact same spot and others still that I encountered at the other swimming holes. Apparently, they love night swimming as much as I do and perhaps, they don't have water like that wherever they're from and they're forced to come here to enjoy that element. Of course, I don't have any real definitive answers or tangible evidence, but I know what I saw and that's good enough for me, which in my opinion, is all that matters in the end anyway.

CHAPTER EIGHTY-SIX

I DON'T REMEMBER a time as a little boy, whether I was playing in the woods behind my house, camping with my family or out for a stroll through some woods with my friends when bigfoot wasn't a part of the conversations we were having. My grandfather and my great grandfather were loggers in Tennessee for most of their lives and I would listen to the stories they would talk about all the times they either just spotted or had an actual encounter with Bigfoot itself. I was fascinated but in all the time I've spent in the woods throughout my life and from a very early age, I didn't have my first encounter with one until I was in my mid-twenties. It was 1992 and my friend had just bought his first home and had asked me to come and help him clear some land on his property because he wanted to build a small cabin he was going to use for when he went hunting, wanted to camp or to just get away from it all and spend some time in the great outdoors. Though it wasn't my actual occupation at the time, as I already mentioned I do come from a long family line of loggers, and I had helped many times with one family member or another's logging business and knew more about what I was doing than anyone else he knew. So, I decided to help him with the stipulation that once the cabin was built, I could have one weekend in it every summer just for myself. He agreed and I headed out into the middle of nowhere to his new house. Now, where he wanted the land cleared was a bit out of the way from where his home was located on the massive property he had just purchased. That meant we had to hike into the woods, and it was hard to get a lot of the equipment out there and much of it had to be done "the old-fashioned way" which would make the job take much longer. However, that's how he wanted it done and we decided to camp out there for a few days while we worked. We got to talking about bigfoot, as we always did, because he said he had been hearing some strange sounds, especially at night, that didn't sound like any animals he was familiar with and that he knew lived in the forests in that area.

We were deep in the forest but that was nothing new and I was happy to be spending some time with this friend because he had moved across the country a few years before living with a girlfriend. They broke up and he came home and spent the money he was planning on spending on that wedding and honeymoon on the house and property that we were there to clear. I loved the idea of having access to a legitimate cabin in the middle of the forest in the middle of nowhere and I was excited to get the job done so that the construction of the cabin could begin. I questioned him a little bit about how he planned on making sure no one ended up breaking into the cabin or roaming around on his property, but he was right when he reminded me how far away from civilization his house was in general, let alone the miles one would have to hike to get to where he was planning on building the cabin. I am a nature lover, but it didn't occur to me that we would be disturbing anything out there by clearing so much of the land. I honestly think that's why we had the encounter we did but I can't be sure. We set up our tents, built a fire and called it a night so we were able to get up bright and early the next day to start the clearing project. Our first night passed without any incidents or strange things happening and we got a lot of work done the next day. It wasn't until around eleven on the second night we were there that we started to hear something weird.

It sounded like it was coming from about one hundred feet away and further into the woods. It was some sort of bizarre howling, and it was something I hadn't ever heard before, but my friend explained it was exactly what he had been telling me he had been hearing ever since moving into the main house on that land. I stood up because I wanted to walk a little bit further into the forest to see if I could figure out what was making the sounds but as soon as I did, not only did the noises get even louder, but they started coming from the same distance in the opposite direction as well. It was almost like two of the same creatures, which was still unknown to use, were communicating across the forest to one another. They either didn't know or didn't care that we were there. As soon as the second entity started howling, the other one that we heard first howled back and it went on and on for several minutes with them going back and forth. They were taking turns howling, almost like two people in a conversation that are talking waiting for the other one to finish their sentence before they themselves speak again. Once I stood up my friend followed suit and that's also when we noticed the otherwise loud and incessantly droning sound of the cicadas had completely stopped as well. Aside from the seemingly communicative howling sounds, the forest was dead silent.

The sounds seemed to be not only getting closer and closer to us, but they also somehow sounded more and more aggressive as the minutes ticked by to the point, we were both feeling vulnerable and somewhat exposed. We briefly discussed just going back to his house for the night and venturing back out the following morning to clear some more of the woods, but we had worked almost fourteen hours that day clearing, and we were exhausted. We decided to just go into our tents, try to get some sleep and mind our own business. After all, we reasoned, if it was some sort of animal, even if it were predatory, it was unlikely in our opinions that it would come right up to a human and open a tent. Also, we were comforted by the fact that we both had brought guns with us in case we were attacked by anything out there. Neither of us particularly enjoyed hunting and we also didn't like using guns at all, but we were comforted by the fact that the option was there should we need it. We said goodnight after another five minutes where we waited to see if we would hear those noises again, but we didn't. The minute we started discussing it and talking about possibly leaving, the strange howling noises stopped completely. The forest stayed completely silent though and that's how we knew we weren't in the clear yet. Whatever had been making those noises was still out there somewhere and still somewhat close because nothing else in the forest was moving or making any sounds. I had a hard time falling asleep because it kept occurring to me that the only thing separating me from whatever was in those woods was a thin nylon tent. I eventually fell asleep about an hour later though.

I jumped up in the middle of the night after hearing my friend scream at the top of his lungs. I was trying to get my bearings and I was looking around for my flashlight to grab my gun and go running out of my tent to see what the problem was. I only heard one scream from him and then I heard that same howling we had heard earlier in the night only much closer, much louder, and seemingly much angrier. I heard what sounded like something smashing into the trees all around us and though I was only there in the tent listening to it all for maybe two to three minutes, before I even had a chance to try and comprehend what was going on, let alone to find my gun and flashlight, my friend came running into my tent. I screamed and he immediately told me to shut up. He looked terrified, and I tried to ask him what the hell was going on, but he just looked at me. He was sweating profusely despite the night being cool, his eyes were wide, and terror filled, and he just kept shushing me and trying to peer out of the flap of my tent. Suddenly and without warning my tent just got ripped up from the ground and we were completely exposed. Both of us were stunned and just sitting there and as I quickly looked around, trying to gauge the situation and figure out what was happening, I saw that his tent was no longer where it had been when we went to sleep as well. I looked all around and so did he, trying to see what in the world had yanked our tents up out of the ground as though picking up something as light and inconsequential as a feather or a leaf, but I couldn't see anything. It was very dark out there, even with all the trees we had cleared throughout that day. I saw my flashlight and turned it on and as soon as I did, we started hearing the howls, growls and banging on the trees around us again. I shined my flashlight all around and that's when we both saw what we were dealing with.

There was a gigantic beast running back into the woods and it looked like it was trying to hide its massive frame behind a rather skinny little tree. It was about eleven feet tall and covered in reddish brown fur from head to toe. It hid for a minute and then must've realized how ridiculous that was or something because it then stepped out from behind the tree, back into full view of us, and started banging on the trees next to it. It just reached its arms out and each massive hand was able to pound a tree. I realized there were others and that was the noise we had been hearing that sounded like something crashing through the trees. It started making that awful howling noise and we heard at least two others making the same types of noises somewhere in the area very close to where we were. We were absolutely panicked, terrified and didn't know what to do. We couldn't hike out of there right then, but we thought that if we stayed, we would have been killed. The creature that had pulled my tent up from around us was staring straight at me, right into my eyes, and it's the strangest thing but I swear despite being overly large and black, they looked human. Something about its eyes and face was reminiscent of a human being and I did the only thing I could think of. I started talking to it.

I put my hands out in a gesture I was hoping meant no harm and started telling it we would leave in the morning, first thing, and never bother it again. It cocked its head to the side and huffed a little bit and we heard the other ones that were then surrounding us fall silent as well. It took a few steps towards me, as my friend shone the flashlight on it, but then it howled, and I jumped and ducked for cover. I was cowering in fear on the ground in front of it. Another one howled lowly in response to that one and then it just turned around and walked back into the woods. The other ones did too and while I didn't ever see them, I knew they were there, and I could hear something huge moving away from us in several spots in a circle around where we were. We didn't know what to do so we just set one of the tents back up as best as we could, and we each watched for three hours while the other one kept watch. We left the following morning as soon as the sun came up and he hired a crew from my uncle's business to go in during the day and clear the land. He had the cabin built by professionals who only worked during the day, and we never saw them again. He has heard them almost nightly during certain seasons and sees a lot of evidence around the cabin that they are still out there. When I go and visit him, I stay out of the woods at night and when I have the cabin to myself, I leave food out. That's all there is too it but they're still out there all these years later and they never hurt us, showed themselves or became aggressive towards us or anyone else ever again after that first night. Maybe now they know we won't hurt them or something, I honestly don't know and that's all there is to say about my encounter.

CHAPTER EIGHTY-SEVEN

TWENTY YEARS AGO, during my time at a summer camp as a Boy Scout, I had an unforgettable encounter. It happened during an overnight camping experience, where we were tasked with spending a night in the wilderness with nothing but our sleeping bags and the vast expanse of stars above.

One might think that such an experience would be peaceful and serene. We were led into the woods by our scout leaders, and I was instructed to find a spot, set up my camp bed, and settle in for the night. Fate placed me next to a sturdy pine tree, accompanied by a young sapling growing beside it. I diligently arranged my bed using pine straw and prepared myself for a night under the open sky. The stars were particularly brilliant that night, and I could clearly make out constellations, even catching a glimpse of the Milky Way. The forest was bathed in a gentle glow, making flashlights unnecessary. However, I must admit that this style of camping always made me slightly uneasy. Your senses become incredibly alert in such a situation. Eventually, exhaustion overtook me, and I drifted off to sleep, although not without some tossing and turning and a few instances of sleep-talking.

Suddenly, I was jolted awake by the sound of wings flapping and a rush of wind passing over me. To my surprise, a massive owl had perched itself on the fallen sapling just above me. Its presence startled me, and as I gazed at the owl, it appeared to be staring back at me. It was then that a pungent odor, reminiscent of a poorly maintained rest stop, assaulted my senses. Nonetheless, I remained fixated on the owl as it swiveled its head, scanning the surroundings. Its gaze seemed to focus on the standing pine tree for a brief moment before it swiftly took flight and disappeared into the night. Curiosity got the better of me, and I turned my attention to the tree, only to notice something peering at me from behind it. Strangely enough, I didn't feel a surge of panic as my scout training had taught me to remain calm in such situations. A panicked mind solves nothing. I distinctly recall that the eyes behind the tree had a pale yellow hue. Though it was possibly more than 10 feet away, I instinctively shuffled back to where I had set up my camp.

My heart pounded fiercely, reverberating in my ears with each beat. And then, the mysterious figure emerged from behind the tree. It stood an astonishing 7.5 feet tall, a measurement I confirmed the following morning. The way it crouched down reminded me of Spider-Man, adopting an unusual posture. Surprisingly, as I started to calm down, the rational side of my brain kicked in, and I began to observe the finer details. It became apparent to me that this creature was female, with a flat chest and no visible male genitalia. I sensed a certain remorse in her demeanor, as if she felt guilty for frightening me. To ease my nerves, she began humming softly, as if trying to comfort me. Time seemed to stretch on endlessly, although I cannot recall the exact duration of the encounter. Throughout the whole ordeal, I never felt threatened by her presence. It was as if she was merely curious about this strange intruder in her domain. I believe she happened upon my campsite after hearing my sleep-induced ramblings and had come to investigate. However, I chose to keep this encounter to myself, knowing that Bigfoot was often dismissed as mere folklore. Who would believe a 14-year-old recounting such a tale?

Looking back on that extraordinary night, it remains etched in my memory as a remarkable and otherworldly experience, one that defied logic and conventional beliefs.

CHAPTER EIGHTY-EIGHT

SPENDING MOST of my childhood camping and playing in the bush, it wasn't farfetched to say that most of my teenage years were spent doing the same. I grew up in a small town and it was a little after my fifteenth birthday. The house I lived in with my mother and father was on the edge of this thick and lush bush. This was the main reason I spent most of my free time exploring and playing amongst the trees. Making friends with the odd squirrel and rabbit. But ever since what happened, I have never been able to go into the forest again.

It was a normal Sunday, I woke up in my small windowless room and crawled out of bed, stretching, I walked across the hall to the bathroom splashing some water in my face. I dried it and made my way up to the kitchen for some breakfast. My mom was already in the kitchen, getting ready for mass, her and my father went every Sunday. I went most Sundays, but that day I had plans to explore a deeper part of the woods than I had ever been in. My mom had taken out the cereal and so I grabbed a bowl to eat with her. We were very close, and she wished me luck on my exploration, telling me to be careful and that she was excited to hear about everything I discovered. She put her bowl in the sink and left with my father. I finished my cereal and washed up the dishes.

I went back down to my room, changing out of my pajamas, I prepared my pack with everything I needed. A rope, a trusty knife I was given as a gift on my tenth birthday, a box of matches, a water bottle, a bunch of snacks, and my phone. I put on my nice hiking shoes and made my way out of the house. Locking up, I started across the lawn towards the bush, the huge opening that was our driveway made it fun to drive on the quads and dirt bikes.

Once I reached the edge of the bush, I double checked I had everything, made sure the straps were properly placed before heading in. The soft crunch of leaves underfoot mixed with the moss felt natural to me, making the trek through the underbrush more enjoyable. A little further in, I noticed a long sturdy stick on the ground. I picked it up and used it like a staff, every step leading me deeper into unchartered territory. I wasn't sure how long I had been walking before I took a break and was surprised to see an hour had already passed. I slowly turned in a circle and it was at this point that I realized I had gotten so enamored in the walk, that I was lost. I took out my water and took a drink. I tried looking around but didn't recognize anything around me.

I took a few deep breaths and got my bearings, that wasn't the first time it happened, and I was certain if I was careful, I could find my way out. After I finished drinking some water, and eating one of the multigrain bars I had, I marked the tree I was at and began walking in a direction I believed was the right direction and started pushing through the heavy brush. As I continued to look around, I noticed the sun starting to rise higher and higher into the sky, but even with the visible passage of time, I still didn't recognize any of my surroundings. I was just about to stop and turn around when a rustling to my right caused me to stop moving completely.

I caught my breath. The rustling was far too profound to be something small. A deer would be ideal. If it was a bear though, I could be in trouble. I slowly lifted my walking stick. Taking a step forward, I swung the stick at the bush to ward off what was there. I fell back as a deer burst from the bush; I watched as it charged past me. But as it did, I couldn't help but notice fear in its eyes. I looked back towards the shrubs, curious as to what it was running from. I had never seen a deer act like that and got up, making my way through the overgrowth, the stick in front of me in case something jumped out. The thicket was much longer than I expected, and I was caught by surprise as I took another step but this time my foot met air. I cried out as I lost my balance and fell in. I spun in the air, trying to cushion my fall, but as I met the ground, my head smacked hard against something, and I felt my vision start to spin before completely fading into nothingness.

I don't know how long I was out. As I started to wake up, I groaned, my head pounding. I spun on my side, reaching up, I felt the back of my head and I felt nauseous when I looked at my hand and saw blood. I rolled onto my back. Looking up at the sky, I could barely see anything past the trees above. I could no longer see the sun anymore. The light had faded, leaving dark shadows everywhere. I managed to work my way into a seated position. Looking around the pit, I felt extremely woozy. Swaying as I tried to get my bearings. I felt fear creeping up inside me as I saw what I hit my head against. I grabbed it and lifted it to be sure, my fear engulfing me fully as I came face to face with the skull of a deer. I tossed it across the pit, scuttling backwards till my back hit a wall. I felt a sharp pain in my ankle, looking down at it, I noticed my ankle was twisted at a bad angle. I didn't notice it before because of the throbbing in my head. But when I did it made me feel sick. Even to this day, I still have problems with my ankle.

So, I took a few deep breaths and collected myself. I looked around the clearing properly for the first time and started to see a lot of animal bones strewn about. I also noticed a tunnel to my right. I knew that I would not be able to climb out, and so lifted my leg with my bad ankle up. I closed my eyes, took a few deep breaths as I grabbed my ankle and quickly twisted it back into place. I whimpered at the pain, cursing at the searing pain that ran up my leg. I searched the ground, finding a couple of sturdy bones, I took off my backpack and pulled out some rope I always brought along. I began binding my ankle in a makeshift cast to keep it stable during the walk. I took out my water and started to drink when I heard a strange sound above me. I lifted my head, my eyes locking with the eyes of a creature I had never seen before.

Its bear-like visage mixed with another animal, more humanistic than other animals, its brown eyes full of intelligence. The sounds I could hear were coming from it, sort of like a soft growling, I was worried it was going to attack if I did anything, sitting silently without even blinking. After what felt like an eternity, it grunted and disappeared. I waited just in case, and I am glad I did, since a moment later it returned and tossed down a deer carcass, the one from earlier, into the pit. I winced slightly, but tried my best to stay still, the creature stood there for a bit longer before turning and vanishing again as though it was never there. The only proof being the dead deer. I grabbed my phone and took a couple pictures of the pit before slowly climbing to my feet. I put pressure on my foot a few times to test how it was, but the pain was nearly unbearable. This is when I noticed my walking stick from earlier. It survived the fall as I slowly limped along the wall to grab it. I took a few more drinks of water, eating a couple of the Nutrigrain bars that got crushed.

Once I was fully prepped, I took a few tentative steps with the help of the stick as a crutch. The pain was still immense, but it was doable. I made my way into the tunnel. It was too dark to see anything, so I had to pull out my phone to use as a flashlight. My heart was pounding loudly in my ears. I swore I could hear movement around me, keeping me on edge the entire time, which helped with the pain if only a little. There were a few branch offs in the tunnel, I flashed my light to see down the tunnels but there were no changes and so, I continued making my way through the main tunnel. I don't know how long it took me to limp my way through the entirety of the tunnel but felt a surge of relief when I finally saw an opening. I picked up the pace slightly, all I could manage, wanting to get out of the darkness. But my hope was short lived when I heard a growl at the opening. I stopped dead in my tracks and quickly shut off the light. Falling sideways into a smaller side tunnel. I was breathing heavily and put a hand over my mouth to muffle the sound. I was worried as my heartbeat began pounding again, I could hear something large shuffling towards me and thought I would be discovered. I watched in horror as a huge bipedal creature began to walk by. I could barely make out its massive outline in the darkness. It stopped next to the tunnel I was hiding in. I could see as it sniffed around. Silently praying that it wouldn't find me. It turned towards the tunnel. I tensed, expecting the worst when it snorted abruptly and began walking away.

I waited till I could no longer hear it and a little longer before finally getting up and dragging myself out of the tunnel and back into the forest. I began limping as quickly as I could to escape the tunnel and the beast. Once I got to the point where I could no longer walk, I tripped and landed onto the soft moss. Taking deep breaths and simply laying there. I slowly curled into a fetal position, never in my life had I been so afraid or in such pain. I began to cry. Unable to hold my composure now that I had gotten away. Staying like this as the light began to fade even more. Once it was dusk, I was finally able to calm myself enough to push myself back up to my feet. I looked around to figure out where I was and was happy to recognize the tree I marked earlier. Without realizing it, I made my way back to my starting point.

I took a short break and headed off in the opposite direction I went before. Working slowly as the pain had gotten much worse compared to before. I checked my head and luckily the blood had fully dried, although I still had a massive headache. I kept checking behind me every so often, worried I was being followed and it wasn't till I began recognizing more of the forest around me that I heard a roar behind me, the sound unlike anything I had ever heard before. My thoughts began to run wild at the thought of having to face off against that creature, what would happen to me if it caught me. I tried to think of other things but was unable to get it out of my head. I stumbled almost falling but I managed to catch myself. I recognized a rock outcropping and realized I was close to home. The prospect of being out of the forest gave me a new burst of energy, picking the pace back up. I heard that awful sound from behind me again, but this time it was much closer. I began stumbling, limping awkwardly to move faster.

I heard rustling behind me, my hairs stood on end, feeling as though a hot breath was brushing against my neck, I yelled out, practically leaping forward as I burst out of the forest abruptly. I crashed to the ground and turned towards the bush. Crawling backwards as I waited for the creature to come out and grab me, to drag me back to that hole. My hand gave way as I crawled. I fell back and felt my head smack against the ground, worsening the already awful pounding. My vision became spotty, and I could hear my name being called. The last thing I saw before passing out was my dad leaning over me, looking extremely worried, trying to get my attention. I tried to say something but couldn't form any words as the world faded to black once more.

I woke up in a hospital bed. Every part of me was aching. I couldn't move my foot. I didn't even have the strength to lift my head. I turned it slightly and saw my mom asleep, holding my hand, her face was red from crying. I groaned and she slowly stirred awake. When she opened her eyes and saw me, a new wave of crying began. Leaping forward, she hugged me in her arms and called me her baby as she did when I was hurt. She asked me what happened and why I was like this. I explained to her about getting lost and falling into the hole, the creature I witnessed and making my way back out. She kept coddling me as I explained everything, saying oh my baby otherwise not saying much else. I asked how I got there, and she explained how they heard me yelling, my father ran out and found me, quickly bringing me to the hospital. The doctors had to quickly take care of my ankle; it was broken in eight places. They ended up having to put 3 pins in and a cast. They found the bleeding on my head and bandaged it. They believe I got a concussion from my fall. The doctor came to check on me now that I was awake. Saying I was very lucky to be alive after everything. He explained that I would have to stay for a few days for observation, otherwise, I had to take it easy and no more trips into the forest for a while. I thanked the doctor and they left. My mom gently squeezed my hand, finally stopping the tears. My father showed up shortly after with some food he went to get for him and my mom. He quickly ran over and hugged me, saying how terrified he was when he found me on the ground. I asked him if he saw the creature and he looked confused. Explaining how when he found me, it was just me, there was nothing else. I was confused, but also happy that it didn't hurt my father. I showed them the photos I took of the pit and the deer carcass. My father said that he would contact the wildlife services to go look.

We ate and I fell asleep shortly after. The years following the incident were very difficult. Pain, nightmares, rehab, a break from school filled my days. As my father said, he contacted the wildlife services and after describing where I went, they went to investigate. They found the hole and the tunnels, but nothing was ever said about the creature I encountered. Everyone believed I simply saw a bear and was disoriented from the concussion. I tried to explain that it wasn't a bear, but no one believed me and eventually I started to believe it too, if only to help stop the nightmares. Now that I am an adult and have a life and family, I look back and recall the truth, that it wasn't a bear, but something far more sinister and mythological. Even if no one believes me, I know what I saw and hope that no one else ever goes through what I had to go through.

CHAPTER EIGHTY-NINE

BACK IN THE summer of '80, our little family embarked on a weekend camping trip to Roscoe, NY. The journey from middle Long Island was quite the adventure, as we eagerly drove up on a Friday afternoon. Now, Roscoe, at that time, was a small town with only the Roscoe Diner as its prominent landmark, conveniently located off Route 17. We had visited this particular camping spot twice before, spending a week each time with just my mom, our beloved dog Gypsy, and me. Needless to say, I was quite familiar with the area and felt a sense of security.

Our chosen camping spot was approximately a mile from a gate along a forest road, roughly three miles away from the Roscoe Diner. Upon arrival, we parked our car just off the road and embarked on multiple trips to transport all our gear from the car to the campsite. With my mom's boyfriend accompanying us, we were able to carry double the load, making the task easier. Within three trips, we were nearly done, with only my pillow and some miscellaneous items left to bring. I eagerly volunteered to make the last trip with Gypsy by my side.

As we made our way back to the car, halfway through our journey, we encountered a picturesque creek adorned with boulders and hemlock trees cascading down a steep embankment. The creek trickled under the road, flowing through a low-lying area, and eventually joining a nearby creek that, back then, boasted cold, crystal-clear water teeming with trout. These trout were no bigger than 8 inches, with most measuring around 3 to 4 inches. Their beauty was akin to precious jewels, as if they were crafted by the famed jeweler Fabergé himself.

During the summer, the little creek that passed beneath the road would often dry up, while the larger creek it fed into, about three miles away from our camp, flowed year-round. This larger creek ultimately emptied into the Battenkill River, a renowned trout haven along the East Coast. As I walked towards the car, an unpleasant stench assaulted my nostrils. It was a repugnant combination of decaying animal flesh and urine, causing me to gag and choke momentarily.

The road, covered by a canopy of trees, allowed me to spot Gypsy and meandering towards the car. We gathered my belongings, securely locked up the car, and started our journey back to camp. Gypsy, my loyal seven-year-old companion, and I were inseparable, especially during our adventures in the great outdoors. She would often trot ahead of me, only to run back and alert me upon reaching camp, eventually joining me for the remaining stretch. However, as we approached the halfway point, I noticed Gypsy standing there, eerily silent and trembling. Something was amiss. I positioned myself to her left, and it was then that I witnessed her shivering in fear. Glancing up, all I could see were towering raspberry bushes and the meandering creek.

To my surprise, not a single sound reached my ears, not even the gentle babbling of the creek. Suddenly, a low growl resonated through the air, permeating my entire being, paralyzing me with terror. Without moving an inch, I glanced down at Gypsy, only to discover her cowering and relieving herself in fear. Initially, I thought it might be a bear, as I had encountered them during my time in Vermont a few years prior. In fact, Gypsy would often give chase to bears fearlessly. However, this time was different. Out of the corner of my eye, I caught a glimpse of a black face amidst the raspberry bushes. It certainly wasn't a bear. In that moment, as the growling ceased, I snapped out of my trance and instinctively sprinted away as fast as humanly possible, with Gypsy closely trailing behind. It was as if we were fleeing from a supernatural force.

Once we reached the campsite, I couldn't contain my shock and fear, and thus began screaming and crying about the monstrous being we had encountered. Unfortunately, my mom's boyfriend, who would later become my stepfather, initially teased me about the incident. However, as I continued insisting that we leave, he grew increasingly annoyed and angry with me. Nothing else eventful occurred throughout the rest of the trip, but the incident left an indelible mark on our relationship. From that day forward, our bond was never the same, and it's safe to say that our connection deteriorated into something far from positive.

CHAPTER NINETY

I'M GOING to tell you a story that I've kept to myself for a long time, and to be honest, I'm a bit apprehensive about sharing it. I know that once people hear this tale, they'll probably laugh me right out of the country. Even I, for many years, would join in the laughter whenever someone brought up the existence of these creatures. But here it goes, the story of an encounter that took place in Northeast Texas, not far from Texarkana, where I've been living for quite some time now.

You see, I used to be an avid coonhunter, but as life got busier and my business demands increased, I found it harder to dedicate time to my beloved sport. Coonhunting requires a significant investment of time, and unfortunately, I just didn't have enough to spare. Eventually, I had to part ways with my trusted Walker hounds. There was a time when I was deeply immersed in the sport, holding hunting licenses in three different states and boasting several Night Champion titles to my name.

It was several years ago, on a bitterly cold night in January or February—I can't recall the exact date. I was out coonhunting in Miller County, Arkansas, in an area the locals refer to as Thornton Wells. This particular night, we found ourselves hunting in the midst of flooded timber. The dogs had split up, with some of them treed on the other side of the swamp. I headed towards my dogs, while the other guys went to tend to their own.

Reaching the tree where my dogs had treed, I examined the coon they had cornered and caught my dogs. Everything seemed fine, so I decided to make my way back towards the others. Faintly in the distance, I could hear their dogs still treeing on the other side of the bayou. However, as I made my way back, I started hearing the sound of something moving through the flooded timber. Now, picture this entire area submerged under 8 to 15 inches of brackish swamp water. Despite the challenging conditions, I could discern the distinct gait of someone navigating the flooded woods. Assuming it must be one of my hunting companions, I called out to them. But instead of a familiar voice in response, all I heard was a deep, guttural growl and an overpowering putrid smell.

Let me try to describe the stench to you—it was like the odor you encounter when you've killed a wild hog and grab it by the hind leg, then drag it along as the pungent smell overwhelms you. Alongside the revolting odor, I heard a peculiar whining, almost whistling sound. My dogs, who were usually courageous and fierce, were now whimpering, huddling behind my legs. You have to understand, these were no ordinary dogs; they were Lipper-bred Walkers from the UKC, weighing close to 100 pounds. They were capable of tearing a 20-pound coon apart, and yet here they were, displaying uncharacteristic fear.

Though perplexed by their behavior, I wasn't too concerned at that moment. I gathered my dogs and started making my way back across the swamp. But after a few minutes, the sound of movement in the water caught my attention once again. I stopped and turned around, only to find myself face-to-face with an enormous creature. It must have stood at least 8 or 9 feet tall, completely covered in dark hair. When my coon light shone into its eyes, they glowed like a deer caught in a spotlight. I can tell you, the hairs on the back of my neck stood on end, and I was overcome with fear like I had never experienced before.

This creature emitted a hissing sound and reached down to scoop up water, flinging it in my direction while making deep, guttural noises. My dogs, having regained their bravery, began growling and straining against their leashes, desperately wanting to confront this entity. Sensing the urgency, I seized their leashes and bolted across the swamp, terrified beyond measure. In my panic, I ended up heading in the wrong direction for a while until I stumbled upon a large Cypress knee, where I finally caught my breath.

The thing that had been following me was still audible, trailing behind about a hundred yards or so. Eventually, it began to move away, emitting mournful moans across the bayou. I regained my composure, consulted my compass to ensure my bearings, and embarked on the journey back to the truck. When I finally reached my companions, I didn't utter a word about what I had witnessed and heard. I feared they would ridicule and mock me relentlessly. Needless to say, I never returned to Thornton Wells, nor do I have any intention to do so. For a long time, I kept this terrifying ordeal to myself, haunted by nightmares of that encounter.

The only person I ever shared this story with was an old coon-hunter, who has since passed away. I recall his advice vividly. He told me, "If you're smart, you'll keep this to yourself. People will laugh at you and call you a liar." I had spent countless nights hunting in the Sulphur River bottoms, but never before or since have I witnessed anything like that. I'm not one for tall tales, but I thought I'd share this chilling experience with all of you because it seems we might have something in common.

CHAPTER NINETY-ONE

I LIVE in the southeastern part of Massachusetts in an area known in some circles as the Bridgewater Triangle. It's about a two hundred square mile area that's known for all sorts of strange activity and phenomenon. There's a lot of paranormal and supernatural happenings there and a lot of extraterrestrial activity but the main thing that goes on there in that part of the region are the cryptid sightings and, more specifically, the sightings of bigfoot. It's been going on for decades and while I've been interested in all those above-mentioned things my whole life, I never in a million years thought that I would have had any sort of encounter while I was visiting there. I was thirty-five years old and going through a rough patch in my life. I was taking a cross country trip in my campervan and just cruising through each state in a sort of zigzag pattern and seeing what this great country has to offer. I was born and raised and spent most of my life in northern Maine, so I wasn't immune to hearing a lot of strange stories about a lot of terrifying creatures and phenomenon and I was introduced to all this kind of stuff from a very early age. I had a failed marriage and some issues with my family and decided to just take two years off and travel. I was so happy out there on the open road and I had more than a few strange and scary experiences while out there and in many states but what happened to me while I was visiting the so-called Bridge-water Triangle was by far the most terrifying. I literally thought I was going to die but before I get to that, let me just start at the beginning.

I had come into some money and was able to buy a state-of-the-art camper for the time. I still have it but now it's parked on the property of the house I own and decided to buy a few years ago in Montana. I still hunt, hike, camp, and fish but I am much more aware of not only my surroundings but what's in those surroundings as well. I don't think human beings really comprehend the bulk of what happens in the forests of our world or that we really have any concept of the types of creatures and beings that live in them. I count myself lucky that I only encountered one sasquatch because I honestly think if there had been any more than that I wouldn't be here telling this story. I know a lot of people think of bigfoot and they think of a peaceful being or even some people think of it as enlightened and only afraid of us because of how we are as a species and the fact we are looking to get evidence of its existence by any means necessary. Please understand that my belief in all the above-mentioned things and entities doesn't mean I was out there on the road looking for any of them. I was of the mindset of I will gladly leave it alone and keep myself happy and ignorant than go searching for something I just might regret finding. It didn't work out that way for me though and I have been on a one-man quest to find more evidence these things exist once and for all because I believe they are far more sinister than we humans can ever imagine and that for the most part they have no peaceful feelings when it comes to us at all. I understand as well that many people have had positive experiences with bigfoot and other cryptids and if that's you then more power to you but that was not my experience with them.

I went to a camp where you could park your camper for a nominal fee and how much you paid dictated how crowded it would be where you parked. I planned on staying for about a week and I didn't want to have to deal with a lot of noise or many people. I didn't want to meet anyone new, make new friends or deal with people at all, really, and so I paid as much as I could to get a spot as far away from everyone else as was humanly possible at the time. I know that sounds weird to some folks nowadays but back in the 80s money spoke a lot louder than it does now and there wasn't as much trouble to get into by slip-ping someone an extra hundred bucks or so to be able to be left completely alone. I was in the middle of the wilderness and really felt like I was alone out there, just like I wanted it. I set up a little camp outside of my camper van and hung out there most of the day. I went fishing and hiking and at the end of every day I would retire into my campervan in the large bed I had in the back. There were very dark blackout curtains separating where my bed was, and the front of the camper and I also had them on all the windows. It started out at around midnight on the second night I was there. I had just put out my fire and gone in for the night when I started hearing weird noises outside of my camper. It sounded like something was lightly knocking on the sides of it and it also sounded like nails were scraping the sides as well. I thought maybe it was a bear at first and tried to ignore it, figuring whatever it was it would just go away if I didn't engage with it. However, the knocking seemed very deliberate to me and eventu-ally I angrily stormed out of my camper to confront what I then thought was going to be either some drunk people or some trouble making teenagers. Remember, the fact that I was completely alone out there had only been an illusion that I paid for with a hundred bucks and there were other campers all over the place at the time.

I got outside very quickly but I didn't see anything. I yelled and cussed but still no one came out to heckle me and I also didn't see or hear anyone running away. I stayed outside for a minute but then I went back inside and figured my yelling as I ran out the very loud door must've scared what or whoever it was off. I was an angry man back then and I was mad at the world and thought that it owed me something, so I fired off two shots from my rifle into the air to make sure that everyone knew not to mess with me. I think that is what sealed my fate that night. Who knows? Maybe if I had just left well enough alone, I wouldn't have had to go through what I did. I went back inside, locked the door, put on my shorts for pajamas and laid down to get comfortable in bed. I fell asleep quickly but woke up to my entire campervan shaking to the point it felt like it was going to tip over. I jumped up fast, but it was hard to walk to the front and see what was going on. I was a scrawny guy and though I was tall, I didn't weigh much back then. I tried to steady myself by walking all along one of the walls and I started yelling and cussing again for whoever it was to get the hell away from my camper and my camp or I was going to shoot. As soon as I said that the rocking stopped but I heard very loud hollering that wasn't coming from a human being, but it also wasn't coming from any animal that I was familiar with. Then, whatever it was started banging loudly and aggressively on the side of the van again. I looked out the window on the side where it was coming from, but I didn't see anything.

I ran to the back and peered out of those windows and that's when I saw a twelve-foot tall, hairy, and bipedal hominid beast that looked like it was trying to rip off my back bumper. I banged on the window and yelled for it to get out of there, but it just roared at me. It was covered in blackish gray hair that was long but matted and dirty in some spots and I saw that its teeth were brownish yellow and rotten looking. They weren't sharp or anything though and they looked like big human teeth. The thing's hands were gigantic and probably twice the size of my face and despite how massive it was, it also looked very athletic and muscular. I was intimidated and I was scared but I refused to show it. Again, I feel like if I had just backed down and left it alone then maybe it would have left me alone too. I don't really know though, but I still think that my shooting the gun off is what brought it back there and I say brought it back because there's no doubt in my mind that's what had been there in the first place, hours before when I had just been preparing for bed. The creature had big green eyes that were disproportionate to its face and head, which both seemed to be too small for the massively tall and wide body. It glared at me, and it growled again. I was trying not to panic and trying to think of what to do next. I knew I couldn't just go out and shoot it or shoot at it because I wasn't sure if it was out there by itself or if it had others with it or nearby in the area. I could do nothing but try to get it to stop ripping at my back bumper by yelling and pounding on the window. However, that just seemed like it was making it angrier, so I just stopped and stared.

It looked at me and growled again, very angrily and aggressively and it then started to lift my entire campervan by the back bumper.

The amount of strength that must have taken is unfathomable to me, but I thought for sure it was going to flip the whole thing over on me and then come in and finish me off. However, it lifted it for a full minute, maybe two, and then it just let go. The van slammed down hard and everything in it jumped into the air. My furniture fell over and all the cabinets opened on their own, with the contents of each one spilling out all over the floor. It then looked right at me as I stared once again out the window. I was horrified and terrified and didn't know what to even think at that point. The creature growled at me, stomped one of its giant feet and then ran off into the woods. I swear it was less than a minute before I started hearing people screaming all throughout the camp. I couldn't believe that it had been running right through camps and showing itself to people. I was so exhausted and mentally overloaded that I just left everything how it was and went to sleep. I figured I would go and see the proper authorities in the camp the next day. I woke up bright and early, got dressed and went out to check the damage on my van. The damage was extensive by way of deep scratches that went well beyond the topcoat of paint all over the one side of the van. The back bumper was destroyed but there were giant handprints in the dust and several giant footprints on the ground. I had a camera with me and went back inside to grab it to get some photographic evidence for my insurance company and for the camp officials. I needed proof but it wasn't like I was trying to capture proof of bigfoot because it wasn't cool or trendy to say you saw one back then and I planned on saying I didn't see what happened because I had been in bed and unable to get up because of how the van had been shaking and rocking and also because of how scared I was at what could have possibly been outside my campervan causing those disturbances.

As I walked back out the door, I literally slammed into two gentlemen who looked like they were government officials and they asked if I would go and talk to them about what I had seen. I told them I needed to get some pictures for insurance, but they grabbed my camera and told me it could wait. I was annoyed but figured it didn't matter because I was going to tell them I didn't see anything anyway. I went with them, and they had me in some little room somewhere far out of the way of the rest of the camp for twelve whole hours. They didn't believe I didn't see anything but after all that time, and after being interrogated for most of it, they seemed somewhat satisfied and escorted me back to my campervan. I went right inside to calm down because I was upset at the ordeal I had just been through. I realized something just as I turned and locked the door behind me and when I went back outside those men were nowhere to be seen. It had been less than a minute but who knows, maybe they disappeared behind some trees. The forest was extremely dense after all. I don't know if I really believe that or not, but I have no evidence one way or another. I walked around the side and to the back of the van and I swear to you now, all the damage on my van had been fixed and there was no evidence left whatsoever as to what had happened to me out there and what that thing had done to my vehicle. I went back out the next morning but by light of day I knew I was right. They hadn't wanted to interrogate me at all but they were distracting me so they could clean up after the animal. I don't know what happened to any of the other campers, but I knew a lot of them saw it because I heard them screaming. That's the extent of my terrifying encounter but I have plenty more I'm going to share with you soon as well. Thanks

CHAPTER NINETY-TWO

BACK IN THE summer of 1966, when I was just a 15-year-old teenager, I had a remarkable encounter in Albion, Mendocino County, California. You see, my father worked as a commercial fisherman, and his boat was docked up the Albion River, a mere 250 to 300 yards away from the boat docks. We lived in Ukiah at the time, but we would make the trip over to visit my dad and bring him supplies at least twice a week. Eventually, we decided to set up a trailer near the boat dock and make the coast our permanent home. It was during this time that my extraordinary experience took place, on an evening just as the sun was setting over the hill, casting a soft glow.

On that particular night, my parents, younger sister, and younger brother were on the boat, preparing to go to bed. It was still before 8 p.m., and my older sister and I had to sleep in the car since there weren't enough bunks on the boat for all of us. We made ourselves comfortable on the car seats, using blankets and pillows to create makeshift beds. Our car was a 1957 two-door Pontiac Chieftain, and even though it was early and the daylight lingered, we weren't quite ready to drift off to sleep. As teenagers do, we started chatting and passing the time. The windows were rolled down, allowing the pleasant summer air to flow through.

Our conversation was abruptly interrupted by a series of unsettling sounds. We heard the sheep on the steep, rolling hillside across the river crying out and baaing in a manner that seemed far from normal for sheep. Curiosity and concern got the better of us, and we both sprung up, leaning over to peer out of the right-side windows, attempting to catch a glimpse of what was causing the commotion among the sheep. What we witnessed was nothing short of astonishing. The sheep, in a state of panic, were running frantically towards the western side of the pasture, dispersing in different directions, forming smaller groups. And there, in the left upper part of the field, we spotted two colossal, hairy creatures chasing after the frightened sheep.

At first, we believed these creatures to be bears, but their behavior puzzled us. They ran on their hind legs, as if they were trained animals performing tricks. It was both shocking and distressing to witness these massive animals terrorizing the defenseless sheep. We estimated that we were approximately 150 yards or more away from the scene. We watched, utterly captivated, as these imposing beings chased the sheep for what felt like an eternity, although in reality, the entire chase lasted around 20 to 30 minutes.

As darkness settled in, fear gripped our hearts, and we became convinced that the bears would swim across the river and come for us next. We swiftly locked the car doors and sought refuge under the blankets, anxiously waiting for morning to break. It felt like an eternity until dawn arrived, and we could finally emerge from the car and reunite with our parents on the boat. We recounted the harrowing events of the previous night to them, but deep down, we knew they thought we had spent the entire night conjuring up a fanciful story. To our surprise, that morning, while at the post office near the site of the attack, we overheard people discussing the incident, mentioning that a pack of wild dogs had killed the sheep. The sheriff, Sam Costa, remarked on the unusual nature of the attack, noting that the dogs had solely focused on consuming the belly and internal organs of the sheep. In the years that followed, we would frequently hear about these wild dogs whenever reports emerged of livestock being killed and mutilated by a predator. However, my sister and I knew in our hearts that what we had witnessed that night was not the work of bears or wild dogs.

The attack had resulted in the loss of several sheep, and while everyone else seemed convinced that wild dogs were to blame, my sister and I held a different belief. We firmly held onto the notion that the creatures responsible for the carnage were, in fact, bears that had somehow mastered the art of walking, running, and hunting exclusively on their hind legs. That unforgettable night forever etched itself in my memory, serving as a constant reminder that there are mysteries in this world that may never be fully explained.

CHAPTER NINETY-THREE

ONE TIME, my 10-year-old son and I went deer hunting not too far from our house, just about a mile away. We decided to hunt on a small cattle farm located on the outskirts of our town. To attract the deer, we had planted food plots and set up elevated blinds around the fields. This particular plot we were hunting was surrounded by thick pines, creating a cozy and secluded environment. The evening was clear and cool, setting the stage for our hunting adventure.

As darkness approached, I took a shot at a deer, and it darted back into the dense pines. We gathered our hunting gear and climbed out of the blind, determined to track down the wounded deer. Armed with flashlights, we cautiously ventured into the pines, following the trail of blood for about 50 yards. Suddenly, from right in front of us, there came an incredibly loud "whoop" that startled us both. We stopped in our tracks and exchanged puzzled glances, asking each other, "What was that?" The sound seemed to emerge from the ground, about 20 yards away, and its intensity reverberated through my chest, sending an unsettling sensation throughout my body.

I swiftly scanned the surroundings with my flashlight and caught sight of the deer, lifeless, lying just 15 yards ahead. My son was visibly frightened at this point, so I put on a brave face, pretending that it was nothing out of the ordinary to keep him calm. However, deep down, I was quite shaken myself. A sense of unease washed over me, compelling me to get out of there as quickly as possible. We grabbed the deer and made our way back to the field, with an eerie feeling that we were being trailed, although we never heard or saw anything else.

We had to retrieve my truck, so we left the deer in the field momentarily. I fully expected that when we returned, the deer would be gone. Surprisingly, it was still there when we came back. Throughout the process of loading the deer into the truck, it felt as though we were being watched from the nearby woods. Even as I type this account, I can't help but feel a chill run down my spine. It almost seemed as if something or someone was approaching the deer from a different direction, and our arrival coincided with theirs. The whooping sound I heard reminded me of the monkeys at the zoo, yet it possessed a deeper and louder resonance. Despite my 40 years of hunting experience and familiarity with the sounds of animals in the area, I couldn't identify the source of that peculiar sound.

Furthermore, I've had two encounters with ghost lights on the same property just before daybreak. Initially, I brushed it off as trespassers with flashlights, but upon closer inspection through binoculars, the light appeared to be floating on its own, moving through the trees. It had a bluish-white hue and emitted a soft, muted glow that intermittently dimmed and brightened as it traversed the woods. The light seemed to be about the size of a softball. On both occasions, I was approximately 200 yards away from it. Strangely enough, these incidents occurred during deer seasons prior to 2013. At the time, I didn't necessarily connect the sightings of these lights with the whooping sound that could potentially be attributed to Bigfoot. However, having heard numerous accounts of people witnessing Sasquatch sightings in conjunction with strange lights, I felt compelled to include these experiences as well.

A few weeks after we heard the distinctive whoop, the property changed hands, and sadly, that marked our final hunting season there. I do know that at least one other person had also witnessed the mysterious lights while hunting on the same property, but nobody ever mentioned anything else out of the ordinary.

Thanks for allowing me to share this story. I've also noticed some trees broken off about 15 feet above the ground, forming an "X" shape across two different logging roads on another property we are currently hunting. It's located just down the road from the previous one, so I'm keeping a watchful eye for any other peculiarities in that area. Who knows what else we might come across.

CHAPTER NINETY-FOUR

BACK WHEN THIS INCIDENT OCCURRED, I was a 15-year-old who had grown up surrounded by the woods. I considered myself well-versed in the inhabitants of the wilderness and could easily identify them. It happened around 3:00 PM as I was making my way home from school, cutting through the dense woods. During my walk, an uneasy feeling began to creep over me, prompting me to scan my surroundings. However, I brushed it off as mere figments of my imagination, attributing it to my mind playing tricks on me.

Without giving it much thought, I continued my journey with my head down, disregarding the lingering unease. But then, by chance, I happened to glance up and saw "someone" standing right in the middle of the trail, roughly 70 to 80 yards away. Initially, I dismissed the figure, assuming it was just one of those individuals who would sneak off after school to smoke cigarettes or indulge in illicit substances in that area. I reasoned that the person I saw was simply engaging in one of those activities. However, something nagged at me, suggesting that what I witnessed wasn't quite right. The spot where this individual stood was where the trail met the swamp, a location where nobody ventured so deep just to smoke. As I lifted my gaze, I froze. An inexplicable fear washed over me. Although I had encountered deer, bears, bobcats, and cougars in this particular patch of land without feeling scared, what I saw before me was unlike any of those creatures. The being in front of me displayed a uniform color, either dark brown or black, with arms that extended almost down to its knees and remarkably broad shoulders. It stood upright on two legs and peered at me from around a tree before eventually moving onto the trail itself. Despite my inability to move or utter a sound, my mind continued to work. I did my best to etch an image of this creature into my memory. I distinctly recall thinking that the head seemed too small for the body, and I couldn't discern any variation in skin tone on its face. It appeared as though the skin blended seamlessly with the rest of its body. The final detail that caught my attention was a branch positioned just above the creature's head.

I noted that the branch hovered only a few inches above the creature's head. I observed this enigmatic animal for no more than a minute when it pivoted on its hind foot, took a single stride into the swamp, and vanished from sight. After about ten minutes, the paralyzing sensation released its grip on me, and I returned to normal. At that point, I felt compelled to investigate further. I approached the spot where the creature had stood, searching for any sign of its presence. However, the ground there was incredibly hard, with no visible tracks. The creature's stride was at least five feet long. As mentioned earlier, the creature initially peered at me from behind a tree but eventually stepped out onto the trail. I estimated that the distance from where the creature stood to where I last saw it at the edge of the trail and swamp was roughly five feet. In just a single step, it disappeared from view.

Now, I stand at around six feet tall and have a stride of three feet. Whatever I saw would have to be significantly larger than me. Keeping this in mind, I also sought out the tree branch that the creature had been standing beneath. To my astonishment, I found it right above my head, confirming that I was indeed in the correct location. The branch sat at a height of about nine feet, implying that whatever I had encountered was just a hair under nine feet tall. To this day, I possess no definitive proof that what I witnessed was a Bigfoot. However, I struggle to find any other suitable explanation. The specific location, at the edge of the swamp, was not a place commonly frequented by people. Furthermore, the creature's physical structure differed greatly from that of a human, and it was far too large to be mistaken for one. As I write this account, I have not experienced any other incidents in that particular area. However, I have had a peculiar encounter in another part of Northern Michigan. While I don't believe the creature intended me harm, I rarely venture into that area of the woods alone.

CHAPTER NINETY-FIVE

LET me tell you a story that happened not too long ago, about a year and a half back. It was early August, and my buddies invited me to join them for a weekend camping trip. We headed to Mottet Campgrounds in Oregon's Umatilla National Forest, a stunning area with ample hiking opportunities. Little did we know that this trip would be etched in our memories forever.

As the evening wore on, after indulging in a delectable meal of venison, elk, and moose that one of our friends had brought along (which, in hindsight, might have attracted some unexpected attention), it was just my pals Jordan, Josh, and me who remained awake by the crackling fire. Nearby, other campers were already fast asleep in their tents, unaware of what was about to unfold.

I had settled on a cot about five feet away from the fire, positioned roughly 20 feet from the edge of the woods where an unexpected noise was about to emerge. The time was around 11:30 PM when Jordan got up from his chair to relieve himself at the nearest tree line. But in the midst of his business, an abrupt growl or snorting sound emanated from about 15 yards deep into the trees. This unexpected interruption startled Jordan, causing him to abandon his task and rush back to the safety of the fire. In an instant, both Josh and I were on our feet, our adrenaline pumping. Without conscious thought, I instinctively grabbed the knife strapped to my side. We exchanged bewildered glances, questioning whether we had all heard the same inexplicable noise. What on earth could have produced such a sound?

Having grown up in the town of Dixie, nestled in the vicinity of the Blues, we were well acquainted with the wildlife one might encounter during nights spent in the mountains. We were all sober, having enjoyed a few wild nights leading up to this camping trip and needing to rise early the next day. After a minute or so of stunned silence, Jordan and I dashed back to our tent to fetch the machete and a large flashlight. With trepidation, we peered into the woods from a distance of about five feet. Initially, we saw nothing, prompting us to start banging on trees and shouting, creating a ruckus in case the source of the noise happened to be a cougar or some other creature. We hoped that enough noise and commotion would scare it away. With that in mind, we stoked the fire, ensuring that some branches stuck out, just in case we needed them as makeshift weapons.

After approximately 20 minutes, our anxiety subsided, and we returned to our usual chatter. However, an hour and 15 minutes later, out of nowhere and from the exact same spot where we had heard the initial noise, we were assaulted by a resounding roar. It was accompanied by the violent smashing of what sounded like large hammers on wood, snapping of tree branches, and a series of thuds. THUD... THUD... THUD. Then, as suddenly as it had begun, silence enveloped the forest. In the span of those six audible thuds, whatever was causing the disturbance had traveled a distance of about 35 to 40 yards. We all sprang to our feet, screaming in shock and confusion, incapable of venturing anywhere near the edge of the woods. One of our fellow campers, who had been sleeping in a tent nearby, bolted out, shrieking and desperate for answers.

This commotion prompted the guy with the .44 to emerge from his slumber, but by the time he arrived, there was little left to be done. After about half an hour, he reluctantly returned to his tent, accompanied by Kaci, the camper closest to the disturbance, who had finally managed to calm down. The three of us remained seated around the fire, shaken by the experience. Twenty minutes later, we heard faint thudding sounds, growing more distant as they moved away. Exhausted and drained, we made the decision to try and get some sleep. It just so happened that all three of us were sharing a four-person tent, and, unluckily, the zipper on the door was broken, leaving it flapping open throughout the night.

When we awoke the next morning, we found ourselves surrounded by two to five pine cones each, positioned around our heads. Yes, the tent door was broken, but there was no conceivable way that we could have inadvertently dragged in that many pine cones near our sleeping heads.

Outside the tent, I discovered an exceptionally large footprint, and upon examining the area where all the commotion had taken place, we spotted two broken spots on two different trees, each measuring approximately 10 and 15 feet in height. It seemed as though something with incredible strength had gripped these trees with both hands, effortlessly bending them.

From that moment on, I became a firm believer in the existence of Bigfoot. Despite the fear that had consumed me during that unforgettable night, I felt an undeniable urge to return to the woods and seek further evidence. One day, I hope that one of us who believes in Bigfoot will obtain the concrete proof we have all been tirelessly searching for.

CHAPTER NINETY-SIX

SO, here's the thing. I had lent my trusty pickup truck to a friend who was moving. To show their gratitude, they offered me a delicious dinner and an intriguing proposition—to prove to me that Bigfoot actually roamed around their property. Now, they lived in this quaint little three-room building near their parents' cabin, and the area had a reputation for being great for mushroom hunting. Intrigued, I asked if we could take a stroll around their property and see what we could find.

We embarked on our adventure, trudging along a muddy tractor path. Along the way, my friend had to guide a calf towards the barn. As we made our way back to the house, carefully navigating the muddy path to avoid a rather large mud puddle, something caught my eye. Lo and behold, right there in the mud was a footprint. It was astonishingly wider and longer than my own foot.

Initially, I suspected that my friend was pulling a fast one on me, trying to scare me with a prank. I voiced my doubts, but my friend encouraged me to create a footprint myself if I thought they had faked it. Well, let me tell you, I couldn't quite replicate the same effect in the puddle. My own track was much smaller, and I struggled to make the toes stand out as prominently. That's when my friend suggested using some plaster they had in the cow barn. We wasted no time and went to mix the plaster, pouring it into the intriguing footprint. With no sign of anyone at the small house they were living in, we made our way up to the cabin.

On the porch, we found my friend's in-laws, along with his wife and their two little kids, happily enjoying the outdoors. My friend's mother-in-law inquired about our little detour down by the rabbit pens, and we excitedly informed her about the discovery of the foot-print, now filled with plaster. To our surprise, she simply requested that we stay out of the rabbit pens. Meanwhile, my friend's father-in-law handed me a pair of binoculars and my friend a shotgun, advising us to use it to scare away any unwanted visitors. As we chatted and sipped our coffee, my friend's wife decided it was time to feed the rabbits, and she headed towards the back of the property.

Suddenly, she burst through the back door, visibly frightened. She claimed to have heard heavy breathing just outside the rabbit shed while she was in there, tending to the cages. Her fear was palpable, and it was in that moment that I began to question whether this was the most elaborate practical joke I had ever encountered or if some-thing truly extraordinary was happening. Determined to find out, my friend and I ventured down to investigate the shed. To our dismay, we found nothing out of the ordinary. I was ready to call it a day, but then the rain started pouring down, leaving us with no choice but to stay put.

Restless, my friend and I began fooling around with the binoculars, scanning the area beyond the cabin, where the woods opened up to reveal a wheat field. And then, it happened. In that golden sunlight, I spotted a figure that resembled a human, completely cloaked in dark-ness, clutching a tree limb. It bobbed up and down in an uncanny, ape-like manner.

A chill ran down my spine, and I pointed towards the figure, ques-tioning my friend about what we were witnessing. To my astonish-ment, he confirmed that he, too, saw the same entity, swaying and bobbing while holding onto a tree limb that was easily ten feet off the ground. Determined to investigate further, he began inching closer to it. But in the corner of my eye, something else caught my attention.

Partially obscured by weeds, I glimpsed a movement down the tractor path. Peering through the binoculars, I could make out flowing, fox-colored hair on a hand that was touching the plaster of Paris we had poured into the footprint. The hair only covered the top of the hand, extending just over the knuckles and back to the wrist.

What struck me as peculiar was that the skin color appeared human-like but tinged with a yellowish hue. The hand seemed to lack thumbs, yet it possessed an unusually elongated shape. Unfortunately, the head remained hidden among the thick weeds. I quickly alerted my friend, and together we retreated towards the rabbit shed, with him carrying the shotgun for our protection. Despite our thorough search, we found no trace of anything unusual down there. We decided it was time to head back to the safety of the cabin. As we walked up the path, backs turned to the mud puddle, a sudden rush of rustling sounds emanated from the weeds, accompanied by the distinct slapping of bare feet on the wet, muddy ground, mere feet away from us.

I didn't hesitate. Fear gripped me, and I sprinted towards my truck, not looking back. As I drove away, I mustered the courage to wave goodbye, but I made a promise to myself that I would never set foot in that place again, except for the occasional drive-by. The memory of that surreal encounter with Bigfoot would forever be etched in my mind, leaving me with a lingering sense of awe and curiosity.

CHAPTER NINETY-SEVEN

MY ENCOUNTER HAPPENED about ten years ago and it's still as fresh in my memory as though it happened yesterday. I never gave much thought to bigfoot because even though I live in the upstate part, I still live in New York and that's not a place I thought the so-called king of the cryptids would ever be found lurking. I was twenty-five years old at the time and had just moved into my own place with my then girlfriend. It was our place as far as we lived there by ourselves, but it belonged to my grandparents and the real reason I was given the go ahead to move in there with my girlfriend was because my grandparents had let it sort of fall to pieces and become overrun and disheveled. They hadn't even been to the home or the property in at least ten years before that. They wanted to sell the house and the property, and they needed someone to do a lot of work on the house and to the woods surrounding it. A lot of it was overgrown and desperately needed to be cleared and so I jumped at the chance to do the work for them to have the opportunity to live there rent free with my significant other. Now that I'm older and that relationship has long since ended, I realize we were simply playing house, but we tried our best I suppose. The strange feelings started the first night we moved in there, so I guess I'll start with that.

It was a very snowy and cold winter, and I knew I wouldn't be able to do any of the trimming or other landscaping until the springtime, but I had a lot to do on the inside as well and figured I would start there. It had snowed a lot more than usual that year and it was cold. We got everything turned back on and despite how raggedy and run down the house was, she and I were happy with it because neither one of us had ever lived on our own before or with anyone other than our parents and we just couldn't wait to start "real life." We finished unloading all our stuff at around nine at night and decided to call it a night early so that we could get up bright and early and start putting things away and cleaning everything. We set up an air mattress on the floor of the living room for the first night and only unpacked our blankets and pillows. We both fell asleep rather quickly and I woke up at around two in the morning to my girlfriend screaming in terror at something I couldn't see. I was so confused, and she just kept pointing to one of the windows in the living room and hollering. I went over to the window, but she wouldn't let me turn any lights on and I didn't see anything. Finally, she calmed down enough and told me she had seen a face there and that it had been some sort of monster. I wasn't going to argue with her and so I just did my best to calm her down. Over the course of the next month there were no more faces in the windows but several times we would wake up to hear loud growling on the side of the house and in the morning our garbage cans would be thrown clear across the yard, which was about a hundred yards. They looked like they had been thrown when they were filled with garbage most of the time too. We slept in the master bedroom on the second floor and despite there being no faces to speak of there were often gigantic tracks of some animal's huge foot all over the place outside in the snow. Again, it never occurred to me it could have been bigfoot until one night I saw him.

My girlfriend and I had been living in the house for about a month and we had gone on several snowy walks in the surrounding woods. The forest was always completely quiet, and we never understood why but she was always suspicious that it was whatever had been leaving the footprints and she attributed all of it to the "creature" she had seen in the window on that first night we were there. The forest on the property was dense and led to several different places all throughout the town we lived in if you walked through it from one side to another in any direction. One night we had gone out to dinner and a movie just to get out of the house for a little while. The little renovations we were able to do while it was snowing out were coming along nicely but she and I weren't getting along that well for a myriad of reasons. I remember she was driving, and we had gotten into a heated discussion about something when she turned and slapped me across my face. I was stunned and wasn't going to stand for it, but I was also taught not to hit women and certainly wasn't going to hit her back, so I demanded she let me out of the car. She slammed on the brakes, and I got out, but she circled back around and kept pestering me to get back in the car and saying she was sorry. I hadn't calmed down sufficiently enough but she wouldn't leave me alone. When she drove off again, I turned and decided to cut through the woods to get back to the house so she wouldn't be able to harass me and so I could properly calm down before having to be in the same house as her.

I was a ten-minute walk through the woods away from my house and from the second I entered that forest I knew something was wrong. It wasn't just the usual eerie silence of the woods but there was something else. I just felt a sense of danger. I had been hanging out in the woods in my town for most of my life, but I hadn't ever been in them in the snow like that and I just couldn't shake the feeling that something was very wrong. I felt like I was being watched and when I looked down, I saw those same giant footprints I was always seeing around my house, specifically all over the place on the nights we would wake up to the garbage all gone through and the can tossed clear across the yard. I was beyond curious at that point and my girl-friend wasn't there to talk me out of further investigating what they might belong to for once and so I decided to take a little detour and follow them. I wish I had just left well enough alone, but I didn't, and I started following the footprints. At first, they led in the direction I was already headed, towards my house but they suddenly veered off and seemed to be going in the direction of the stream that ran through that part of the woods. I expected the water to be completely iced over but it looked like the ice had been broken and the water was somewhat flowing. I didn't understand what was going on and figured maybe I should just turn around and go back towards my house. No sooner had I thought that than something that sounded very big seemed to be coming up from behind me. I heard the snow crunching under the feet of whatever it was, and it was breathing very heavily. I turned around and was face to face with a giant animal of some sort. I hadn't ever seen anything like it, and it took a minute or two for it to register, while we stared at each other, that I was faced to face with bigfoot. I gasped.

The creature in front of me seemed like it was sizing me up, looking me up and down and grumbling, and it was standing in a somewhat aggressive stance. It made a disgusted, snorting type of sound and turned to walk over to the water. It was huge. It was covered all over its body with black fur, but it had gray patches all over it too. It looked wet and smelled like a wet dog and rotting garbage. Its face looked somewhat human but also like it belonged to an animal and it had large green eyes that looked somewhat human as well. They were bright green and where humans have whites on their eyeballs, so did it. I just stood there, stupidly watching it turn from me, walk to the water and crouch down. Then, it let out a loud holler that seemingly reverberated through the entire forest and shook a lot of the snow off the trees. I jumped but still didn't move even though it no longer seemed to be interested in or paying attention to me. However, the minute the sound it had just made came back to it, meaning there was another one somewhere in those woods and close, I turned and made a run for it. It hollered and screamed after me, but I didn't dare stop or look back.

I barely knew where I was going and fell several times on the way back to my grandparent's property and my house, but I eventually made it there in one piece. The bigfoot didn't seem like it had followed me, but I couldn't be sure. I ran into my house and started yelling but my girlfriend thought I was still angry about our earlier argument and that's what I was yelling about and so she started yelling back. Finally, I calmed down enough and calmed her down enough to tell her what I had just seen and what had happened to me. At first, she thought I was joking with her but then I reminded her of the giant footprints, tossed garbage cans and that scary face that had terrified her that had been looking at us through the window our first night there. She was shocked and I could tell she was extremely scared. I was nervous, I'll admit, but I was more excited than anything else. As she made her way through the house, locking the doors and closing all the blinds, I followed closely behind her, peeking through all the closed blinds to see if I could spot the animal again. I didn't see anything right then, but I started to develop a theory. I thought that perhaps because of its familiarity with our home, our garbage, and our faces- from looking in our windows- the bigfoot somehow knew or sensed I wasn't a threat and that's why it didn't attack me but why it first looked mean and aggressive. I thought maybe it was going or attempting to show me something with the water, but I ran off before it had the chance and that's why it started screaming when it noticed I was no longer standing there. Of course, I have no way of knowing if any of that is true, but I still wonder if it is to this day.

My girlfriend and I broke up not long after that encounter happened, and I ended up living in that house alone for another two years. Eventually I bought it from my grandparents and was able to do so because they let me slowly pay them off. I have done all the work and I still live here. I have encountered a bigfoot a few times in the last ten years, but I don't go out into the woods looking to catch "proof" because I respect them and their privacy as living beings. I think they sense that about me because I haven't been attacked and I started leaving the lid off my garbage in the winter and they haven't ever been damaged or thrown again. I love knowing they're there but don't tell too many people because I feel like they might try and go after the poor things, and I think they're peaceful and just want to be left alone. That's been my experience with them at least.

CHAPTER NINETY-EIGHT

I LIVED ALONE in a modest two-bedroom residence situated about a quarter mile north of US Hwy. 199, nestled on a gentle wooded slope. The property encompassed roughly three acres, featuring two horse pastures—one located below the house and another above it. Both pastures were enclosed by active hot-wire fences, allowing the two horses to freely roam between the lower and upper areas.

On that particular evening, I found myself engrossed in the completion of a research paper for one of my college classes. Sitting at the kitchen table, a solitary light illuminated the room. Outside, my friend's dog, a small brown heeler, was tethered to the porch with a 35-foot wire.

As I focused intently on my schoolwork, I suddenly became aware of the dog outside erupting into a frenzy of barks. Naturally, I became alarmed and immediately shifted my attention to the dog's actions. The cacophony that followed will forever be etched in my memory. Dogs and horses from neighboring residences, situated quite a distance away across various hills and ridges, joined in with ceaseless, piercing shrieks. Sensing the need for caution, I retrieved a large caliber pistol and a powerful flashlight from my gun safe, preparing to investigate the situation.

Dimming the lights in the house, I cautiously opened the front door, brandishing the flashlight and pistol, scanning the area before stepping outside. What I witnessed filled me with unease. The little heeler was fixated on the lower horse pasture, emitting a low, menacing growl. The two horses had moved to the upper pasture, their usual movements replaced by an eerie restlessness and peculiar neighing. Kneeling beside the dog, who seemed unusually indifferent to my presence, I pointed my flashlight in the direction he was facing. What I saw next nearly froze my heart in my chest—a large figure crouched down in the tall grass just outside the outer hot-wire, next to a telephone pole. The light from my flashlight reflected off two small circular markers on the pole, further diffused by the light fog, making it difficult to identify the creature initially. My immediate thought was "bear."

But to my utter astonishment, the dog suddenly let out a blood-curdling scream, leaping into the air with its hair standing on end. It landed and promptly darted under a nearby pickup truck, whimpering like a frightened pup. In those fleeting seconds, while this unfolded before my eyes, the figure outside rose up on two legs and began moving along the hot-wire. Rising to my full height, I aimed my pistol directly at it. Thoughts raced through my mind, desperately trying to make sense of what I was witnessing—"Is it a bear? No, maybe a horse? Wait, a person? No, wait, what the hell is this thing?!" With my pistol sights and flashlight fixed on the creature (my military police training from my five years of service flooding back to me in that intense moment), I tracked its every move for at least two seconds. And then, to my horror, I watched this colossal entity take off in a full, bipedal run, the unmistakable sound of its footfalls echoing in a rhythmic "thud-thud" as its two legs propelled it forward. I've never felt more fear in my entire life (and yes, I'm a grown man!). I sprinted back to the safety of my house, grabbing more substantial weapons and immediately calling my friend's father in Grants Pass, urging him to come and help search for this enigmatic being. When he arrived, we drove down to the road outside the hot-wire fence, where I believed the creature had been. Unfortunately, the gravel road offered no clues except for disturbed grass, as if something massive had passed through it—no footprints were found. Throughout the night and into the next morning, the animals in our small community near Wilderville, Oregon remained agitated and restless, with the little heeler being the most affected, refusing to calm down for an entire day.

I hope this information proves useful for your research, and I fervently hope that one day, as a society, we can gather enough evidence to confirm the existence of whatever inexplicable entity I encountered that fateful night in Southern Oregon.

CHAPTER NINETY-NINE

I'VE ALWAYS BEEN FASCINATED by this particular incident, and I've shared the story with my parents and a few close friends over the years. I even contemplated submitting it to a website dedicated to strange encounters, but I hesitated because the incident took place on an island, and I thought people might consider me crazy for sharing it. However, when I stumbled upon a report on the same site about an incident on Hartstene Island, a shiver ran down my spine, and I felt compelled to finally share my own experience.

It was back in 1984 when my parents would travel to California to sell Christmas trees. During that time, I was a junior in high school, and I would be left home alone for approximately three weeks. Fortunately, my older brother and his wife lived across the street, so I never felt completely isolated. Our residence was a spacious one-story house situated on a farm within an old fruit orchard. We had horses, chickens, and pigs, and Charlie, our loyal German Shepherd, was always around, except for that one night when this peculiar incident occurred. Her absence was noticeable because her barking would have surely woken me up. Sometimes she would vanish at night, and we attributed her barking fits to deer passing through. Occasionally, we could even hear the snapping of twigs in the woods behind our house. Those woods stretched far, having been previously logged, and the regrowth spanned extensively with no houses in sight at that time.

On this particular occasion, my parents were in California selling trees, and I was left alone in our large, window-filled house. At night, I often felt a disquieting sensation of being watched, prompting me to close most of the curtains around the house. Beyond the glow of the yard light, darkness enveloped everything. The shape of our house formed a T, and my bedroom occupied the far left end, while the kitchen resided in the middle of the top section of the T. A sliding door opened from the kitchen onto a covered deck, which had two gates. Interestingly, one of the gates was located merely two feet from one of my bedroom windows, positioned about five feet above the ground.

I had fallen asleep, but suddenly, around 2:30 AM, I jolted awake for no apparent reason. I turned my gaze to the bedroom window on the right side of my bed and observed a dark figure outlined against the glass. All I could discern was a head, as though it was attempting to peer into the window rather than standing directly in front of it. At that moment, it seemed as if whatever it was became aware of my presence and hastily retreated from the porch, causing a clattering noise as it knocked something over (wooden objects colliding). At the time, I speculated that it might have been the sound of deer hooves, but why would a deer be leaning over the fence on our porch, peering into my window? The figure swiftly vanished from the porch, racing around the side of the house where my room was located, which meant I could hear it sprinting through the side yard and into the back yard. Its speed was astonishing, accompanied by the thunderous crashing of branches as it tore through the woods.

The pace was so rapid that I honestly cannot recall whether the sounds indicated a bipedal movement or not. Nevertheless, I highly doubt that a deer would stand upright against the side of a house to peer into a window at night—such behavior simply didn't make sense to me. My instincts led me to believe it was an unfamiliar animal rather than a human. Filled with fear, I closed my eyes and offered a prayer because I couldn't comprehend why a deer would exhibit such behavior. I thought it might have been a person, but their incredible speed contradicted that assumption. Moreover, it unnerved me to think that someone would sprint through the woods behind our house at 2:30 AM when they could have just retraced their steps down the driveway. Needless to say, from that night onward until my parents returned, I sought refuge at my brother's house.

CHAPTER ONE HUNDRED

BACK IN 1954, when my mother was just 14 years old, she resided near Elkhorn City, Kentucky, in a small community nestled at the base of a mountainous region. It was an idyllic setting, with nature enveloping their surroundings. One sunny afternoon, my mom and her sister decided to take a short trip across the road from their home to a modest general store in search of a refreshing soda. After making their purchase, they settled on a bench along the walkway to indulge in conversation and admire the picturesque view of the mountains that extended to the edge of their backyard.

While engrossed in their conversation, my mother's sharp eyes detected movement in a meadow atop one of the hills. This meadow, a quaint expanse nestled between two ridges adorned with lush vegetation, caught her attention. Initially, she assumed it was a man, leisurely venturing into the woods, following an old sheep trail. However, the distance made it difficult to confirm her suspicion. As she focused her gaze, the figure gradually emerged onto the sheep trail, steadily progressing from right to left. It was at this moment that my mother experienced a jolt of astonishment. The figure she observed was none other than a man covered entirely in hair—long tresses gracing its head and shorter strands adorning its body. The sight startled her to the core, prompting her to let out a piercing scream while urgently pointing out the mysterious being to her sister.

As the scream pierced the air, the figure halted its movements, fixating its gaze upon my mother and aunt. In a state of panic, my aunt rushed into the store to seek the assistance of the owner. The store owner promptly joined them outside and witnessed the enigmatic figure firsthand. Bewildered by the sight, they turned to him, seeking answers. The store owner, still shaken, responded with a phrase that echoes in my mother's memory to this day: "I don't know what that Goddamn thing is! It's some kind of wild man!" With that, the figure continued its path, disappearing around the mountain and vanishing from sight.

Interestingly, preceding this unusual encounter, my grandmother had developed a habit of leaving the house doors open during the sweltering heat of the day, as trust among neighbors was paramount in those times. However, she encountered an unnerving incident. Returning home on one occasion, she discovered the oven door ajar and half a pan of freshly baked biscuits devoured. Perplexed, she questioned each family member, yet no one claimed responsibility for the mysterious biscuit thief. Two days later, the scenario repeated itself— an open oven door and a partially consumed pan of biscuits. This time, no family members were present, leaving my grandmother deeply concerned. It was at this point that my grandfather insisted on locking the doors whenever they left the house, determined to ward off any further intrusion.

Another strange occurrence unfolded when my grandfather's smokehouse fell prey to an unseen intruder with an apparent penchant for smoked pork. The incident left them puzzled, unable to fathom who or what had infiltrated the smokehouse and indulged in their preserved meats. However, the strangeness did not end there. On a separate occasion, late at night around 10:00 PM, the chickens in the coop began to raise a ruckus, squawking and causing a commotion. My grandmother's little dog, fiercely protective, began barking incessantly toward the edge of the bank. My father happened to be visiting my mother at the time (their date night, as it were), and both he and my grandfather ventured to the back of the property to investigate the source of the birds' distress. Armed with a sizable flashlight, they combed the area surrounding the coop, shining their light to uncover any possible culprits. Though they searched diligently, they found no evidence of intrusion within or near the pen. However, my father's sharp eyes noticed peculiar scratch marks etched onto a nearby sassafras tree. The scratches, about half an inch wide and spaced an inch apart, stretched to a height of approximately nine feet. Curious about this unusual find, neighbors were summoned the following day to examine the enigmatic markings. Surprisingly, despite the intrigue surrounding these events, nobody thought to search for tracks or pursue the elusive "wild man." As my mother explained, such matters were unfamiliar to the community at the time.

Reflecting on these incidents from long ago, it is astounding how times have changed. Today, with a wealth of information at our fingertips and a heightened awareness of the mysterious and unexplained, we approach such encounters with a different perspective. Yet, for my mother and her family, those events remain vivid memories, forever etched in their minds, testaments to the extraordinary experiences they once encountered in the tranquil hills of Elkhorn City, Kentucky.

————

Continue with
The Big Bigfoot Book: Volume 2

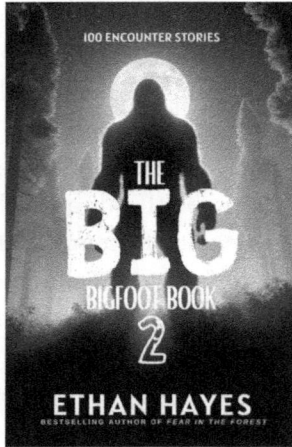

THE MEGA MONSTER BOOK
NOW AVAILABLE!

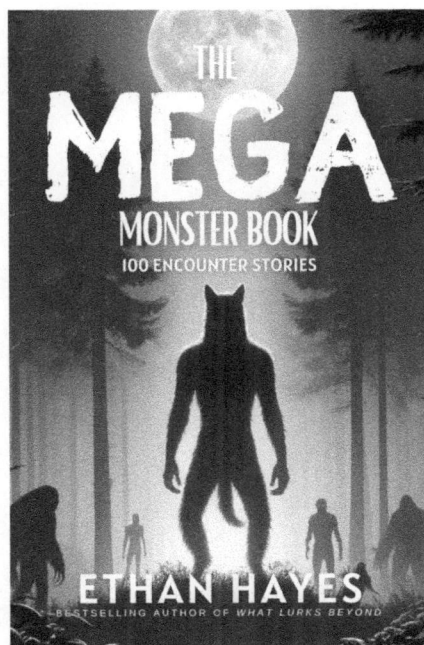

ABOUT THE AUTHOR

Ethan Hayes grew up in Oklahoma and moved to Texas when he attended Texas A&M. Upon graduation he was hired by Texas Parks and Wildlife and remained there until he retired twenty-two years later. He currently lives in southeast Texas with his wife and two dogs. When he's not spending time enjoying the outdoors and writing, he sips a cold beer on his front porch while listening to Bluegrass music.

———

Send in your encounter story: encountersbigfoot@gmail.com

ALSO BY ETHAN HAYES

ALSO BY FREE REIGN PUBLISHING